KNOWLEDGE MANAGEMENT IN LIBRARIES

Chandos
Information Professional Series
Series Editor: Ruth Rikowski
(Email: Rikowskigr@aol.com)

Chandos' new series of books is aimed at the busy information professional. They have been specially commissioned to provide the reader with an authoritative view of current thinking. They are designed to provide easy-to-read and (most importantly) practical coverage of topics that are of interest to librarians and other information professionals. If you would like a full listing of current and forthcoming titles, please visit www.chandospublishing.com.

New authors: we are always pleased to receive ideas for new titles; if you would like to write a book for Chandos, please contact Dr. Glyn Jones on g.jones.2@elsevier.com or telephone + 44 (0) 1865 843000.

KNOWLEDGE MANAGEMENT IN LIBRARIES
Concepts, Tools and Approaches

MOHAMMAD NAZIM

BHASKAR MUKHERJEE

ELSEVIER

AMSTERDAM • BOSTON • CAMBRIDGE • HEIDELBERG
LONDON • NEW YORK • OXFORD • PARIS • SAN DIEGO
SAN FRANCISCO • SINGAPORE • SYDNEY • TOKYO
Chandos Publishing is an imprint of Elsevier

CP
CHANDOS
PUBLISHING

Chandos Publishing is an imprint of Elsevier
50 Hampshire Street, 5th Floor, Cambridge, MA 02139, USA
The Boulevard, Langford Lane, Kidlington, OX5 1GB, UK

Notices

Knowledge and best practice in this field are constantly changing. As new research and experience broaden our understanding, changes in research methods, professional practices, or medical treatment may become necessary.

Practitioners and researchers must always rely on their own experience and knowledge in evaluating and using any information, methods, compounds, or experiments described herein. In using such information or methods they should be mindful of their own safety and the safety of others, including parties for whom they have a professional responsibility.

To the fullest extent of the law, neither the Publisher nor the authors, contributors, or editors, assume any liability for any injury and/or damage to persons or property as a matter of products liability, negligence or otherwise, or from any use or operation of any methods, products, instructions, or ideas contained in the material herein.

Library of Congress Cataloging-in-Publication Data
A catalog record for this book is available from the Library of Congress

British Library Cataloguing-in-Publication Data
A catalogue record for this book is available from the British Library

ISBN: 978-0-08-100564-4 (print)
ISBN: 978-0-08-100568-2 (online)

Publisher: Glyn Jones
Acquisition Editor: Glyn Jones
Editorial Project Manager: Harriet Clayton
Production Project Manager: Debasish Ghosh
Designer: Victoria Pearson Esser

Typeset by SPi Global, India

CONTENTS

LIST OF FIGURES

LIST OF TABLES

ABOUT THE AUTHORS

Mohammad Nazim is an assistant professor at the Department of Library and Information Science, Aligarh Muslim University, Uttar Pradesh, India. He has more than 10 years professional and teaching experience in the library profession. He holds a Ph.D. in Library and Information Science from Banaras Hindu University and a Master's degree in Library and Information Science from Aligarh Muslim University. Prior to joining the teaching profession in Apr. 2015, he spent 9 years at Banaras Hindu University as Assistant Librarian. He has had 25 research papers published in journals of international repute. He is a member of the editorial board of the *Journal of Information* and a reviewer for Chandos Publishing/Elsevier, UK. His research interests include open access to scholarly communication, knowledge management, and information storage and retrieval.

Bhaskar Mukherjee is an associate professor at the Department of Library and Information Science, Banaras Hindu University, Varanasi, Uttar Pradesh, India. A young science graduate with a doctorate in the field of library and information science, he has been working in this profession for 16 years in various positions. He has experience of various theoretical technical aspects of library and information science teaching, as well as having worked in various types of library and information centers. He has had 64 research articles on library and information science published in a number of various highly reputed journals, including *JASIST*, *Scientometrics*, *LISR*, *IFLA*, *Journal of Academic Librarianship*, etc. He received a Raja Rammohun Roy Foundation award for best contributing article. He is also a reviewer for a number of highly reputed journals in this field and allied fields. His research interests are in webometrics, open access, information storage and retrieval, knowledge organization, etc.

PREFACE

There is an increasing recognition of the value of knowledge and information to individuals, organizations, and communities. Individuals are more adept at identifying, locating, interpreting, and using knowledge. As knowledge has become a central productive and strategic asset, the success of all types of organizations is increasingly dependent on their ability to acquire, create, store, share, and utilize knowledge. That is why developing procedures and routines to optimize the acquisition, creation, protection, and sharing of knowledge and information in organizations has become an important undertaking.

In this age of globalization and increased worldwide competition, organizations are looking for new ways to gain a competitive advantage. In doing so, they are trying to protect and use their intellectual capital. Knowledge management (KM) is an emerging discipline with the potential to capitalize on organizations' intellectual capital. In recent years, KM has become an interesting subject of discussion. Both business and academic communities believe that by leveraging knowledge, an organization can sustain its long-term competitive advantages. KM deals with the process of creating value from an organization's intangible assets. These assets or knowledge resources can be classified either as tacit or explicit. The distinction between these two types of knowledge is relevant because the management of each type of knowledge requires the use of different tools, systems, and strategies.

The advent of the Internet and related technological developments has not only increased stocks and flows of information, but also has transformed the nature of library and information services. Technological changes, along with the external pressure of market forces, has motivated libraries to transform their structures and implement new managerial processes. These changes can help them to become more flexible and thereby stimulate innovation and performance in the face of competition from emerging groups of information suppliers and an ever increasing level of user expectations. KM is one of these processes and is recognized worldwide as a very useful solution for the survival and success of libraries. Libraries embrace huge amounts of knowledge in various areas and its use can help libraries to improve quality of services, to make better decisions as well as to improve their overall performance. In libraries, explicit knowledge is either generated within the organization, in the form of reports, memos, guidelines, theses, minutes of meetings, etc., or acquired from external sources, including books, journal articles, databases, external reports, government information, etc. Tacit knowledge, on the other hand, resides in senior and experienced employees with a sound knowledge of work procedures, rules and regulations, etc. and the unarticulated knowledge of the librarians themselves. Both types of knowledge (explicit and tacit) are regarded as key knowledge sources of a library which is managed appropriately. The success of KM initiatives in every organization depends on creation, sharing, and utilization of knowledge because transfer and use of knowledge within an organization reduce the chances of duplication of work, improve productivity, and lead to considerable cost savings, while lack of transfer and use can lead to information overload and confusion, as well as wasted manpower.

KM is a concept that has emerged very rapidly in the business community over the last three decades. During the last few years, a body of literature has emerged that explicitly addresses KM from the perspective of librarianship and information science. However, there is an ongoing debate among library and information science (LIS) professionals on whether KM is a completely new discipline or simply a rebranding of librarianship or information management. Perceptions about KM, as they have emerged in the literature, are varied. This has resulted in, among other things, a lack of universal consensus on some of the key issues of KM, including the concept of KM and its implications for libraries.

When something is not clearly defined, it becomes difficult to apply. Academic institutions, particularly universities, have significant opportunities to apply KM practice to support every part of their mission. According to Kidwell et al. (2000), there are five key areas of KM application in universities, including research, curriculum development, administrative services, alumni services, and strategic planning. However, the concept of KM is relatively new to libraries; therefore it is important to explore its implications for libraries and for LIS professionals. Although there are several benefits of application of KM in libraries, as have emerged in the professional LIS literature, it is important to know how librarians perceive the benefits of KM. It is also unclear whether traditional skills of librarianship among LIS professionals are relevant for the management of knowledge or whether other types of skills and competencies are needed in order for them to perform their task in knowledge-intensive organizations in their capacity as knowledge managers. Therefore it is important to examine the requirements of KM skills and competencies for LIS professionals. Identification of required KM skills and competencies would help the academic community to reconsider LIS curricula and teaching methods, and modify existing curricula to impart a wide range of competencies among LIS students to enable them to perform their job more effectively in knowledge-intensive organizations. Moreover, a need for the inclusion of KM education in professional LIS educational programs has been asserted by many academics, but there remains a degree of uncertainty as to the extent to which this is to be incorporated into existing LIS educational programs.

Over the years, several conventional and information technology (IT)-based KM tools and systems have evolved. They are being used to support the processes of knowledge capture, codification, and sharing. Intranets, web portals, blogs, wikis, social media, groupware, knowledge directories, and communities of practice are increasingly used in different types of organizations as KM tools and systems. But there is uncertainty about what tools and systems will suit the requirements of libraries and how they may be used in libraries for the management of knowledge.

The success or failure of KM implementation is largely dependent on systematically integrating three basic pillars of KM: people, processes, and IT. Integration of these essential components of a KM needs a well-planned KM strategy. In addition to the formulation of a well-planned KM strategy, creation and development of a favorable environment for communication, collaboration, knowledge creation, sharing and transfer, as well as easy identification of the organization's knowledge assets, are essential for KM to succeed. Since KM is an emerging field in the area of libraries, it is important to develop a better understanding of those factors which are critical to the success of KM in libraries.

Some of these issues are addressed in *Knowledge Management in Libraries: Concepts, Tools and Approaches*. This book is an analysis of the concepts of KM that prevail in the LIS community. It explores the concepts and approaches of KM from the perspective of LIS professionals. Furthermore, unlike most books on KM, which address the subject almost exclusively in the context of helping a firm or an organization to gain a competitive advantage, this book looks at KM in the context of not-for-profit organizations such as libraries.

This book is divided into 11 chapters. Chapter 1 provides an overview of KM, along with the concept of knowledge and its relation to data and information. The importance of KM for academia and for libraries is described, together with the emerging KM roles and responsibilities needed to ensure successful KM implementation in libraries. Chapter 2, "History and Evolution of Knowledge Management Systems," includes a brief history of KM. Brief descriptions of different systems of KM are provided to give the reader an indication of how the practice of KM developed. Chapter 3 examines the concept of KM from the perspective of LIS professionals. Chapter 4 discusses the various approaches used in KM in libraries. Chapter 5 provides an overview of different types of organizational knowledge, along with the strategy for managing each type of knowledge in libraries. In Chapter 6, different KM tools and techniques are discussed. KM tools are categorized as IT-based KM tools and conventional or non-IT-based KM tools. In Chapter 7 the requirements of different skills and competencies for LIS professionals involved in KM practice are discussed. Chapter 8 provides an overview of KM education and examines its relevance in LIS educational courses. The role of KM, its potential implications and benefits for libraries are examined in Chapter 9. Chapter 10 presents an exploration of the potential utilization of different information and communication technologies as KM solutions in libraries. Chapter 11 aims to identify and analyze a set of factors critical to the success of KM in libraries.

REFERENCES

Kidwell, J.J., Linde, K.M.V., Johnson, S.L., 2000. Applying corporate knowledge management practices in higher education. Educ. Q. 23 (4), 28–33.

ACKNOWLEDGEMENTS

First, and above all, we praise God, the almighty, for providing us with the insight and knowledge to write this book.

We would like to express our gratitude to all those people who provided support in the writing of this book. We wish to personally thank Prof. Shabahat Husain, Prof. S.C. Biswas, Prof. H.N. Prasad and the late Professor B.N. Juyal for their contributions to our inspiration and scholarly guidance throughout the journey.

Many thanks go to our colleagues and friends who have generously given their support during the writing of this book. We are also indebted to Chandos Publishing/Elsevier for the opportunity to undertake this book project. Special thanks go to Dr. Glyn Jones and Harriet Clayton who worked enthusiastically with us from beginning to end.

Last, but by no means least, we would like to thank our families for their understanding, unstinting moral support and encouragement.

CHAPTER 1

An Introduction to Knowledge Management

INTRODUCTION

Tony Blair (former Prime Minister of the UK), while speaking at an e-summit in Nov. 2002, stated that:

> *The fundamental challenge is to create a knowledge-driven economy that serves our long-term goals of first-class public services and economic prosperity for all. To do so we need to innovate. We need to use ideas and intelligence in new ways that create higher value-added products and better quality services ... and we must extend the opportunities of the information age to all.*
>
> ***(cited in Hayes, 2004, p. 231)***

The idea of knowledge management (KM) has been around since Plato, but the phrase "knowledge management" was formally used by Carl Wiig in 1986 at a Swiss conference sponsored by the United Nations—International Labor Organization. Over the past 30 years, there has been a great deal of new terminology added to this concept. The growth of the knowledge economy is being driven by business change and has put greater emphasis on the need for better management of organizational knowledge. Its fundamental premise is that an enormous amount of knowledge about customers, processes, products, and services exists at all levels of an organization, and if this cumulative knowledge can be captured and communicated, it can help organizations become more productive, effective, and successful. Although the concept of KM emerged as a business trend in the corporate world in the 1990s, it is now being applied in public sector organizations, including academic institutions and their libraries.

EMERGENCE OF THE KNOWLEDGE AGE

Human societies have passed through three transitional stages of development. In addition to the role of different sources of wealth in each stage of the development of human societies, knowledge has always been a factor of production and a driver of economic and social development. The lives of the early ancestors of mankind was dependent on hunting and gathering. The shift from a hunter-gatherer society to an agricultural society was driven by the knowledge of how to use seeds to sow and harvest food. Ownership of land was the main source of wealth during the agricultural age. The next shift, from an agricultural to an industrial society, occurred in the 18th century. The Industrial Revolution was also driven by knowledge of how to use capital, machines, and other fossil fuels. In the industrial age, ownership of land, fossil fuels, equipment, and capital were the primary factors of production as well as the sources of wealth.

The Industrial Revolution continued this enormous material development throughout the 20th century. The late 20th century saw a period of major social, economic, and political changes, particularly with the advancement in information and communication technologies (ICT). It was also a time of transition from the Industrial Revolution to the knowledge revolution, with substantial changes in how people acquired knowledge and how they used it. Hayes (2004) points out three major drivers of this change:

- *Globalization.* Geographical boundaries are no longer important and, as developed countries cannot compete on production costs, they are competing in industries based on knowledge, where "know-how" and reputation are important.
- *Technological advances and ICT.* Connectivity and networking are enabling new and greatly enhanced products to supplement and replace existing products and achieve new markets using electronic delivery, and existing products are offered to a much wider market via the Internet.
- *Recognition of the importance of information and knowledge in the economy.* All business development relies on information and know-how. Over 70% of workers in developed countries are knowledge workers, from authors to librarians, teachers to zookeepers. Governments are keen to boost economies by educating knowledge workers and creating new opportunities through knowledge creation.

In the knowledge age, the source of wealth is based upon the ownership of knowledge and the ability to use that knowledge to create or improve goods and services. It was predicted in 1996 that, in the knowledge age, 2% of the working population will work on the land, 10% will work in industry, and the remainder will be knowledge workers (Savage, 1996). The concept of "knowledge workers" was first introduced by Peter Drucker in 1959 in his book *The Post-Capitalist Society*. He argues that knowledge is displacing capital, natural resources, and labor as a basic economic resource (Drucker, 1993).

Today, it is widely recognized that we are living in a knowledge society, by which is meant that knowledge has become the social and economic basis of the society. According to Bedford et al. (2015), "a knowledge society is one in which all members of a society engage in knowledge transactions in the business environment, in the social sphere, in civic activities, and in everyday environmental actions" (p. 81). A knowledge society, according to the United Nations Economic Commission for Africa (2010):

> *[...] is based on the creation, dissemination and utilization of knowledge, in which case knowledge assets are deliberately accorded more importance than capital and labour assets and the economy relies on knowledge as the key engine of economic growth. It is an economy in which knowledge is acquired, created, disseminated and applied to enhance economic development (p. 5).*

In a knowledge-based society, people are expected not only to have access to information and knowledge, but are able to locate, assess, and represent new information and knowledge quickly. They are also expected to communicate this to others, and to work productively in collaborations with others. The process of sharing and communication of knowledge would certainly help people to be creative and innovative. Most importantly, the process of knowledge access and use can help a nation or society to fulfill the social needs of its people, create wealth, and enhance quality of life in a sustainable manner. Addressing the 90th Indian Science Congress, the great visionary and former president of India, A. P. J. Abdul Kalam, stressed that:

> *Efficient utilization of existing knowledge can create comprehensive wealth of nations and also improve the quality of life – in the form of better health, education, infrastructure and other social indicators. Ability to create and maintain the knowledge infrastructure, develop knowledge workers and enhance their productivity through creation, growth and exploitation of new knowledge will be the key factors in deciding the prosperity of this knowledge society. Whether a nation has arrived at a stage of knowledge society is judged by the way the country effectively deals with knowledge creation and knowledge deployment in all sectors like agriculture and food processing, IT, industries, healthcare and education.*
>
> ***(Abdul Kalam, 2003, para 7)***

This view of the knowledge society presents new opportunities for societies and organizations to leverage their intellectual capital by creating an environment of knowledge creation, dissemination, and utilization. An organization in the knowledge age is one that learns, remembers, and acts based on the best available information, knowledge, and know-how. The ability to manage knowledge is becoming increasingly more crucial in today's knowledge economy. The creation and diffusion of knowledge have become ever more important factors in competitiveness. In the age of globalization and increased worldwide competition, every organization is looking for new ways to gain competitive advantage over its rivals. Today, KM is being recognized worldwide as the most useful solution for the survival and success of an organization.

WHAT IS KNOWLEDGE?

In order to define KM, it is important first to understand the concept of knowledge and its value for organizations.

Any discussion on KM needs an understanding of the concept of knowledge and its relationships to information and data. Several authors have explained the similarities and differences between these concepts. Data, information, knowledge, and wisdom are viewed by information technology (IT) practitioners as part of a continuum, one leading to another, each the result of actions on the preceding, with no clear boundaries between them. However, there seems to be a kind of knowledge hierarchy in a continuum proceeding from data (facts and figures) to information (data with context) to knowledge (information with meaning) to wisdom or intelligence (knowledge with insight). Data represents information in its elementary and crude form; information represents data endowed with meaning; knowledge represents information with experience, insight, and expertise (Zins, 2007); and wisdom represents the ability to use knowledge and experience to make good judgments.

The Merriam-Webster Online Dictionary and Thesaurus (2008) includes the following definitions:

- data is factual information (measurements or statistics) used as a basis for reasoning, discussion, or calculation;
- information is the communication or reception of knowledge or intelligence;
- knowledge is the condition of knowing something gained through experience or the circumstance or condition of apprehending truth or fact through reasoning; and
- wisdom is knowledge of what is proper or reasonable—good sense or judgment.

Fleming (1996) explains the concept of data, information, knowledge, and wisdom, and concludes the following:

- Data comprises facts or observations, which are unorganized and unprocessed and have no meaning or value unless they are converted into information by analysis (numbers, symbols, figures).

- Information relates to description, definition, or perspective (what, who, when, where). Knowledge comprises strategy, practice, method, or approach (how).
- Wisdom embodies principle, insight, moral, or archetype (why).

According to Davenport and Prusak (1998):

> *[Data are] objective facts about events with no inherent meaning.*

Davis and Olson (1985) define information as:

> *[...] data that has been processed into a form that is meaningful to recipient and is of real or perceived value in the current or the prospective action or decision of recipient (p. 200).*

According to Davenport and Prusak (1998):

> *Knowledge is a fluid mix of framed experience, values, contextual information, expert insight, and grounded intuition that provides an environment and framework for evaluating and incorporating new experiences and information. It originates and is applied in the mind of the knowers. In organizations it often becomes embedded not only in documents or repositories, but also in organizational routines, practices and norms (p. 5).*

From the definitions above, it may be said that knowledge is the highest order manifestation of information and includes both data and information. The hierarchal relationships of data, information, knowledge, and wisdom are based on the increasing levels of added value that each provides as we go from data to information to knowledge to wisdom. Each entity (from data to wisdom) represents an increasing level of added value, complexity, abstractness, integration context, usefulness, meaningfulness, and interpretability (Alavi and Leidner, 2001; Kebede, 2010). Data is the rawest form of facts without any meaning. Information is organized, analyzed, and meaningful within particular connections or contexts. When information is combined with experience, context, interpretation, and reflection, it becomes knowledge. Thus knowledge is the combinations of collected information, personal experiences, insights, expertise, and logical reasoning in an actionable context.

Data, Information, and Knowledge: Conceptual Difference

The concept of knowledge and information is often used interchangeably. Therefore, in order to understand the concept of knowledge, it is important to recognize how knowledge is different from data and information. The difference between data, information, and knowledge is illustrated in Table 1.1.

Table 1.1 Conceptual difference between data, information, and knowledge

Data	• Scattered, unrelated facts, writings, numbers, or symbols • Usually data is static in nature • It can represent a set of discrete facts about events • Data is a prerequisite to information • Data alone is not significant, as is does not relate to other data • An organization sometimes has to decide on the nature and volume of data that is required to create the necessary information
Information	• Selected, organized, and analyzed data • When data is organized in a logical, cohesive format for a specific purpose, it becomes information • Information is considered as facts and data organized to characterize a particular situation • When data is made meaningful by being put into a context it becomes information • Information is data transformed by the value-adding processes of contextualization, categorization, calculation, correction, and condensation (Davenport and Prusak, 1998)
Knowledge	• Information combined with the user's ability and experience that is used to solve a problem or to create new knowledge • Human understanding of a subject matter that has been acquired through proper study and experience • Knowledge is usually based on learning, thinking, and proper understanding of the problem area • Knowledge is viewed as an understanding of information based on its perceived importance and relevance to a problem area • Knowledge is derived from information in the same way as information is derived from data • Knowledge is also considered as the integration of human perspective that helps to draw meaningful conclusions • Knowledge is the application of information and mind. Knowledge is more complex than data or information; it is subjective, often based on experience, and highly contextual

Modified from Awad, E.M., Ghaziri, H.M., 2004. Knowledge Management. Pearson Education International, Upper Saddle River, NJ.

Everything that exists in the "real world" is either data or information, and everything that is embodied within a person is knowledge. The process of informing amounts to converting data into knowledge. Knowledge that originates from and becomes embodied in the mind of the knower (Rowley, 2007) is called personal (tacit) knowledge, which remains confined to the knower. When personal knowledge is expressed in lectures or in recorded form, it becomes information (explicit or public knowledge). Nonaka and Takeuchi (1995) explained the difference between information and knowledge as follows:

> *Information is a flow of messages, while knowledge is created by that very flow of information anchored in the beliefs and commitments of its holder (p. 58).*

Knowledge is valued over information because it is closer to action, while information by itself does not make any decisions; it is the transfer of information into people's knowledge base that leads to decision-making and thereby to action. Knowledge gives certainty to acts and also helps people to take informed decisions (Parboteeah et al., 2009). Information is tangible in nature and easily available to anyone who wants to seek it out, whereas knowledge is intangible in nature and not accessible to everyone as it resides in the minds of people. Data or information has a chance to be lost, as they are tangible in nature, whereas knowledge, which exists only within one who knows, cannot be lost suddenly. Blair (2002) describes it as:

> *[the] essential difference between data, information and knowledge [is] that when we lose data or information, we often lose something that we can physically possess, something tangible. But when we lose knowledge, what we lose is an ability to do something (p. 1020).*

Organizational Knowledge

Knowledge is one of the most important assets of an organization. In an age of globalization and increased worldwide competition, many organizations are looking for new ways to gain competitive advantage. For this, organizations are trying to use a variety of organizational resources. Today, knowledge, as an intangible asset, has taken precedence over traditional organizational resources such as capital and labor.

Scholars have classified knowledge into different categories. However, Janiffer Rowley classified knowledge into two broad categories: individual knowledge and organizational knowledge. Individual knowledge resides in an individual mind, whereas organizational knowledge is formed through interactions between technologies, techniques, and people (Rowley, 2003).

According to Myers (1996), "organizational knowledge is processed information embedded in routines and processes that enable action. It is also knowledge captured by the organization's system, processes, products, rules, and culture." Thus organizational knowledge, in an organization, often becomes embedded not only in the minds of workers, documents or repositories, but also in routines, processes, practices, and norms.

A widely accepted classification of organizational knowledge was proposed by Polanyi in 1966, which was later adopted and elaborated by Nonaka (1991), Nonaka and Takeuchi (1995), and Nonaka and Konno (1998). They classified knowledge in an organization into "explicit knowledge, which can be documented, and implicit or tacit knowledge, which resides in the minds, cultures and the experiences within the organization" (Rowley, 2003, p. 434). Explicit knowledge is defined as formal and systematic knowledge; codified in the product specification or scientific formula or a computer program; and stored in textbooks, journal articles, business records, documents, databases, web pages, intranets, e-mails, etc. It can easily be captured in repositories, systems, or operating technologies, and also made available to all the members of the organization with high quality, reliable, and fast information-retrieval systems (Ralph and Tijerino, 2009). Tacit knowledge, on the other hand, is defined as informal knowledge; difficult to capture and codify; and never easy to communicate to and share with others. Davenport and Prusak (1998) assert that tacit knowledge represents great value to an organization, because it is embedded in activities such as problem-solving and creativity, but is more difficult to capture, articulate, and diffuse.

Chun Wei Choo classified organizational knowledge into three categories: explicit knowledge, tacit knowledge, and cultural knowledge. An organization's cultural knowledge, according to Choo (2000), consists of the beliefs that an organization holds to be true based on experience, observation, and reflection about itself and its environment. The cultural knowledge in an organization includes shared beliefs about the nature of its main business, core capabilities, markets, competitors, etc. Like tacit knowledge, cultural knowledge is also not written down, but it may be conveyed in stories, histories, and reward or evaluation systems. It remains with the organization even after its inventors or authors leave the organization.

Organizational knowledge, according to Brooking (1996), includes: (1) the collective sum of human-centered assets, (2) intellectual property assets, (3) infrastructure assets, and (4) market assets.

The Delphi Group Inc. (2000) identified four components of organizational knowledge: (1) employee's brain, (2) paper documentation, (3) electronic documentation, and (4) electronic knowledge, with the share of each type of knowledge in the organization as shown in Fig. 1.1.

Uriarte (2008) divided organizational knowledge into two categories: (1) core knowledge and (2) enabling knowledge. Knowledge that is critical to the attainment of the organization's goal and the fulfillment of its

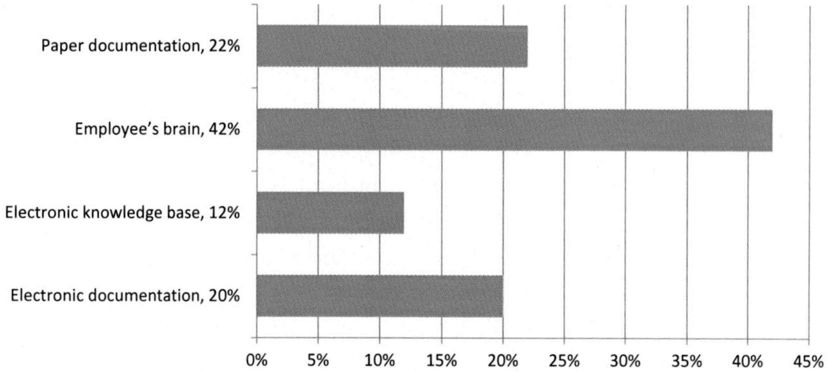

Fig. 1.1 Primary repository of an organization's knowledge. *(Source: From The Delphi Group Inc., 2000. Centering the Business Desktop. The Delphi Group, Boston, MA.).*

strategy is called "core knowledge," whereas knowledge that can maintain the effectiveness of the organization is known as "enabling knowledge." In an organization, certain areas of knowledge are more important than others. Because core knowledge is critical to the organization, the management of core knowledge must be kept within the organization. It must be developed and nurtured inside the organization. However, core knowledge alone cannot fully support an organization and make it competitive. When enabling knowledge is combined with core knowledge, it leads to the development of new products, processes, and services. By its very nature, the management of enabling knowledge can be outsourced.

KNOWLEDGE CREATION AND CONVERSION PROCESS

Despite the differences between tacit and explicit knowledge, Nonaka and Takeuchi (1995) believe that these two types of knowledge complement each other and have common relationships and engagements. Nevertheless, tacit knowledge can sometimes be communicated through a shared understanding between individuals. In other cases, tacit knowledge must be converted into explicit knowledge before it can be shared. Nonaka and Takeuchi (1995) proposed a set of four core processes, namely socialization, externalization, combination, and internalization, which has become the cornerstone of knowledge creation and transfer theory.

Socialization is a process of sharing tacit knowledge between individuals through apprenticeship, mentoring, or collegiate relations. In socialization, the tacit knowledge of one person is shared and transmitted to another person and it becomes part of the other person's tacit knowledge.

Externalization is the process of expressing tacit knowledge in an explicit form. Through externalization, an organization extends its knowledge base by codifying the experiences, insights, or judgments of its employees into a form which can be reused by others in the organization.

Combination is a process of converting explicit knowledge into more complex sets of explicit knowledge through systematization, standardization, communication, and dissemination.

Internalization is a process of broadening and extending the tacit knowledge base by internalizing new or shared explicit knowledge. Explicit knowledge that is available as text, sound, or video facilitates the internalization process. The use of operating manuals for various machines or equipment is a quintessential example of explicit knowledge that is used for internalization.

The interplay of these four knowledge processes constitutes the essence of converting tacit knowledge to explicit knowledge and vice versa.

KNOWLEDGE MANAGEMENT

KM has become increasingly important in recent years. The concept of KM emerged during the mid-1990s and received considerable attention from scholars and practitioners in several fields. The term "knowledge management" was first used by Carl Wiig in 1986 at a Swiss conference sponsored by the United Nations—International Labor Organization. However, today KM is being practiced in a number of fields associated with information systems, business and management, library and information science (LIS), computer science, communications, etc. Wen (2005) traces its emergence first in the business sector, then in higher education, and now in library management.

Since the concept of KM is used in many disciplines, it has come to mean different things to different people, and there is no single agreed on definition of KM. This is likely because of the multidisciplinary nature of KM, drawn from various disciplines and technologies including, but not limited to, artificial intelligence, LIS, technical writing, document management, relational and object databases, simulation and organizational science. Moreover, there is a tendency among different professions interested in KM to present and interpret what constitutes KM from their own perspective. Consequently, developments in KM are influenced by the different professions interested in knowledge. This has resulted in, among other things, lack of universal consensus on some of the key issues of KM, including conceptualizations, processes, systems, and enablers.

Definitions From the Literature

The phrase "knowledge management" "is used to describe the process of locating, organizing, transferring, and using information" (Duffy, 2000, p. 10). However, there are numerous definitions of KM, which are characterized by many different concepts, perspectives, and approaches. Some definitions emphasize the process of KM. Others focus on the objective of KM. Some definitions of KM that certainly help to understand the notion of KM in a better way are given below.

According to Wiig (1994):

> *KM is a conceptual framework that encompasses all activities and perspectives required to make the organization intelligent-acting on a sustained basis. KM includes activities gaining overview of, dealing with, and benefiting from the areas that require management attention by identifying salient alternatives, suggesting methods for dealing with them, and conducting activities to achieve desired results.*

According to Brooking (1997), KM is:

> *an activity, which is concerned with strategy and tactics to manage human center asset (p. 364).*

According to Hibbard (1997):

> *KM is the process of capturing a company's collective expertise wherever it resides in databases, on paper or in people's heads, and distributing it to wherever it can help produce the biggest payoff.*

According to Rastogi (2000):

> *KM is a systematic and integrative process of coordinating organization-wide activities of acquiring, creating, storing, sharing, diffusing, developing and deploying knowledge by individuals and groups in pursuit of major organizational goals.*

According to Du Plessis (2006) KM is a:

> *planned and structured approach to manage the creation, sharing, harvesting and leveraging of knowledge as an organizational asset, to enhance an organization's ability, speed and effectiveness in delivering products or services for the benefit of clients, in line with its business strategy (p. 1).*

According to Sousa and Hendriks (2006):

> *KM addresses policies, strategies and techniques aimed at supporting an organization's competitiveness by optimizing the conditions needed for efficiency improvement and collaboration among employees.*

According to Skyrme (2011):

> *Knowledge Management is the explicit and systematic management of vital knowledge—and its associated processes of creation, organisation, diffusion, use and exploitation—in pursuit of business objectives.*

Although there are various beliefs and methodologies that are applicable to KM, certain themes exist that are common in the definitions of KM. These themes are:

(a) management of information—explicit/recorded knowledge
(b) management of processes—embedded knowledge
(c) management of people—tacit knowledge
(d) management of innovation—knowledge conversion
(e) management of assets—intellectual capital.

Ruggles and Holtshouse (1999) identified the following key attributes of KM:

(a) generating new knowledge;
(b) accessing valuable knowledge from outside sources;
(c) using accessible knowledge in decision making;
(d) embedding knowledge in processes, products, and/or services;
(e) representing knowledge in documents, databases, and software;
(f) facilitating knowledge growth through culture and incentives;
(g) transferring existing knowledge into other parts of the organization;
(h) measuring the value of knowledge assets and/or impact of KM (p. 13).

A careful review of the definitions of KM shows a changing view of its focus, resulting in different levels of technological support. However, a common theme is the emphasis on managing and leveraging organizational knowledge. Initially the focus of KM was on empowering knowledge workers, which was later shifted towards the use of specific processes and activities with the support of IT-based systems and a change in organizational culture.

In its early conceptualization stage, the focus of KM was on empowering knowledge workers and providing support to organizations starting to adopt its methodology. As KM gained popularity, this focus shifted towards a practical approach—finding better ways to manage organizational knowledge. Therefore definitions of KM during the 1990s include lists of specific manageable activities, such as knowledge creation, identification, codification, sharing, reuse, and application facilitated by IT-based systems. Most of the KM research during this time therefore focused on specific IT solutions to support KM activities: knowledge creation, codification, transfer, and application. Examples of specific IT-based KM systems include knowledge discovery and mapping tools, knowledge repositories, e-learning suites, meta-search systems, enterprise knowledge portals, and collaboration tools.

In recent years, there has been a shift towards a knowledge-based view of an organization. This view puts knowledge at the center of the organization, and stresses that intellectual capital (tacit knowledge) is the organization's key asset. Acquiring, integrating, and leveraging an individual employee's knowledge has become an important KM activity. Thus, today, the focus of KM research is on managing knowledge as an organizational resource together with other resources, including IT-based systems, learning systems, and human resource. In this perspective, IT plays a revised role in supporting KM. Now IT-based systems such as intranets, web portals, groupware, video-conferencing, wikis, and blogs are often used to facilitate the sharing of knowledge among employees in an organization because of their capabilities in extending the reach as well as enhancing the speed of knowledge transfer. In addition to the role of IT as facilitator, the focus of KM research today is on people and organizational culture that values, contributes, and supports knowledge sharing and development, which includes continuous learning, knowledge exchange, and communication. The creation of a favorable environment for formal or informal communication, collaboration, knowledge sharing and transfer has become an essential strategy of KM implementation.

Now, KM cannot be seen as a stand-alone application but should be integrated with all aspects of business. There is a growing realization that technological and social processes interact in complementarities to shape KM efforts.

Different Perspectives on KM

KM is concerned with the management of information, knowledge, processes, systems, and enablers. Management of knowledge includes recorded (explicit) knowledge, personal (tacit) knowledge, and cultural knowledge. Management of processes includes capturing, storing, and sharing knowledge. Management of systems includes knowledge repositories or databases, e-learning tools, etc. Management of enablers (or KM enablers) includes organizational culture, technology infrastructure, etc. Thus there are several different perspectives of KM. Wiig (1993) considers KM in organizations from three perspectives, each with different horizons and purposes:

Business perspective—This focuses on why, where, and to what extent the organization must invest in or exploit knowledge. Strategies, products and services, alliances, acquisitions, or divestments should be considered from knowledge-related points of view.

Management perspective—This is associated with something that has connotations of systemizing, providing structure, and contributing an overall sense of coherence to an organization to achieve the desired business strategies and objectives.

Hands-on perspective—This is concerned with applying expertise to conduct explicit knowledge-related work and tasks.

Uriarte (2008) identified two major perspectives of KM, namely information management (IM) and people management. Viewed from this perspective, KM is about information on one hand, and people on the other. This IM perspective focuses on the management of knowledge related to objects that are identified and handled by information systems, whereas the people management perspective focuses on the management of tacit knowledge that resides inside the heads of people.

Beckman (1999) described six perspectives of KM:

Conceptual perspective—This deals with defining and describing the foundations and frameworks for managing different types of organizational knowledge.

Process perspective—This is concerned with the specific steps involved in generating, creating, or acquiring knowledge; codifying and organizing knowledge to facilitate easy access; making knowledge available to others through communication or publications; facilitating access to, and retrieval of, knowledge; and using and applying knowledge to solve problems, support decisions, improve performance, coach, and analyze situations and processes to support business activities.

Technological perspective—This perspective of KM concerns the use of IT for implementing a KM program in the organization. It includes development of IT infrastructure, representation of knowledge objects within the system, creation of knowledge repositories and databases, combining these repositories into integrated performance support systems, and knowledge transformation (using techniques like data mining, data warehousing, etc.). Technologies such as relational database management systems, document management systems, the Internet, intranets, search engines, workflow tools, performance support systems, decision support systems, data mining, data warehousing, e-mail, video-conferencing, bulletin boards, news groups, and discussion boards can play a pivotal role in facilitating the management of knowledge.

Organizational perspective—This perspectives of KM is concerned with the internal organization that is created for superheating, evangelizing, and implementing KM.

Strategic management perspective—The strategic management perspectives deals with measurement and evaluation of the benefits of implementing a KM program, and the resulting rewards/incentives/motivational systems. This perspective relates KM implementation explicitly to business goals, sets assessment criteria, and therefore monitors the KM programs. These perspectives also clarify the personal advantages that a KM program can offer to people who participate.

Implementation perspective—This perspective is focused on specific issues encountered in the implementation process: development of IT infrastructure, identification of knowledge assets and core competencies of employees, identification of critical success factors for implementing KM, understanding the prerequisites and challenges, and integration of KM business and corporate strategies.

OBJECTIVE OF KM

Although there is a lack of consensus on a definition of KM, there is widespread agreement as to the goals of KM. The objective of KM is to continuously improve an organization's performance through the improvement and sharing of organizational knowledge throughout the organization (ie, the aim is to improve the organization's ability to execute its core processes more efficiently and ensure that the organization has the right knowledge at the right time and place). Based on a study of 31 KM projects in 24 different organizations, Davenport et al. (1998) identified four business objectives of KM systems in practice as:

(a) creating a knowledge repository
(b) improving knowledge assets
(c) enhancing the knowledge environment
(d) managing knowledge as an asset.

The goal of creating knowledge repositories is to store knowledge, including that embedded in memos, reports, articles, and presentations, so it can be easily retrieved. When access is provided to the stored knowledge and its transfer is facilitated among individuals, knowledge access is improved. Enhancing the knowledge environment involves the creation of an environment which is more conducive to knowledge creation, transfer, and use. When knowledge is managed like any asset on the organizational balance sheet, it is considered as an asset. Some organizations incorporate their intellectual capital on the balance sheet; others leverage their knowledge assets to generate new income from or to reduce costs with their patent base.

Dalkir (2005) identified five objectives of knowledge:

(a) Facilitating a smooth transition from those retiring to their successors who are recruited to fill their positions.
(b) Minimizing loss of corporate memory due to attrition and retirement.
(c) Avoiding reinventing the wheel.
(d) Identifying critical resources and critical areas of knowledge so that the corporation "knows what it knows and does it well—and why."
(e) Building up a toolkit of methods that can be used with individuals, with groups, and with the organization to stem the potential loss of intellectual capital.

Organizations mostly implement KM systems for different reasons. Havens and Knapp (1999) proposed that organizations implement KM systems for one of the following reasons:

(a) solving problems and seizing opportunities;
(b) increasing responsiveness and innovation;
(c) saving costs;
(d) supporting decision-making;
(e) facilitating collaboration;
(f) increasing employees' productivity; or
(g) reducing the negative impact associated with knowledge attrition, ie, knowledge loss when employees leave the job.

One of the important objectives of KM is to make appropriate knowledge available from providers to receivers when and where needed. Knowledge providers and receivers may be internal or external to an organization. The providers may be individuals or other forms of sources of knowledge, eg, store houses or knowledge repositories. Stewart and Kaufman (1995) believe that the purpose of KM is to turn an organization to learning and sharing by linking people together and creating a flow between the buckets of information generated by people in different units of finance, operations, competitive intelligence, etc. However, Gandhi (2004) pointed out that organizations engage in KM to achieve one or more of the following tasks:

(a) enhancing collaboration;
(b) improving productivity;
(c) enabling and encouraging innovation;
(d) coping with information overload and delivering only the essentials;
(e) facilitating the flow of appropriate knowledge from providers to receivers without the constraints of time and space;
(f) facilitating information sharing among employees and preventing them from having to reinvent the wheel every time;

(g) capturing and recording the knowledge of employees before they leave the company, ensuring that valuable expertise does not leave when an employee leaves;

(h) increasing an organization's awareness of the gaps in its knowledge, and helping companies stay competitive by increasing their awareness of strategies, products, and best practices of their competitors; and

(i) improving customer service.

BENEFITS OF KM FOR INDIVIDUALS, COMMUNITIES, AND ORGANIZATIONS

KM allows employees to save time when searching for information and expertise, thereby making highly paid professionals concentrate on their areas of expertise. In addition, effective KM processes make it possible for employees to expand the resources immediately available to them to make more intelligent decisions, thus leading to improved performance and employability. Liebowitz (2011) explains the benefits of KM for individual employees, communities of practice, and organization.

For individual employees, KM:

- helps people do their jobs and save time through better decision-making and problem-solving
- builds a sense of community bonding within the organization
- helps people to keep up to date
- provides challenges and opportunities to contribute.

For the community of practice, KM:

- develops professional skills
- promotes peer-to-peer mentoring
- facilitates more effective networking and collaboration
- develops a professional code of ethics that members can adhere to
- develops a common language.

For the organization, KM:

- helps drive strategy
- solves problems quickly
- diffuses best practices
- improves knowledge embedded in products and services
- cross-fertilizes ideas and increases opportunities for innovation
- enables organizations to better stay ahead of the competition
- builds organizational memory.

CHALLENGES IN MANAGING KNOWLEDGE

A great deal of the knowledge in an organization is created and stored at an individual level. It is in the heads of people and groups of people who work in the organization—the employees, managers, and top executives. Unfortunately, very few organizations are able to harness this asset in a meaningful way. Even fewer are organizations that are able to optimize the use of this important asset.

Proper utilization of knowledge in an organization reduces duplication, improves productivity, and cuts cost (Clarke, 2004). On the other hand, lack of transfer leads to information overload and confusion, as well as wastage of manpower. The challenge of managing explicit knowledge is one of handling the sheer volume of information that is available. On the other hand, while tacit knowledge potentially represents great value to the organization, it is by its very nature far more difficult to capture and diffuse. But to make KM efforts successful, it is essential to capture and utilize both tacit and explicit knowledge. While much of the organizational knowledge is available in explicit form, a significant portion of core and enabling knowledge remains tacit. The willingness to share this tacit knowledge is influenced to a large extent by the managerial approaches used to identify, capture, and integrate that knowledge. These approaches include award and punishment systems and organizational procedures for assessment of individual performance. The effective implementation of these approaches can contribute to wider sharing of tacit knowledge within the organization. Organizations contain vast reservoirs of untapped core knowledge and enabling expertise. The problem is that top management usually does not know who has what information. Few top executives are aware of where core and enabling knowledge reside and how to enable this knowledge to flow throughout the organization.

New knowledge always begins with an individual. When an individual's personal knowledge is transformed into organizational knowledge it becomes valuable to the whole organization, and the process of transforming an individual's knowledge into shared or organizational knowledge is the major challenge. But at a practical level the challenges are very different. Explicit knowledge can be adequately transferred with the help of electronic tools. For tacit knowledge, the challenge is to formulate the knowledge into a communicable form. Face-to-face interaction and use of practices such as apprenticeships, mentoring, community of practice, and network analysis are some important methods of communicating tacit knowledge throughout the organization. KM addresses these problems directly and pointedly.

KM, ACADEMIA, AND LIBRARIANSHIP

KM, as a business concept, has received considerable attention from many scholars and practitioners. KM has already been practiced in the business, government, financial, and health care information sectors (Blair, 2002; Chua, 2009). Recently, academic institutions have also developed an interest in KM. The first significant article on KM in higher education was published in the open access journal *Ariadne* by Sheila Corrall in 1999. This article raised many aspects of KM as to how it could be applied to higher educational institutions.

Profound changes in competition forced academic institutions to think like businesses. They are being forced to operate in much more business-like competitive environments, characterized by tighter education funding, increased interest in information-sharing practices, greater accountability, and increased information needs of teachers, faculty, staff, and administrators (Petrides and Nodine, 2003). Like business organizations, academic institutions need better access to the best internal and/or external information and knowledge for effective decision-making and the ability to innovate and adapt (Martin, 2000). The academic community believes that by leveraging knowledge, an academic institution can sustain its long-term competitive advantages.

Academic institutions, particularly universities, have significant opportunities to apply KM practice to support every part of their mission. Kidwell et al. (2000) identified five key areas in universities where KM may be applied. These areas are research, curriculum development, administrative services, alumni services, and strategic planning. Furthermore they argued that, if applied effectively, it can lead to better decision-making capabilities, reduced product development cycle times (eg, curriculum development and research), improved academic and administrative services, and reduced costs.

Librarianship often used to be described as the organization of recorded knowledge. In this sense, KM has a long history in library practice because librarians have been managing codified or recorded knowledge for a long time. Lastres (2011) described the involvement of librarians in managing knowledge as:

> *Librarians have served as knowledge managers since the earliest days of libraries by maintaining the scrolls at the library of Alexandria and creating the catalogue for the House of Wisdom (a Ninth Century Islamic Library).*

In recent decades, a body of professional literature has emerged that explicitly addresses KM from the perspective of LIS. The LIS community has welcomed the challenges and opportunities offered by KM; for more than a decade most of the leading figures in LIS education have contributed to the debate on these issues (Broadbent, 1997; Corrall, 1998; Abell and Oxbrow, 2001; Koenig and Srikantaiah, 2002).

There is a key assumption reflected within the LIS literature that, since the organization of knowledge has always been the strongest suite of librarians, they must not only engage in, but also actively spearhead KM initiatives (Gandhi, 2004). However, Jantz (2001) considers KM primarily a business activity where librarians have no choice to take on a new title such as "knowledge manager." Broadbent (1998) also stated that:

> *KM is not about managing or organizing books or journals, searching the Internet for clients or arranging for the circulation materials, rather she considered these activities as parts of KM spectrum and processes in some way.*

Now the question arises: what does KM mean to libraries and LIS professionals? According to Jantz:

> *KM within libraries involves organizing and providing access to intangible resources that help librarians and administrators carry out their tasks more effectively and efficiently.*
>
> ***(Jantz, 2001, p. 34.)***

So librarians need active management of their organization's knowledge assets rather than passively responding to the requests of users. But where do libraries fit into this highly business-intensive field? It is not clear how either the work experience or educational background of most LIS professionals would equip them to operate within this highly business-intensive field. KM is a wide and multidisciplinary field that incorporates various aspects of the management of key organizational resources. There is an acknowledgment within the LIS literature that, although LIS professionals with potential IM competencies are likely to be significant players in KM, they need to develop additional skills and overcome a number of obstacles if they want to extend their roles into the KM domain. In order to equip LIS professionals to be ready for a range of roles across the KM spectrum, any existing and potential gaps between their current and future needs for education must also be addressed. Some of these issues will be addressed in this book.

KM AND ACADEMIC LIBRARIES

The ultimate aim of KM is to increase the effectiveness and the sustainable growth of an organization. Although KM was originally developed for profit organizations, its practice has spread to the nonprofit sectors, including libraries, as there are general benefits that can be derived from KM in each kind of organization. The goal of KM is to make full use of the knowledge existing in an organization to increase the productivity and/or operational efficiency to gain a competitive edge. But what is the driving force for academic libraries to adopt KM?

The main functions of an academic institution are education and research. To achieve these functions there is a need to use all of their knowledge and information accurately, precisely, and systematically. Academic libraries, now known as information centers, have been established in support of the mission of their parent institutions to generate knowledge, and to equip people with knowledge in order to serve society and advance the well-being of mankind. In the digital age, academic libraries face challenges both from within (academia) and outside (the business sector). To prove their relevance and value, academic libraries must strive to provide the right amount of information to the right clientele with appropriate financial and human resources to improve organizational performance.

Due to reduced budgets and increasing demand from library users, librarians have been forced to think about implementing KM. However, adoption of KM in libraries is mainly driven by its mission rather than by the competition from Internet-based sources and services (Wen, 2005). Providing the right amount of information from a huge volume of information at the right time is more critical than ever to the fulfillment of the mission of academic libraries and their parent institutions (Ghosh and Jambekar, 2003). KM, therefore, is the only alternative for academic libraries to operate more efficiently with reduced financial and/or human resources to achieve their aims. KM is a tool that can help in this regard and offers libraries the opportunity to improve effectiveness, both for themselves and their parent institutions (Townley, 2001).

The role of KM in academic libraries today has become more vital, along with the development of the knowledge economy. The roles of librarians in libraries are described largely in "traditional" terms, such as library management; general library work; information or user services; research; information literacy instruction; records management; data and document control management; website, intranet, and content management; and KM initiatives. However, the main roles and functions of librarians, as identified by Ferguson et al. (2008), in today's knowledge environment include the following:

- fostering knowledge-sharing culture and practices, including use of communities of practice;
- IM, including content management, information and records management, information retrieval, analysis and critique of information sources, and information auditing;
- education and training;
- information systems and technology management, including information systems support, provision of infrastructure, harnessing of new technologies to enable knowledge sharing, and intranet and website management;
- provision of information services, including the collection, organization, analysis, and dissemination of business information;
- management of an organization's "intellectual capital";
- research support, including the provision of a research evidence base for decision-making.

Academic librarians can benefit their institutions, their libraries, and themselves by undertaking a campus-wide role in managing organizational knowledge. They can use KM as a way to expand the library's role in areas such as administration or support services, where libraries have had little impact in the past. Moreover, they can develop cross-functional teams with units in areas such as computing, instructional technology, institutional planning, and personnel to create collaborative organizations that have major institutional missions and responsibilities (Townley, 2001). Academic libraries are also considered as learning organizations; if KM occurs within libraries, this can be of great value for creating and maintaining a learning culture. KM also benefits internal communication; when employees share their expertise with each other, they simultaneously learn from each other to fulfill the needs of their users.

KM provides new opportunities for academic librarians to expand existing roles and utilize the skills they have acquired to meet corporate objectives (Hayes, 2004). Shanhong (2000) suggests that the objective of KM in libraries is to promote knowledge innovation, closer relationships in and between libraries, and between a library and its users, to strengthen knowledge internetworking and to quicken knowledge flow. KM can help employees to produce outputs that tap into their skills, talents, thoughts, and ideas, so that decision-making is improved concerning strategic issues, competitors, customers, distribution channels, products, and services. Libraries need to adopt KM for one or more of the following reasons:

- improving the future prospects of the library;
- improving library operation and services;
- better decision-making capabilities;
- reducing processing time by avoiding duplication of work;
- enhancing collaboration within different units of the library;
- enabling and encouraging innovation;
- facilitating information sharing among employees and preventing them from having to reinvent the wheel every time;
- capturing and recording the knowledge of employees before they leave the library, ensuring that valuable expertise does not leave when an employee leaves;
- increasing an organization's awareness of the gaps in its knowledge;
- helping libraries to survive by increasing their awareness of strategies, information products and services, and best practices of their competitors; and
- improving user services.

Over the last few years, several IT-based systems, such as intranets, Internet, web portals, blogs, wikis, social media, groupware, and knowledge directories, have evolved. They are being used to support the processes of knowledge capture, codification, and sharing in all types of organizations. How can these systems help in the management of knowledge in libraries? These issues will be discussed in the remaining chapters of this book.

SUMMARY

Although knowledge has always been the driving force of change in human societies, today an increasing fraction of economic output and innovation is knowledge-intensive, and involves proportionately more use of knowledge than tangible resources, such as land or machines and capital. Knowledge is more complex than data or information, as it is subjective, often based on experience, and highly contextual. The concept of KM is not completely new, as it has been practiced for a long time in a wide variety of settings. Despite the lack of a commonly accepted definition of KM, most professionals and practitioners believe that KM treats both tacit and explicit knowledge with the objective of adding value to the organization. However, before initiating KM each organization needs to define it in terms of its own business objectives. KM is all about applying knowledge in new, previously unencumbered, or novel situations. KM has its roots in a variety of different disciplines, including librarianship. The goal of KM is to make full use of the knowledge existing in an organization to increase productivity and/or operational efficiency to build a competitive edge. Application of KM in libraries is a useful solution for promoting knowledge innovation, making relationships in and between libraries, and between a library and its users, strengthening knowledge internetworking and expediting knowledge flow. KM provides an opportunity for librarians to expand the library's role to areas such as administration or support services, where they have had little impact in the past.

REFERENCES

Abdul Kalam, A.P.J., 2003. Vision for global space community: prosperous, happy and secure planet earth. In: Speech Delivered at 90th Indian Science Congress, Jan. 4, 2003, Bangalore. Available at: http://neo.jpl.nasa.gov/1950da/1950DA_Kalam_90th_Indian_Congress.pdf (accessed 13.03.15).

Abell, A., Oxbrow, N., 2001. Competing with Knowledge: The Information Professionals in the Knowledge Management Age. Library Association Publishing, London.

Alavi, M., Leidner, D., 2001. Knowledge management and knowledge management systems: conceptual foundations and research issues. MIS Q. 25 (1), 107–136.

Beckman, T.J., 1999. The current state of knowledge management. In: Liebowitz, J. (Ed.), Knowledge Management Handbook. CRC Press, New York, NY.

Bedford, D.A.D., Donley, J.K., Lensenmayer, N., 2015. The role of librarians in a knowledge society: valuing our intellectual capital assets. In: Woodsworth, A., David Penniman, W. (Eds.), Current Issues in Libraries, Information Science and Related Fields. Advances in Librarianship, vol. 39. Emerald Group Publishing Limited, Bingley, pp. 81–113. http://dx.doi.org/10.1108/S0065-283020150000039011. Published online: 15.06.15 (accessed 15.12.15).

Blair, D.C., 2002. Knowledge management: hype, hope, or help? J. Am. Soc. Inf. Sci. Technol. 50 (12), 1019–1028.

Broadbent, M., 1997. The emerging phenomenon of knowledge management. Aust. Libr. J. 46 (1), 6–24.

Broadbent, M., 1998. The phenomenon of knowledge management: what does it mean to the information profession? Inf. Outlook 2 (5), 23–34.

Brooking, A., 1996. Introduction to Intellectual Capital. The Knowledge Broker, Cambridge.

Brooking, A., 1997. The management of intellectual capital. Long Range Plan. 30 (3), 364–365.

Choo, C.W., 2000. Working with knowledge: how information professionals help organizations manage what they know. Libr. Manag. 21 (8/9), 395–403.

Chua, A.Y.K., 2009. The dark side of knowledge management initiatives. J. Knowl. Manag. 13 (4), 32–40.

Clarke, R., 2004. KM in the main library of the University of West Indies, Trinidad. Inf. Dev. 20 (1), 30–35.

Corrall, S., 1998. Knowledge management: are we in the knowledge management business? Ariadne 18. Available at: http://www.ariadne.ac.uk/issue18/knowledge-mgt/ (accessed 13.11.15).

Dalkir, K., 2005. Knowledge Management in Theory and Practice. Elsevier Butterworth-Heinemann, Burlington, MA.

Davenport, T.H., Prusak, L., 1998. Working Knowledge: How Organizations Manage What They Know. Harvard Business School Press, Boston, MA.
Davenport, T.H., DeLong, D.W., Beer, C., 1998. Successful knowledge management project. MIT Sloan Manag. Rev. 39 (2), 43–57.
Davis, G.B., Olson, M.H., 1985. Management Information Systems: Conceptual Foundations, Structure, and Development, second ed. McGraw Hill, New York, NY.
Drucker, P.F., 1993. The Post-Capitalist Society. Butterworth Heinemann, Oxford.
Du Plessis, M., 2006. The Impact of Organizational Culture on Knowledge Management. Chandos Publishing, Oxford.
Duffy, J., 2000. Knowledge management: what every information professional should know. Inf. Manag. J. 34 (3), 10–16.
Ferguson, S., Hider, P., Lloyd, A., 2008. Are librarians the ultimate knowledge managers? A study of knowledge, skills, practice and mindset. Aust. Libr. J. 57 (1), 39–62. http://dx.doi.org/10.1080/00049670.2008.10722440 (accessed 29.06.15).
Fleming, 1996. Copying with a Revolution: Will the Internet Change Learning. Lincoln University, Canterbury.
Gandhi, S., 2004. Knowledge management and reference services. J. Acad. Librariansh. 30 (5), 368–381.
Ghosh, M., Jambekar, A., 2003. Networks, digital libraries and knowledge management: trends and developments. DESIDOC Bull. Inf. Technol. 23 (5), 3–11.
Havens, C., Knapp, E., 1999. Easing into knowledge management. Strateg. Leadersh. 27 (2), 4–10.
Hayes, H., 2004. The role of libraries in the knowledge economy. Serials 17 (3), 231–238.
Hibbard, J., 1997. Knowing what we know. Information Week. October, 46–64.
Jantz, R., 2001. Knowledge management in academic libraries: special tools and processes to support information professionals. Ref. Serv. Rev. 29 (1), 33–39.
Kebede, G., 2010. Knowledge management: an information science perspective. Int. J. Inf. Manag. 30, 416–424.
Kidwell, J.J., Linde, K.M.V., Johnson, S.L., 2000. Applying corporate knowledge management practices in higher education. Educ. Q. 23 (4), 28–33.
Koenig, M.E.D., Srikantaiah, T.K., 2002. Business world discovers assets of librarianship. Inf. Outlook 6 (4), 14–18.
Lastres, S.A., 2011. Knowledge management in changing world. Available at: futureready365.sla.org/02/28/knowledge-management-in-a-changing-world/ (accessed 16.01.15).
Liebowitz, J., 2011. Introduction to knowledge management. In: Dalkir, K., Liebowitz, J. (Eds.), Knowledge Management in Theory and Practice. MIT Press, Cambridge, MA, pp. 1–30. Available at: http://www.jstor.org/stable/j.ctt5hhhx9.4 (accessed 12.01.16).
Martin, B., 2000. Knowledge management within the context of management: an evolving relationship. Singap. Manag. Rev. 22 (2), 17–37.
Merriam-Webster Online Dictionary and Thesaurus, 2008. Available at: http://www.merriam-webster.com/ (accessed 17.06.15).
Myers, S.P., 1996. Knowledge Management and Organizational Design. Butterworth-Heinemann, Boston, MA.
Nonaka, 1991. The knowledge creating company. Harv. Bus. Rev. 6 (8), 96–104.
Nonaka, I., Konno, N., 1998. The concept of "Ba": building a foundation for knowledge creation. Calif. Manag. Rev. 40 (3), 40–54.
Nonaka, I., Takeuchi, H., 1995. The Knowledge-creating Company: How Japanese Companies Create the Dynamics of Innovations. Oxford University Press, New York, NY.
Parboteeah, P., Jackson, T., Ragsdell, G., 2009. Using autopoiesis to redefine data, information and knowledge. Paper Presented at 20th Australasian Conference on Information Systems, Melbourne, 2–4 December.

Petrides, L.A., Nodine, T.R., 2003. Knowledge management in education: defining the landscape. ISKME Monograph. Available at: http://iskme.path.net/kmeducation.pdf (accessed 25.03.15).
Polanyi, M., 1966. The Tacit Dimension. Routledge, London.
Ralph, L.L., Tijerino, C., 2009. Knowledge management and library culture. Coll. Undergrad. Libr. 16 (4), 329–337.
Rastogi, P., 2000. Knowledge management and intellectual capital: the new virtuous reality of competitiveness. Hum. Syst. Manag. 19, 39–49.
Rowley, J., 2003. Knowledge management-the new librarianship? From custodians of history to gatekeepers to the future. Libr. Manag. 24 (8/9), 433–440.
Rowley, J., 2007. The wisdom hierarchy: representations of the DIKW hierarchy. J. Inf. Sci. 33 (2), 163–180.
Ruggles, R., Holtshouse, D., 1999. The Knowledge Advantage. Capstone Publishers, Dover, NH.
Savage, C.M., 1996. Fifth Generation Management: Dynamic Teaming, Virtual Enterprising and Knowledge Networking, second rev. ed. Butterworth-Heinemann, Boston, MA.
Shanhong, T., 2000. Knowledge management in libraries in the twenty-first century. In: Paper Presented at the 66th IFLA Council and General Conference, Jerusalem, August 13–18, 2000.
Skyrme, D., 2011. Definition. Available at: http://www.skyrme.com/kmbasics/definition.htm (accessed 08.12.15).
Sousa, C.A.A., Hendriks, P.H.J., 2006. The diving bell and the butterfly: the need for grounded theory in developing a knowledge-based view of organizations. Organ. Res. Methods 9, 315.
Stewart, T.A., Kaufman, D.C., 1995. Getting real about brainpower. Fortune 132 (11), 201–203.
The Delphi Group Inc., 2000. Centering the Business Desktop. The Delphi Group, Boston, MA.
Townley, C.T., 2001. Knowledge management and academic libraries. Coll. Res. Libr. 62 (1), 44–55.
United Nations Economic Commission for Africa, 2010. Science and Technology and the Knowledge Society in Africa, Addis Ababa, Ethiopia. Available at: http://www.gesci.org/assets/files/Science%20and%20Technology%20and%20the%20Knowledge%20Society(1).pdf (accessed 14.05.15).
Uriarte, F.A., 2008. Introduction to Knowledge Management. ASEAN Foundation, Jakarta.
Wen, S., 2005. Implementing knowledge management in academic libraries: a pragmatic approach. In: 3rd China-US Library Conference, Shanghai, March 22–25, 2005.
Wiig, K.M., 1993. Knowledge Management Foundations. Schema Press, Arlington, TX.
Wiig, K.M., 1994. Knowledge Management: The Central Management Focus for Intelligent-acting Organizations. Schema Press, Arlington, TX.
Zins, C., 2007. Conceptual approaches for defining data, information and knowledge. J. Am. Soc. Inf. Sci. Technol. 58 (4), 479–493.

CHAPTER 2
History and Evolution of Knowledge Management Systems

EARLY CIVILIZATIONS

The history of knowledge management (KM) can be traced back to the earliest civilizations. The palace archives of Sumer and Akkad and the extensive Cuneiform archives recently discovered in Ebla in Syria (all more than 4000 years old) were attempts to organize the records of civilization, of government and commerce, so that the information contained therein could be used to guide new transactions and to prevent the loss of knowledge from generation to generation. This imperative to preserve knowledge eventually led to the great libraries of antiquity, the most notable being the library of Alexandria in Egypt, which was founded in the 3rd century BC and lasted almost 1000 years. The library had more than 500,000 handwritten works, copies of which were made and disseminated throughout the world (Knowledge Associate Ltd., 2002). KM also has deep roots in library practice as librarians have been managing codified or recorded knowledge for a long time. As mentioned by Lastres (2011), librarians have served as knowledge managers since the earliest days of libraries by maintaining the scrolls at the library of Alexandria and creating the catalog for the House of Wisdom (a 9th century Islamic library).

Knowledge, including knowing and reasons for knowing, has been documented by Western philosophers for millennia. Eastern philosophers have an equally long documented tradition of emphasizing knowledge and understanding for conducting spiritual and secular life. Many of these efforts were directed to obtain theoretical and abstract understandings of what knowledge is about (Wiig, 1999).

The condition for preservation of knowledge and ideas was mnemonic during the prewriting oral tradition. Verbal and musical rhymes were used as methods for promoting memory, instruction and knowledge preservation. These rhymes, however, had several limitations. The epic poets did not memorize actual content verbatim due to the heavy memory load, and as a consequence they created new versions from a set of possibilities as they went along. However, the concept of an original version that could be preserved did not evolve until after written text. Advances in communication and learning technology expanded the possibilities of knowledge capture and distribution.

Monks were one of the first knowledge specialists. As older civilizations passed, great efforts were made to preserve the knowledge gained through experience and reflection over long periods of time. Much of the knowledge of Greeks and Persians, falling to an expanding Islamic empire, was preserved in Arabic translations. This knowledge eventually made its way into the monasteries of Europe, where knowledge specialists (monks) were dedicated to seeking truth and viewing all knowledge as an expression of God and His creative Act. They preserved and translated these works for contemporary scholars and for those yet to come. During this time the skills of translation and techniques (libraries) of knowledge preservation were developed to a very high degree, yet the knowledge itself was disseminated with the greatest of physical efforts as everything was still copied and preserved manually.

The Persian poet, Ferdowsi, described knowledge and wisdom in his well-known poem as the foundation of power. Francis Bacon has gained global recognition for his statement "Knowledge is power" in his first publication, *In Praise of Knowledge* (1592). He defined the individual by his/her knowledge (Asl and Rahmanseresht, 2007). Peter Drucker, when describing the historical trends of knowledge management in his book *The Post-Capitalist Society*, believes that the social intentions of knowledge have evolved in three phases:

- The first phase was before AD 1700, when an attitude of knowledge, wisdom, and enlightenment was pursued.
- The second phase occurred between AD 1700 and 1800. In this era, by stressing technology creation, knowledge was shifted to an organized, systematic, and goal-oriented entity.
- The third phase commenced in about AD 1800 and reached its peak with Fredrick Taylor's principles of scientific management. Scientific management made some attempts to formulate the skills and experiences of its employees to scientific and goal-oriented knowledge, which reflects the era of applying knowledge for knowledge (Nguen, 2002, cited in Asl and Rahmanseresht, 2007).

INVENTION OF THE PRINTING PRESS

The invention of the printing press is often considered to be one of the greatest revolutions, as it accelerated the distribution of knowledge exponentially and lowered the cost, bringing knowledge to ordinary people.

Since the 15th century, the sheer quantity of information has steadily increased as technologies for creating and preserving knowledge have progressed. Print literacy not only allowed people to think in new ways, but provided new means of instruction and allowed advances in distance education and knowledge distribution. However, it posed new challenges for handling huge amounts of knowledge. As the volume of information increased due to the invention of the printing press, many great thinkers pondered the problem of making information more accessible and converting it into knowledge. With the evolution of digital computers, enormous progress has been made in solving several distinct knowledge capture and distribution limitations.

EMERGENCE OF THE KM CONCEPT

The concept of knowledge management has been around for much longer than the actual term has been in use. Denning (2000) mentioned in his blog that from "time immemorial, the elder, the traditional healer and the midwife in the village have been the living repositories of distilled experience in the life of the community" (Denning, 2000, cited in Dalkir, 2005, p. 12). Narrative repositories have also been in existence for a long time and people used to share their knowledge through meetings, workshops, seminars, and mentoring sessions. According to Dalkir (2005):

> *some form of narrative repository has been in existence for a long time, and people have found a variety of ways of sharing knowledge in order to build on earlier experience, eliminate costly redundancies, and avoid making at least the same mistakes again. For example, knowledge sharing often took the form of town meetings, workshops, seminars, and mentoring sessions. The primary "technology" used to transfer knowledge consisted of the people themselves. Indeed, much of our cultural legacy stems from the migration of different peoples across continents.*
>
> ***(Dalkir, 2005, p. 12)***

Although the term "knowledge management" was first used by Carl Wiig in 1986 at a Swiss conference sponsored by the United Nations International Labor Organization, KM has been around for many decades. Its roots had begun in 1938 when H. G. Wells described a similar concept in his vision of the "World Brain." Although Wells has never used the actual term "knowledge management", but the term World Brain, according to Wells (1938), represents "a universal organization and clarification of knowledge and ideas" (p. xvi), which would allow the intellectual organization of the sum total of our collective knowledge. Wells's vision of the

"World Brain" encapsulates many of the desirable features of today's World Wide Web, where the entire world can easily be applied within an organization in the form of an intranet. According to Dalkir (2005), the World Brain of Wells:

> *encapsulates many of the desirable features of the intellectual capital approach to KM: selected, well-organized, and widely vetted content that is maintained, kept up to date, and, above all, put to use to generate value to users, the users' community, and their organization (p. 13).*

Comparing the concept of the "World Brain" of Wells with knowledge management, Dalkir (2005) further mentioned that:

> *[. . .] we are now able to simulate rich, interactive, face-to-face knowledge encounters virtually through the use of new communication technologies. Information technologies such as an intranet and the Internet enable us to knit together the intellectual assets of an organization and organize and manage this content through the lenses of common interest, common language, and conscious cooperation. We are able to extend the depth and breadth or reach of knowledge capture, sharing, and dissemination activities, as we had not been able to do before, and we find ourselves one step closer to Wells' (1939) "perpetual digest . . . and a system of publication and distribution" (pp. 70–71) "to an intellectual unification . . . of human memory" (pp. 86–87) (p. 13).*

Librarians, philosophers, teachers, and writers have long been making use of many similar terms and techniques. However, the concept of KM had begun to flourish during the 1960s and continued in the 1970s when businesses in the United States started focusing on the improvement of performance and application of total quality management (TQM). During the early 1960s, the terms "knowledge work" and "knowledge worker" were used by Peter Drucker in discussions of the role of knowledge in organizations. He was the first to coin the term "knowledge worker" and pointed out that the economy of the United States has shifted from an economy of production to a knowledge economy, where the basic resource is knowledge, not capital (Drucker, 1969). This was the starting point of an emerging market-driven economy as opposed to a product-driven economy.

In the early 1970s, researchers at MIT and Stanford University were analyzing the possibility of creation, use and diffusion of knowledge in companies. This was the first essential step in the evolution of the concept of KM, as known today. The idea of knowledge being a corporate asset had not yet caught on, and it was not until the 1980s that companies truly began to value knowledge. During the 1980s and early 1990s, companies introduced the concept of reengineering. This concept was a fundamental rethinking and radical redesign of business processes in order to achieve dramatic improvements in critical areas such as cost, quality, service, and speed. Thus reengineering radically changed the way work was perceived and organized. It utilized collaboration, cross-training, and technology. However, the emphasis was on technology development that led to a de-emphasis on people, and downsizing and delayering were put into practice (Ralph, 2008).

In 1990, Peter Senge focused on the "learning organization" as one that can learn from past experiences stored in corporate memory systems. During the early 1990s, companies in the United States discovered the importance of knowledge embedded in their employees. They realized that during the period of downsizing and delayering, some of the people who left an organization took with them significant knowledge that could not easily be replaced. They began to find ways to manage knowledge through such technologies as artificial intelligence and expert systems (Awad and Ghaziri, 2004). In 1995, Leonard-Barton's book *Wellsprings of Knowledge: Building and Sustaining Sources of Innovation* was published by Harvard Business School. In this book, she documented her case study of Chaparral Steel, a company which had an effective knowledge management strategy in place since the mid-1970s.

The International Knowledge Management Network (IKMN), which started in Europe in 1989, went online in 1994. Many other KM-related groups and publications started appearing. There was a tremendous increase in the number of knowledge management conferences and seminars as organizations focused on managing explicit and tacit knowledge and leveraging these resources to achieve competitive advantage. It was only in 1995 that knowledge management in its current form first received significant attention among corporations and organizations (Uriarte, 2008). This came about as a result of the publication of the seminal book by Ikujiro Nonaka and Hirotaka Takeuchi, titled *The Knowledge-Creating Company: How Japanese Companies Create the Dynamics of Innovation.* Nonaka and Takeuchi (1995) studied how knowledge is produced, used, and diffused within organizations and how such knowledge contributes to the diffusion of innovation. In Sep. 1995, Arthur Andersen and the American Productivity and Quality Center (APQC) co-sponsored the Knowledge Imperative Symposium in Houston, which was followed by many more similar conferences and publications. Of the many publications that followed, the more popular titles include *Intellectual Capital* by Tom Stewart (1997), *The New Organizational Wealth* by Karl Erik Sveiby (1997), and *The Knowledge Revolution* by Verna Alle (1997).

By the end of the 1990s, organizations had started to recognize the growing importance of organizational knowledge as a competitive asset and they started implementing "knowledge management solutions." A cross-industry benchmarking study published in 1996 by Carla O'Dell, president of APQC, focused on the following KM needs:

- knowledge management as a business strategy
- transfer of knowledge and best practices
- customer-focused knowledge
- personal responsibility for knowledge
- intellectual asset management
- innovation and knowledge creation (APQC, 1996, cited in Dalkir, 2005, p. 13).

With the advent of the information or computer age, KM has come to mean the systematic, deliberate leveraging of knowledge assets. In 1969, the launch of Arpanet in the United States allowed scientists and researchers to communicate more easily with one another in addition to being able to exchange their large data sets. They came up with a network protocol or language that would allow disparate computers and operating systems to network together across communication lines. Next, a messaging system was added to this data file transfer network. In 1991, the nodes were transferred to the Internet and World Wide Web. The emergence of the Internet allowed KM to take off. The Internet facilitated access to publications about the concept of KM and how to implement it. With the help of the Internet, KM became a feasible concept for many organizations. It also has provided many more opportunities for knowledge sharing and knowledge transfer than there had been in the past. Simultaneously, many key developments were occurring in information technologies devoted to knowledge-based systems: expert systems that sought to capture "experts on a diskette," intelligent tutoring systems aimed at capturing "teachers on a diskette," and artificial intelligence approaches that gave rise to knowledge engineering in which someone was tasked with acquiring knowledge from subject matter experts, conceptually modeling this content, and then translating it into machine-executable code (McGraw and Harrison-Briggs, 1989, cited in Dalkir, 2005).

The studies conducted in the late 1970s by Everett Rogers at Stanford on the diffusion of innovation and by Thomas Allen at MIT on information and technology transfer were largely responsible for the current understanding of how knowledge is produced, used, and diffused within organizations. This growing recognition of the importance of organizational knowledge led to an increasing concern over how to deal with exponential increases in the amount of available knowledge and the complexity of products and processes. It was at this point that computer technology, which had contributed heavily to the great abundance of information, started to become part of the solution in a variety of ways. Given the progress made in automating procedures in the 1970s and communications and networking (mostly through e-mail) in the 1980s, the focus of technology in the 1990s was on cognitive computing to augment the knowledge work of human beings. Of these the Internet and intranets have had the most profound impact on spreading know-how among people in different places.

Dalkir (2005) summarized different developmental phases in KM history. The technological revolution started with the industrial era in the 1800s, people started focusing on transportation technologies in 1850, communications in 1900, computerization began in the 1950s, and virtualization in the early 1980s, and early efforts at personalization and profiling technologies began in the year 2000. We have also noticed many key developments in information technologies devoted to knowledge-based systems. These knowledge-based systems include: expert systems that aimed at capturing *experts on a diskette*, intelligent tutoring systems aimed at capturing *teachers on a diskette*, and artificial intelligence approaches that gave rise to knowledge engineering, someone tasked with acquiring knowledge from subject matter experts, conceptually modeling this content, and then translating it into machine-executable code (McGraw and Harrison-Briggs, 1989, cited in Dalkir, 2005). The design and development of such knowledge-based systems have much to offer knowledge management, whose aim is also the capture, validation, and subsequent technology-mediated dissemination of valuable knowledge from experts (Dalkir, 2005). By the early 1990s, books on knowledge management began to appear and the field picked up momentum in the mid-1990s with a number of large international KM conferences and consortia being developed. Today, over a hundred universities around the world are offering courses in KM, and quite a few business and library schools are offering degree programs in KM (Petrides and Nodine, 2003, cited in Dalkir, 2005). Some of these technological developments and KM milestones are summarized in Table 2.1.

Table 2.1 Evolution of knowledge management

Year	Entity/event/development
1800	Industrialization
1850	Transportation
1900	Communication
1950	Computerization
1969	Birth of the Internet
1980	DEC, CMU-XCON Expert System
1986	Dr. K. Wiig coined KM concept at UN
1989	Consulting firms start internal KM projects
1991	Article in *Harvard Business Review* by Nonaka and Takeuchi
1993	First KM book published by Dr. K. Wiig
1994	KM Network sponsored first KM conference
Mid-1990s	Consulting firms start offering KM services
Late 1990s	Key vertical industries implement KM and start seeing the benefits
2000–2003	Academia-KM courses/programs in universities with KM texts
2003 to present	Professional and Academic Certification-KM degrees offered by universities, by professional institutions such as Knowledge Management Consortium International (KMCI)

Modified from Dalkir, K., 2005. Knowledge Management in Theory and Practice, Burlington: Elsevier/Butterworth-Heinemann.

EVOLUTION OF KNOWLEDGE MANAGEMENT SYSTEMS

Organizations started using computers to manage data and information in the 1950s. However, the concept of data management emerged during the 1970s, when punched cards, magnetic tapes, and other record-keeping media were easily available for storage, distribution, backup, and maintenance of a large amount of data. With the proliferation of information technology and the extending reach of information systems in the 1980s and 1990s, management of data and information took on a new form (Venkatraman, 1994). In libraries, computers have been used primarily to automate and efficiently manage processes such as circulation, cataloging, serials, acquisitions, interlibrary loans, and bibliographic information retrieval. However, in the 1990s, dramatic hardware and software improvements significantly enhanced the ability of computers to store, manage, manipulate, and provide access to data and information (Gandhi, 2004). During the period of transition, the concept of managing data has also changed to document management, information management, content management, knowledge management, etc. These improved capabilities of computers have spurred their use for KM activities in organizations.

Data Management Systems

TechTarget (2010) defined data management as "the development and execution of architectures, policies, practices and procedures in order to manage the information lifecycle needs of an enterprise in an effective manner." In a broader sense, it deals with all organizational and technical tasks concerning the planning, storage, and provision of data, both for computer personnel and end users (Schulte, 1987). Schlögl (2005) identified two components for data management: data administration and database administration.

Data administration primarily serves a planning and analysis function. It may be responsible for data planning, accountability, policy development, standards setting, and support. One of the major tasks is the design of the data architecture of an organization. Database administration provides a framework for managing the data on an operational level. Its role may include performance monitoring, troubleshooting, security monitoring, physical database design, and data backup.

Gandhi (2004) mentioned transaction processing systems (TPSs) as one of the earliest examples of computerized data management systems. In the mid-1950s, organizations started using TPSs to automate manual, repetitive processes and collect data associated with daily transactions such as payroll, inventory control, ordering, billing, etc. TPSs were simple applications that provided limited types of information, primarily in the form of lists or summaries of transactions (Blair, 2002, cited in Gandhi, 2004).

Data management systems were first used in libraries for automating circulation and serial records, cataloging, indexing, interlibrary loans, and assisting in the retrieval of bibliographic information. According to a Special Libraries Association survey, by 1966 data processing equipment was being used by 209 libraries, primarily for serials management and acquisitions. In addition, 131 libraries were using data processing systems for reference or document retrieval (Sherrer, 1995, cited in Gandhi, 2004). By the late 1960s, a number of libraries had also begun to develop first-generation online public access catalogs (OPACs) to enhance bibliographic information retrieval. These early OPACs were known as item-finding tools that provided few access points (typically only author, title, and control number) to short nonstandard bibliographic records (Hildreth, 1987, cited in Gandhi, 2004). Since these first-generation OPACs had limited functionality, and did not assist users in discerning patterns or relationships between the various data elements, they are best characterized as data management systems (Gandhi, 2004).

Data management systems were replaced in libraries with more advanced systems such as management information systems (MIS). Recently, a more advanced system of data management has emerged, "big data management," which deals with the organization, administration, and governance of large volumes of both structured and unstructured data (TechTarget, 2010). Corporations, government agencies, and other organizations employ big data management strategies to help them contend with fast-growing pools of data, typically involving many terabytes or even petabytes of information and a variety of data types.

Document Management Systems

The term "document management," often referred to as a document management system, has some overlap with the concepts of content management systems. It is often viewed as a component of enterprise content management systems, and is related to digital asset management, document imaging, workflow systems, and records management systems. Document management systems may be defined as the use of a computer system and software to store, manage, and track electronic documents and electronic images of paper-based information captured through the use of a document scanner. They are designed to help individuals, workgroups, and large enterprises manage their growing number of documents stored in electronic form. Document management systems commonly provide storage, versioning, metadata, security, as well as indexing and retrieval capabilities.

An effective document management system helps an organization to carry out the following specific tasks:

- what kinds of documents and other content are created in an organization
- what template to use for each kind of document
- what metadata to provide for each kind of document
- where to store a document at each stage of its life cycle
- how to control access to a document at each stage of its life cycle
- how to move documents within the organization as team members contribute to the documents' creation, review, approval, publication, and disposition (SharePoint Foundation, 2013).

The document management planning process consists of seven major steps:

- identifying document management roles
- analyzing document usage
- planning the organization of documents
- planning how content moves between locations
- planning content types
- planning workflows.
- planning content governance.

Components of Document Management Systems

Document management systems include the following components:

Creation of metadata: Metadata is typically stored for each document. Metadata may, for example, include the date the document will be stored and the identity of the user storing it. The document management systems may also extract metadata from the document automatically or prompt the user to add metadata. Some systems also use optical character recognition on scanned images, or perform text extraction on electronic documents. The resulting extracted text can be used to assist users in locating documents by identifying probable keywords or providing for full text search capability, or can be used on its own. Extracted text can also be stored as a component of metadata, stored with the image, or separately as a source for searching document collections.

Integration of documents: Document management systems attempt to integrate document management directly into other applications, so that users may retrieve existing documents directly from the document management system repository, make changes, and save the changed document back to the repository as a new version, all without leaving the application.

Capture of data/information: Capture of data/information primarily involves accepting and processing images of paper documents from scanners or multifunctional printers. Optical character recognition (OCR) software is often used, whether integrated into the hardware or as stand-alone software, in order to convert digital images into machine-readable text. Optical mark recognition (OMR) software is sometimes used to extract values of checkboxes or bubbles. Capture may also involve accepting electronic documents and other computer-based files.

Indexing for tracking of documents: Indexing may be as simple as keeping track of unique document identifiers, but often it takes a more complex form, providing classification through the documents' metadata or even through word indexes extracted from the documents' contents. Indexing exists mainly to support retrieval. One area of critical importance for rapid retrieval is the creation of an index topology.

Storage of documents: Storage of the documents often includes management of those same documents—where they are stored, for how long, migration of the documents from one storage medium to another (hierarchical storage management) and eventual document destruction.

Retrieval of documents from the storage: Although the notion of retrieving a particular document is simple, retrieval in the electronic context can be quite complex and powerful. Simple retrieval of individual documents can be supported by allowing the user to specify the unique document identifier, and having the system use the basic index (or a nonindexed query on its data store) to retrieve the document.

Publishing: Publishing a document involves the procedures of proofreading, peer or public reviewing, authorizing, printing and approving, etc. These steps ensure prudence and logical thinking.

Standardization: Many industry associations publish their own lists of particular document control standards that are used in their particular field. The ISO has published the following series of standards regarding the technical documentation:

- ISO 2709 Information and documentation—Format for information exchange.
- ISO 15836 Information and documentation—The Dublin Core metadata element set.
- ISO 15489 Information and documentation—Records management.
- ISO 21127 Information and documentation—Reference ontology for the interchange of cultural heritage information.
- ISO 23950 Information and documentation—Information retrieval (Z39.50)—Application service definition and protocol specification.
- ISO 10244 Document management—Business process baselining and analysis.
- 32000 Document management—Portable document format.

Information Management Systems

In the 1970s and 1980s, the introduction of database management technology provided a major impetus to information management. Relational database management systems enhanced the functionality of TPSs and permitted users to rearrange and present data and information in new and creative ways. With this flexibility, users were able to discover correlations between data elements. For example, users could discover relationships between sales of specific products and the times of the year (Blair, 2002, cited in Gandhi, 2004).

Relational database management systems found several information management applications in libraries. In the 1970s and 1980s, they led to the development of second-generation OPACs, such as the University of Illinois at Urbana Champaign's OPAC, with greatly enhanced bibliographic information retrieval and data manipulation capabilities. Users could search not only by author and title, but could also search by subject headings, keywords, Boolean operators, and cross references. Additionally, they could restrict searches to specified record fields and limit results by date, language, place of publication, etc. (Hildreth, 1987, cited in Gandhi, 2004). They also provide the flexibility of picking and choosing fields to search by enabled users to combine and rearrange data elements in various permutations and combinations, and thus discover correlations between data elements.

During these two decades, a number of information management and retrieval systems for improving access to periodicals, newspapers, and other nonbook sources were developed. Online knowledge management systems, bibliographic databases, indexing and abstracting databases, and full-text databases were introduced and began to proliferate. Databases and online retrieval services such as DIALOG, BRS, OCLC, WILSONLINE, VU/TEXT, MEDLINE, Chemical Abstracts Online (CAS), Info-Trac, Lexis, Nexis, ERIC, NTIS, Dun's Market Identifiers, AGRICOLA, and the electronic edition of the Academic American Encyclopedia appeared and began to be seen in reference work (Sherrer, 1995, cited in Gandhi, 2004).

In the 1990s, the number of online databases containing bibliographic citations, indexes, abstracts, and full-text expanded exponentially. The number of online databases grew from 40 in 1972 to 300 in 1979, 2800 in 1987, 5300 in 1994, and to as many as 12,000 in 2001. This phenomenal growth led to online databases becoming an integral part of reference services in libraries. In addition to online databases, the World Wide Web also became a key component of reference work in the 1990s.

Even though OPACs, online databases, and the World Wide Web have proliferated extensively over the last several decades and have become an integral part of reference work in libraries, they are still essentially information management systems. IT applications in libraries have simply changed the way that libraries package, store, and provide access to information. Instead of card catalogs, libraries now provide access to their holdings through OPACs; instead of print journals, newspapers, directories, and encyclopedias, libraries provide access to this information through online databases and World Wide Web gateway sites. However, OPACs, online databases, and the World Wide Web still deal with the collection, codification, classification, and organization of information. These processes increase the user's access to information but do not provide any value-added or special insights to the user. They do not help a user make inferences, recognize unusual patterns, hidden trends, or exceptions in the data and information they find. As Grogan states, information retrieval systems are little more than a set of elaborate matching routines performed very quickly on a high-speed computer; the system cannot think in the same manner that humans can (Grogan, 1992, cited in Gandhi, 2004).

Content Management Systems

Over the last few years, many content management systems have emerged with an interdisciplinary approach dealing with different aspects of content management, including creation, codification, organization, sharing, and application. Content management is the "art of locating, selection, acquiring, processing, managing, and disseminating content" (Srikantaiah, 2000, p. 149).

The American Productivity and Quality Center (APQC, 2001) defined content management as "a system to provide meaningful and timely information to end users by creating processes that indentify, collect, categorize, and refresh content using a common taxonomy across the organization." A content management system consists of a database which organizes and provides access to all types of digital content files containing images, graphics, animation, sound, video, or text (Grant, 2000).

Content management systems are designed to manage digital assets during the development of digital resources, such as websites or multimedia production. They might be used by staff digitizing images, authors and editors, or those responsible for the management of the content development process (content managers). Content management systems are used to carry out a wide range of tasks. Alice Grant (2000) described the following functions of content management systems.

Holding Information About Digital Content (Metadata)

Content management systems hold information describing digital assets. This information is known as "metadata" (information about other information). The metadata held in a content management system can be used to manage and provide access to digital resources. Metadata held in a content management system include three levels of content descriptions:

1. Capture and creation of information (eg, author, editor, date captured, image resolution, type of scanner used, etc.).
2. Descriptive information (eg, subject, caption, reference to the original document or object, associated people, places or events, etc.).
3. Rights ownership (eg, copyright owner, licensing information, etc.).

Holding Digital Content

Content management systems may store narrative text for publication on the web. Text can be recorded together with author, version and currency information, which enables the publication of information online to be managed more effectively. Systems may also provide direct links to digital assets, enabling users to browse through images, sound or video clips as part of the authoring process.

Process Management

The system should enable content managers and editors to keep a close eye on the digitization process, including monitoring the capture of images, or tracking the authoring and editing of narrative text. This can be done using simple checkboxes or by completing data fields which document progress. Some systems allow the prepublication process to be tracked more visually, using workflow management tools which represent the progress of a piece of text through the authoring process—for example, using colored "traffic lights" to indicate when a piece is ready to be published online, or alternatively by displaying a "route-map" with milestones indicating how far an article has progressed down the editorial route.

Publishing Online

Any content management system should have a mechanism allowing it to make this content available to a website. Depending on the complexity of the system, this might be done in different ways.

Content management is a strategic application and integration of technology, content, and people resources to leverage the business process and create competitive advantage. They allow content to be published once and used many times; thus a portal (intranet) page may consist of several information blocks, while one block (such as name and address) may appear on many pages; as individual information blocks change, this is reflected automatically on many web pages, thus making websites easier to maintain. A content management system offers a way to manage large amounts of web-based information that escapes the burden of coding all of the information into each page in HTML by hand (Seadle, 2006).

Content management systems are important to libraries because the sheer mass of their public web presence has reached the point where maintenance is a problem. Often the web pages grew out of the personal interests of staff members, who have since left for other jobs for other responsibilities or simply retired. These may not be mission-critical pages in the same sense as a library's front page, but often they have a dedicated set of users who regard them as part of the library's service mission. Many libraries also want to customize their look and feel to emphasize consistency and branding. That can be very difficult when it requires multiple authors to agree on fonts, formats, logos, and other limitations on their creativity and individuality. A content management system assists conformity by providing a centrally managed system for displaying the content, which still remains under the control of library staff with appropriate subject expertise.

Academic libraries, and their parent institutions, are increasingly using content management systems for website management. As library websites have evolved over the years, so has their role and complexity. In the beginning, the purpose of most library websites was to convey basic information, such as hours and policies, to library users. As time passed, more and more library products and services became available online, increasing the size and complexity of library websites. Many academic library web designers found that their web authoring tools were no longer adequate for their needs and turned to content management systems to help them manage and maintain their sites (Connell, 2013).

Knowledge Management Systems

During the past few years, knowledge management has emerged as one of the topics of discussion among academicians and professionals of many disciplines. There are several disciplines that took an interest in the research and development of KM, including information technology, strategic management, cogitative science, knowledge engineering, artificial intelligence, sociology, library and information science, economics, and many more. As an established discipline since 1991, KM includes courses taught in the fields of business administration, information systems, management, and library and information science. There are several academic and professional journals that are publishing articles on KM. Professional associations (such as the International Federation of Library Association and institutions (IFLA), Knowledge Management Society (KM pro), Knowledge Management Society of Malaysia and International Society for Information Science (ISI)) are promoting the interests of KM among professionals and practitioners by organizing seminars, conferences, and workshops on KM.

In response to a growing interest of the LIS community in KM, the International Federation of Library Associations gave formal status to KM by creating a new section for KM (47th section) in Dec. 2003 (IFLA, 2012). Since its approval by the IFLA, LIS professionals have been expressing a need for a deeper understanding of the various dimensions of KM and its relevance for the LIS profession.

The University of Texas (2015) defined KM as "the systematic process of finding, selecting, organizing, distilling and presenting information in a way that improves an employee's comprehension in a specific area of interest. Knowledge management helps an organization to gain insight and understanding from its own experience. Specific knowledge management activities help focus the organization on acquiring, storing, and utilizing knowledge for such things as problem solving, dynamic learning, strategic planning, and decision making. It also protects intellectual assets from decay, adds to firm intelligence and provides increased flexibility."

Gandhi (2004) emphasizes that KM is not merely concerned with information collection, organization, presentation, storage, and retrieval. KM comprises of various methods, steps, and strategic efforts of an organization to gain competitive advantage by utilizing its knowledge assets, which reside in its employees, products, processes, and clients. However, the most important step is to identify knowledge which can be considered as an asset for the organization and utilize it to enhance learning and productivity. Though information and data management are important components of KM, KM differs from information and data management due to its emphasis on collaborative learning, capture of tacit knowledge, and the value added obtained through best practices and data mining.

Early IT applications for KM took the form of decision support systems (DSSs) and expert systems (ESs). The goal of these systems was to utilize IT applications to either improve human decision-making or replace it entirely. As KM evolved, it was recognized that human decision-making is a form of individual expertise and cannot be supplemented or replaced by IT (Blair, 2002, cited in Gandhi, 2004). This realization led to a quantum shift to expertise-centered management. The focus of KM shifted from trying to supplement or replace human expertise to encourage and facilitate its sharing (Broadbent, 1998).

KM systems are based on one or more of a host of IT applications such as data warehousing, data mining, enterprise information portals, document management systems, groupware, DSSs, intranets, Lotus notes, search engines, e-mail, content management systems, and collaborative applications. Of these, data-mining applications perhaps have the greatest potential for KM since they can help users identify unusual patterns or hidden trends in data that are not otherwise apparent (Blair, 2002).

Information Management Versus Knowledge Management

Knowledge management has emerged as a multidisciplinary subject, which includes human resource management, information and communication technology, information science, and information management. Information management is often associated with the information technology systems that help to create, store, and share information, while KM:

> *[...] involves the management of explicit knowledge (i.e. knowledge that has been codified in documents, databases, web pages, etc.) and the provision of an enabling environment for the development, nurturing, utilization and sharing of employees' tacit knowledge (i.e. know-how, skills, or expertise).*
>
> ***(Ajiferuke, 2003, p. 1)***

The dimensions of knowledge management are broader than those of information management. One of the important added dimensions of KM, over IM, is its focus on managing tacit knowledge that is embedded in people in the form of their experience, know-how, insights, expertise, competences, and so on (Kebede, 2010). Due to its focus on people, KM also uses cultural means such as face-to-face meetings, socializations, and mentoring as tools for sharing and using knowledge.

Both IM and KM need a high degree of human involvement; however, their objectives are often very different. The ultimate goal of IM is to ensure the storage and retrieval of information, while KM offers an opportunity for an organization to achieve organizational objectives by making the best use of knowledge.

Some scholars believe that IM is a part of KM. However, it provides a foundation for KM because some of the tools and techniques of IM are used in KM. Todd and Southon (2001) argue that IM is a part of KM because one of the ways that knowledge is created and nurtured is through continued exposure to information, that the three manifestations are in a continuum, the higher one involving the lower-level manifestation as we go from data to information to knowledge, thus explaining the overlap we see among the aspects of the management of data, information, and knowledge. KM therefore includes a range of aspects of IM (cited in Kebede, 2010). Blair (2002) noted that "though KM is not the same as data or information management, but data and information retrieval can be important components of it" (p. 1026).

The use of some tools, terminology, and techniques are common to both IM and KM. The overlaps include tools in use (databases, Internet collaborative tools, and so on) and concepts (information audit vs. knowledge audit, information mapping vs. knowledge mapping, and so on). Information management tools allow organizations to generate, access, store, and analyze data, usually in the form of facts and figures. Information management tools enable the manipulation of information but do not capture the complexity of context and the richness of knowledge. While knowledge management systems may include tools that also handle data and information, data and information management tools are not robust enough to truly facilitate knowledge management.

Thus information management is an important pillar of knowledge management. However, knowledge management encompasses broader issues and, in particular, creation of processes and behaviors that allow people to transform information into organizational knowledge and create and share knowledge. The difference between information management and knowledge management is outlined in Table 2.2.

Table 2.2 Differences between information management and knowledge management

Information management	Knowledge management
Emphasizes human involvement in auditing, acquiring, storing, retrieving, and disseminating information	Emphasizes human involvement in capturing, creating, sharing, learning, and contextualizing information
Success depends on the preservation and retrieval of information	Success depends on collection, distribution, and utilization of knowledge
Works with objects	Works with people
Treats information as a resource	Treats knowledge as a resource
Deals with unstructured and structured facts and figures	Deals with both codified and uncodified knowledge. Uncodified knowledge—the most valuable type of knowledge—is found in the minds of practitioners and is unarticulated, context-based, and experience-based
Benefits greatly from technology, since the information being conveyed is already codified and in an easily transferable form	Technology is useful, but KM's focus is on people and processes. The most valuable knowledge cannot effectively be (directly) transferred with technology, it must be passed on directly from person to person
Focuses on organizing, analyzing, and retrieving—again due to the codified nature of the information	Focuses on locating, understanding, enabling, and encouraging—by creating environments, cultures, processes, etc., where knowledge is shared and created
Is largely about know-what, ie, it offers a fact that you can then use to help create useful knowledge, but in itself that facts do not convey a course of action	Is largely about know-how, know-why, and know-who
	Is hard to copy—at least regarding the tacit elements. The connection to experience and context makes tacit knowledge extremely difficult to copy. This is why universities cannot produce seasoned practitioners—there are some things (the most important things) that you simply cannot teach from a textbook (or other codified sources of information/explicit knowledge). These are learnt in the field and understood on an intuitive level. You cannot easily copy or even understand this intuition without the right experience, context, etc.—and it is this intuition that represents the most valuable organizational knowledge

Modified from Jain, P., 2007. An empirical study of knowledge management in academic libraries in East and Southern Africa. Libr. Rev. 56 (5), 377–392; Frost, A., 2014. Information Management vs. Knowledge Management. Available at: http://www.knowledge-management-tools.net/IM_vs_KM.html (accessed 16.12.15).

SUMMARY

KM evolved in the United States as a business activity. Its fundamental premise was that enormous amounts of knowledge about customers, processes, products, and services exist at all levels of an organization, and if the organization was to be successful, then this knowledge had to be managed effectively. Organizations implement KM because it enables them to avoid previous errors, ensures continuity of best practices, and draws on the collective wisdom of its current and previous employees (Nilakanta et al., 2006).

Although the concept of KM emerged in the business sector, its practices are now being applied in the domain of nonprofit and public sector organizations, including academic institutions. Increasingly, library practitioners are acknowledging the importance of KM for libraries. In response to the growing interest in KM among the LIS community, a new KM section was created by the International Federation of Library Associations and Institutions (IFLA) in Dec. 2003 (IFLA, 2012). Since its inception, LIS professionals have been expressing a need for a deeper understanding of KM's many dimensions and its relevance throughout the library and information environment.

Data management, document management, information management, content management, and KM are interrelated but distinct operations. Data management systems automate manual, repetitive processes related to daily transactions within an organization and provide limited types of information. Document management systems are designed to help individuals, workgroups, and large enterprises manage their growing number of documents stored in electronic form. Information management systems allow users to manipulate and rearrange the data to a certain degree and thereby help them discover correlations between data elements. Information management is inextricably integrated into today's libraries in the form of OPACs, online databases, and the World Wide Web. Content management systems assist an organization in managing (locating, selecting, acquiring, processing, and disseminating) content and making the right knowledge available at the right time to users (Srikantaiah, 2000). Even though data management, document management, information management, and content management may be important components of KM, the ultimate objective of KM systems is to promote collaborative learning and knowledge sharing within organizations.

REFERENCES

Ajiferuke, I., 2003. Role of information professionals in knowledge management programs: empirical evidence from Canada. Inform. Sci. J. 6, 247–257.

Alle, V., 1997. The Knowledge Evolution: Expanding Organizational Intelligence. Butterworth-Heinemann Business Books, Boston.

APQC, 1996. The american productivity and quality centre. Available at: http://www.apqc.org (accessed 17.12.15).

APQC, 2001. Managing content and knowledge (best practices report). Available at: https://www.apqc.org/knowledge-base/documents/managing-content-and-knowledge-best-practices-report (accessed 15.12.15).

Asl, N.S., Rahmanseresht, H., 2007. Knowledge management approaches and knowledge gaps in organizations. In: Khosrow-Pour, M. (Ed.), Managing Worldwide Operations and Communications with Information Technology. Idea Group Inc., Hershey, PA, pp. 1427–1431.

Awad, E.M., Ghaziri, H.M., 2004. Knowledge Management. Pearson Education International, Upper Saddle River, NJ.

Blair, D.C., 2002. Knowledge management: hype, hope, or help? J. Am. Soc. Inf. Sci. Technol. 50 (12), 1019–1028.

Broadbent, M., 1998. The phenomenon of knowledge management: what does it mean to the information profession? Inform. Outlook 2 (5), 23–26.

Connell, R.S., 2013. Content management systems: trends in academic libraries. Inform. Technol. Libr. 2013, 42–55.

Dalkir, K., 2005. Knowledge Management in Theory and Practice. Elsevier/Butterworth-Heinemann, Burlington.

Denning, S., 2000. History of knowledge management. Available at: http://www.stevedenning.com/history_knowledge_management.html (accessed 16.12.15).

Drucker, P.F., 1969. The Age of Discontinuity: Guidelines to Our Changing Society. Harper & Row, New York.

Gandhi, S., 2004. Knowledge management and reference services. J. Acad. Libr. 30 (5), 368–381.

Grant, A., 2000. Content management systems. Available at: http://www.ukoln.ac.uk/nof/support/help/papers/cms/ (accessed 17.12.15).

Grogan, D., 1992. Practical Reference Work, second ed. Library Association Publishing, London.

Hildreth, C.R., 1987. Extending the access and reference service capabilities of the Online Public Access Catalog. In: Smith, L.C. (Ed.), Questions and Answers: Strategies for Using the Electronic Reference Collection, Papers Presented at the 1987 Clinic on Library Applications on Data Processing, April 5–7, 1987, p. 18.

IFLA, 2012. KM section brochure. Available at: http://www.ifla.org/files/assets/km/publications/KM%20brochure%202012.pdf (accessed 15.02.15).

Kebede, G., 2010. Knowledge management: an information science perspective. Int. J. Inf. Manag. 30, 416–424.

Knowledge Associate Ltd., 2002. Knowledge management consulting method. Available at: http://www.knowledge-management-online.com/supportfiles/module1.2-a-history-of-km.pdf (accessed 17.12.15).

Lastres, S.A., 2011. Knowledge management in changing world. Available at: http://www.futureready365.sla.org/02/28/knowledge-management-in-a-changing-world/ (accessed 15.03.15).

McGraw, K., Harrison-Briggs, K., 1989. Knowledge Acquisition: Principles and Guidelines. Prentice Hall, Englewood Cliffs, NJ.

Nilakanta, S., Miller, L.L., Zhu, D., 2006. Organizational memory management: technological and research issues. J. Database Manag. 17 (1), 85–94.
Nonaka, I., Takeuchi, H., 1995. The Knowledge-Creating Company: How Japanese Companies Create the Dynamics of Innovations. Oxford University Press, New York, NY.
Nguyen, T.V., 2002. In: Knowledge Management: Literature Review and Findings About Perceptions of Knowledge Transfer in Collaborative and Process-Oriented Teams. Pepperdine University, Doctor of Education in Organizational Leadership Dissertation. p. 227.
Petrides, L., Nodine, T., 2003. Knowledge management in education: defining the landscape. The Institute for the Study of Knowledge Management in Education. Half Moon Bay, CA. Available at: http://iskme.path.net/kmeducation.pdf (accessed 17.12.15).
Ralph, L.L., 2008. An Investigation of a Knowledge Management Solution for Reference Services. Doctor of Philosophy in Information Science, Nova Southeastern University.
Schlögl, C., 2005. Information and knowledge management: dimensions and approaches. Inf. Res. 10 (4), paper 235. Available at: http://www.informationr.net/ir/10-4/paper235.html (accessed 15.12.15).
Schulte, U., 1987. Praktikable Ansatzpunkte zur Realisierung von Datenmanagement-Konzepten. Inf. Manag. (4), 26–31.
Seadle, M., 2006. Content management systems. Libr. Hi Tech 24 (1), 5–7.
SharePoint Foundation, 2013. Overview of Document Management in SharePoint 2013. Available at: https://technet.microsoft.com/en-in/library/cc261933.aspx (accessed 15.12.15).
Sherrer, J., 1995. Implications of new and emerging technologies on reference service. In: Pitkin, G.M. (Ed.), The Impact of Emerging Technologies on Reference Service and Bibliographic Instruction. Greenwood Press, Westport, CT, p. 42.
Srikantaiah, T.K., 2000. A note on content management and knowledge management. In: Koenig, M.E.D., Srikantaiah, T.K. (Eds.), Knowledge Management Lesson Learned: What Works and What Doesn't. Information Today, Medford, NJ, p. 149.
Stewart, T., 1997. Intellectual Capital: The New Wealth of Organizations, Doubleday, NY.
Sveiby, K.E., 1997. The New Organizational Wealth, Managing and Measuring Knowledge-Based Assets. Berrett-Koehler, San Francisco.
TechTarget, 2010. Data management definition. Available at: http://searchdatamanagement.techtarget.com/definition/data-management (accessed 16.12.15).
Todd, R.J., Southon, G., 2001. Educating for a knowledge management future: perceptions of library and information professionals. Aust. Libr. J. 50 (4), 313–326.
University of Texas, 2015. Knowledge management. Available at: http://www.bus.utexas.edu/kman/answers.htm#how (accessed 16.12.15).
Uriarte, F.A., 2008. Introduction to Knowledge Management. ASEAN Foundation, Jakarta, Indonesia.
Venkatraman, N., 1994. IT-enabled business transformation: from automation to business scope redefinition. Sloan Manage. Rev. 35 (2), 73–87.
Wells, H.G., 1938. World Brain. Doubleday, Doran & Co., Garden City, NY.
Wiig, K.M., 1999. Knowledge management: an emerging discipline rooted in a long history: draft of Chapter 1. In: Chauvel, D., Despres, C. (Eds.), Knowledge Management Scheduled for publication Fall.

CHAPTER 3

Knowledge Management From a Library and Information Science Perspective

INTRODUCTION

The advent of the Internet and related technological developments has transformed the nature of library and information services. In the midst of these changes, knowledge management (KM) has emerged as a further significant influence on library practice. KM, as an emerging discipline, focuses on the various management processes that facilitate finding, identifying, capturing, creating, storing, sustaining, applying, sharing, and renewing knowledge to improve an organization's performance. Libraries embrace vast amounts of knowledge in various areas and its management is considered important for providing quality information services, making effective decisions, improving their overall performance, and becoming more relevant to their parent organizations. However, the concept of KM has been unclear among library and information science (LIS) professionals, as reflected within the LIS literature. Therefore this chapter aims to examine the concepts of KM that prevail among LIS professionals.

KM, as a multidisciplinary subject, integrates a range of concepts, theories, and practices from different disciplines. Although the concept of KM emerged in the business community, it has attracted the attention of professionals from other disciplines, including LIS. The growing interest of LIS professionals in KM may be seen in the LIS literature, as it has featured as a major focal theme of many conferences and seminars recently held on LIS (Sarrafzadeh, 2008). An established discipline since 1991, KM includes courses taught in the fields of business administration, information systems, management, and library and information science. In response to the growing interest of the LIS community in KM, the International Federation of Library Associations (IFLA) gave formal status to KM by creating a new section for KM (47th section) in Dec. 2003 (IFLA, 2012). Since its approval by the IFLA, LIS professionals have expressed a need for a deeper understanding of the various dimensions of KM and its relevance in the LIS profession.

This chapter is organized into five sections. The first section is devoted to the concept of knowledge. The second describes the concepts of KM and its relationship with librarianship and information management (IM). The third examines the scope of KM in the LIS profession. In the fourth section, opportunities and threats for LIS professionals, emerging from the origins of KM, are discussed. The fifth section examines the requirements of competencies for LIS professionals in the KM environment. The chapter ends with the main outcomes and a summary.

CONCEPTS OF KNOWLEDGE ASSETS IN LIBRARIES

Knowledge in an organization is classified either as explicit or tacit knowledge. Explicit knowledge is defined as formal and systematic knowledge, which can be expressed in words or numbers and can be documented or stored in databases as electronic records. Some examples of explicit knowledge include commercial publications, a telephone directory, e-mail, the web, databases, intranets, self study material, instruction manuals, and reports of research findings. Tacit knowledge is subjective and experience-based knowledge which is difficult to articulate or write down and communicate (Nonaka and Takeuchi, 1995). Some examples of tacit knowledge are skills, experiences, insights, intuitions, and judgments. Tacit knowledge can be shared between people through face-to-face communications, telephone conversations, e-mails, discussions in formal and informal meetings, communities of practice, mentoring and training, and personal interactions.

Wijetunge (2002) identified four types of knowledge in a library system:

1. *Internal tacit knowledge*, which consists of senior and experienced employees with a sound knowledge of work procedures, rules and regulations, etc. and the unarticulated knowledge of the librarians themselves.
2. *Internal explicit knowledge*, which consists of reports, guidelines, theses, databases, minutes of meetings, and any other type of tangible knowledge content generated within a university.
3. *External explicit knowledge*, which consists of tangible material in the form of books, journals, reports, CD/ROMs, and any other media, produced outside a university.
4. *External tacit knowledge*, which consists of personnel external to a university with expertise knowledge, ie, service personnel, subject experts, and any other person who provides expertise to university libraries.

In libraries, explicit knowledge is either created within the organization, such as reports, memos, policies and guidelines, working process, theses, minutes of meetings, etc., or acquired from external sources, including books, journal articles, databases, external reports, government information, etc. Tacit knowledge, on the other hand, resides in senior and experienced employees with a sound knowledge of work procedures, rules and regulations, etc. and the unarticulated knowledge of the librarians themselves (Wijetunge, 2002). Both types of knowledge (explicit and tacit) are recognized as the key knowledge resources of a university or library that is managed properly (Ajiferuke, 2003).

An infrastructure is essential for bringing explicit knowledge and tacit knowledge together and making KM efforts successful. According to Srikantaiah (2000), this infrastructure may include:

> *[...] simple or sophisticated information technology, top management support, social capital, and a basis of trust, mentoring, benchmarking, training, and employee development, along with the allocation of sufficient budget to invest in KM initiatives (p. 11).*

CONCEPTS OF KM AMONG LIS PROFESSIONALS

The concept of KM from the perspective of librarianship is not well defined, and there is no commonly accepted definition of KM. This has resulted in a lack of universal consensus on some of the key issues of KM, including its conceptualizations, processes, goals, and scope. Kebede (2010) noted that the LIS profession has not played an influential role in comparison to most of the other professions interested in KM, due to the following apparent reasons:

LIS professionals are unable to understand whether KM is a legitimate and distinct field of specialization of LIS: There is a continuous debate among members of the LIS community on whether KM is a new or distinct field of specialization of LIS. They consider KM as another term for what they have been doing for a long time. In fact, they are unable to distinguish KM from IM, and for this reason they obviously avoid purposeful engagement in advancing KM.

Misperceptions towards KM: A group of LIS professionals perceive KM as just another aspect of IM. They consider KM as akin to the IM that they are currently practicing, and fail to see its real value in their profession. They seem to be satisfied with the current status of IM and do not see any particular urgency or reason to engage in KM.

Lack of a new and different skill set, new mindset, and a new professional culture: Some members of the LIS community realize the importance of managing knowledge. However, they believe that the management of knowledge, particularly tacit knowledge, is beyond their current professional remit and therefore they do not see the necessity of acquiring a new set of skills as a prerequisite for their participation in KM.

Lack of understanding of the key concepts and the distinct dimensions of KM: Due to a lack of adequate exposure and knowledge of the essence of KM, some members of the profession feel uncomfortable with KM and remain reluctant to actively contribute in any meaningful way to the ongoing debate or to the advancement of KM.

Lack of readily usable techniques, frameworks, and tools: A group of LIS professionals have been inhibited from engaging in research and practice due to the lack of readily usable techniques, frameworks, and tools developed or promoted by their profession and that are in tune with the existing traditions, philosophy, and theoretical frameworks of LIS. Although they have shown an appreciation and acceptance of KM as a legitimate development in their profession, this group finds itself ill-prepared to actively participate in KM research and practice (Kebede, 2010).

Lack of active participation of LIS professionals in KM initiatives: Some members of the LIS community believe that they are not getting the opportunity to actively participate in KM initiatives in their respective organizations. The focus of these people is to prove their value to their organizations, rather than focusing on and advancing KM. There is little reported evidence to suggest that LIS is one of the main professions contributing to the emergence and further evolution of KM in terms of research findings, conferences, publications, and so on (Jashapara, 2005; Sarrafzadeh et al., 2006). There is also little evidence of the involvement of members of the profession in the KM programs of organizations (Ajiferuke, 2003; Sarrafzadeh et al., 2006).

Definitions of KM in the LIS Literature

White (2004) defined KM as "a process of creating, storing, sharing and re-using organizational knowledge (know-how) to enable an organization to achieve its goals and objectives" (p. 2).

According to the working definition of the IFLA, KM is:

> *a process of creating (generating, capturing), storing (preserving, organizing, integrating), sharing (communicating), applying (implementing), and reusing (transforming) organisational knowledge to enable an organisation to achieve its goals and objectives.*
>
> ***(IFLA, 2009)***

Further, the IFLA clarifies that the term knowledge is not limited to published information; it also covers tacit knowledge (expertise), implicit knowledge, explicit knowledge, and procedural knowledge.

Townley (2001) described KM "as the set of processes that create and share knowledge across an organization to optimize the use of judgment in the attainment of mission and goals" (p. 45). Further, she described the importance of KM for libraries by stating that "librarians can use knowledge management as a way to expand the library's role to areas such as administration or support services, where libraries have had little impact in the past" (p. 51).

According to Kebede (2010), "KM is a purposeful and systematic management of knowledge and the associated processes and tools with the aim of realizing fully the potential of knowledge in making effective decisions, solving problems, facilitating innovations and creativity and achieving competitive advantage at all levels (personal, group, organization, country and so on)" (p. 421).

According to Sydänmaanlakka (2002), KM includes an organization's strategy and objectives, together with its information technology systems, learning systems, and human resource management.

Despite a recent spurt in published output on KM, the LIS community is still debating whether KM is a new discipline or simply a rebranding of librarianship or IM. One school of thought in the LIS community believes that KM is deeply rooted in library practice because librarians have been managing codified or recorded knowledge for a long time. Lastres (2011) mentioned that librarians have served as knowledge managers since the earliest days of libraries by maintaining the scrolls at the library of Alexandria and creating the catalog for the House of Wisdom (a ninth century Islamic library). The librarian's traditional role has always been one of identifying and organizing information, sharing information resources, and connecting people to the information they need (Riccio, 2011), thus playing their roles as intermediaries between people who have knowledge and those who need it (Sarrafzadeh et al., 2010). Several KM techniques have evolved and been applied by librarians in the provision of reference services, cataloging of documents and other library services (Ralph and Ellis, 2009). There seems to be a considerable overlap of the tools, terminologies, and techniques used in librarianship, IM and KM, as described in the literature. This overlap includes the use of tools (databases, Internet, collaborative tools, etc.) and concepts (information audit vs. knowledge audit, information mapping vs. knowledge mapping, etc.) (Martin, 2008; Owen, 1999;

Teng and Hawamdeh, 2002). Thus, from this perspective, KM is not a new concept for librarians but has a long history in library practice. For example, Onyancha and Ocholla (2009) described KM as:

> *[...] comprising largely the management of information resources, services, systems and technologies using various technologies and tools through activities such as information acquisition/creation, information retrieval and storage, data mining, classification and cataloguing, and information use in different information handling institutions or centers such as libraries, archives and museums. These activities are carried out by information professionals (e.g. librarians, archivists, knowledge workers, executives, etc) (p. 15).*

However, one should not lose sight of the fact that the main focus of KM is on tacit knowledge embedded in people via their experience, know-how, insights, expertise, and competence. This embedded knowledge facilitates knowledge-rich relations and ensures ongoing development and innovation in the organization. Broadbent (1998) describes the concept of KM in libraries as not being about managing or organizing books or journals, searching the Internet for clients or arranging the circulation materials, but she considers these activities as parts of the KM spectrum and processes, not owned by any particular group in an organization, or profession or industry. The aim of librarianship is organization of recorded knowledge (Corrall, 1998), while KM:

> *[...] involves the management of explicit knowledge (i.e. knowledge that has been codified in documents, databases, web pages, etc.) and the provision of an enabling environment for the development, nurturing, utilization and sharing of employees' tacit knowledge (i.e. know-how, skills, or expertise).*
>
> ***(Ajiferuke, 2003, p. 1)***

There is also a difference of opinion within the LIS community as to the extent to which KM represents something new. To some it is a completely new discipline, while to others it is simply a rebranding of librarianship or IM. However, there appears to be widespread recognition within the LIS literature that KM is relevant to, and has considerable overlap with, the interests of the LIS profession. In spite of a wide variety of perceptions and attitudes of the LIS community towards KM, most authors consider KM from more positive viewpoints and call for full involvement of LIS professionals in KM. Thus, responding to the exciting and emerging phenomenon of KM, LIS professionals have shown a keen interest in this field, but this demands a deeper understanding of its ramifications and relevance to their work.

Thus KM cannot be confined to any given place or subject; applications of KM are likely to emerge in various places as the demand for knowledge managers will surface in different sectors. LIS professionals must realize that it is the people, and not the information sources, who are the most valuable knowledge asset of their organization. Due to the increased focus of KM on people and their expertise, some researchers (Martin, 2008; Sinotte, 2004; Wilson, 2002) highlight the importance of creating social knowledge networks, such as online forums, discussion groups, and communities of practice for sharing knowledge between librarians and library users. The importance of knowledge sharing and communication as part of KM is further emphasized by Wagner-Dobler (2004), who suggests the use of conversations, storytelling, mentoring, and apprenticeship as important methods of transferring the knowledge of experienced librarians with less experienced professionals. But these techniques, according to Kebede (2010), have not been widely practiced by librarians and they are reluctant to use them in their profession.

FACTORS LEADING TO THE EMERGENCE AND DEVELOPMENT OF KM

The core reasons for the development of the need and desire to manage knowledge are outlined by a number of researchers and writers in the field of LIS (Sinotte, 2004; Kebede, 2010). There are several factors that have contributed to the emergence and development of KM, as outlined below.

Shift From an Industrial Model of Business to an Intellectual Capital Model of Business

KM has emerged due to a shift from an industrial model of business, where an organization's assets were primarily tangible and financial (eg, production facilities, machinery, land, and ever cheaper labor costs), to an intellectual capital model of business, where assets are primarily intangible and are tied up in the knowledge, expertise, and capacity for innovation of its people.

Dramatic Increase in the Volume of Information

Another factor for the emergence of KM has been the dramatic increase in the volume of information, its electronic storage, and increased access to information in general. This has increased the value of knowledge, because it is only by knowledge that this information can be evaluated (Prusak, 2001, cited in Sinotte, 2004). Sinotte (2004) stated that:

> *[...] increased value of knowledge is exemplified by shifts in the LIS field. Once it was sufficient to help people find information; now, because there is so much more information and such wide access to this huge volume, both good and bad, it has become increasingly important that people know how to evaluate what they find (p. 191).*

The Emergence of a Knowledge Society

Some scholars believe that the LIS profession has had to embark on emphasizing knowledge and KM in response to the emergence of the knowledge society—a society that puts knowledge production and use at the heart of its activities—and due to the fact that the inherent qualities of knowledge are receiving increasing appreciation globally (Drucker, 1993, cited in Kebede, 2010). The emergence of a knowledge-based society has also brought with it a new sense of urgency to look into the issues surrounding knowledge with earnest (Kebede, 2010). Oluic-Vukovic (2001) believes that one of the reasons for the current need to intensify the activities involved in the discovery of knowledge is the emergence of knowledge-based societies:

> *The emergence of knowledge-based societies, paralleled by replacement of capital and labor-intensive organizations with knowledge-intensive organizations, where the quality and availability of intellectual capital become critical success factors, allowing business to make proactive, knowledge-driven decision ... (p. 420).*

The Emergence of Information and Communications Technology (ICT)

Some scholars also believe that technological developments are among the factors behind the current interest in KM by the LIS profession (Blair, 2002; Oluic-Vukovic, 2001). Becerra-Fernandez and Sabherwal (2006) state that:

> *Rapid changes in the field of knowledge management (KM) have to a great extent resulted from the dramatic progress we have witnessed in the field of information and communications technology. ICT allows the movement of information at increasing speeds and efficiencies, and thus facilitates sharing as well as accelerated growth of knowledge ... Thus, ICT has provided a major impetus for enabling the implementation of KM applications (p. 230).*

NEEDS AND SCOPE OF KM FOR THE LIS PROFESSION

The professional KM literature indicates that the application of KM contributes to the improvement in organizational performance, economic success in the marketplace, organizational creativity, operational effectiveness, quality of products and services, and economic sustainability. However, KM in libraries is viewed as having the potential to make libraries more relevant to their parent organizations and their users. According to Jain (2007):

> *Academic libraries and their associated institutions can work in close relationship to collaborate, share, and disseminate knowledge (p. 382).*

Successful KM initiatives help an organization to establish internal benchmarks, identify and record best practices, and create an environment of continuous learning (Gandhi, 2004). The value of KM in the LIS profession has been realized as:

- a survival factor for libraries to overcome the challenges library professionals are facing in a changing and competitive environment;
- a solution for the improvement of the future prospects of libraries;
- a method for improving knowledge-based services for internal and external users by creating an organizational culture of sharing knowledge and expertise within the library;
- a solution for the development and application of organizational knowledge to improve library operations and services;
- a means for the transformation of a library into a more efficient and knowledge-sharing organization.

There is a group of scholars who strongly argue that LIS professionals, on the basis of their skill in information handling, can apply and incorporate KM practice in several areas of an academic library, including administrative and support services, technical services (cataloging, classification, indexing, etc.), reference and information services, knowledge resource management, resource sharing and networking, information technology development and application. Gandhi (2004) explains the early efforts of reference librarians in capturing tacit knowledge through old information tools like card-files of frequently asked questions. While these traditional practices in many cases continue to be important, they are no longer sufficient to meet the changing KM needs of libraries and other knowledge-based organizations. Recent developments in Web 2.0 technologies have provided an excellent platform to meet this need. Increasingly, LIS professionals are using blogs, wikis, and other Web 2.0 applications for knowledge-sharing purposes.

OPPORTUNITIES AND NEW ROLES FOR LIS PROFESSIONALS IN KM

KM expands the horizons of LIS and offers a number of opportunities for LIS professionals. An increasing number of job opportunities with new job titles and positions have emerged from the origin of KM. Ferguson (2004) identified some new positions for LIS professionals in the KM environment from the "sample job description" compiled by Bishop (2001), which include competitive intelligence leader, knowledge and information manager, intranet content manager, and knowledge coordinator. Malhan and Rao (2005) argue that the new roles of LIS professionals in knowledge-intensive organizations are more or less the same as the current job titles and activities of librarians and other information professionals. These new roles and functions are: knowledge engineer, knowledge editor, knowledge analysts, knowledge navigator, knowledge gatekeeper, knowledge brokers, and knowledge asset managers. Hayes (2004) remarks that:

> *The knowledge economy and the growth of knowledge management, as an essential competency of organizations, provides new opportunities for librarians and information specialists to expand existing roles and utilize the skills they have honed to meet corporate objectives. The key information management role of both internal and external information, alongside the contribution to information competence and the ability to contextualize information, contributes to organizational excellence, customer benefit and competitive advantage which can be achieved more effectively through collaboration and partnership (p. 231).*

The emergence of KM brings with it new roles for LIS professionals, beyond those traditionally practiced, thus requiring increased intellectual flexibility. Priti Jain (2009) suggests the following roles that LIS professionals are expected to perform in the KM environment:

- *Technology experts*: both in using and training technology.
- *Knowledge mappers/engineers*: representing or mapping tacit and explicit knowledge to enable its classification and dissemination, and identifying gaps in this knowledge.
- *Knowledge gatekeepers*: acting as subject experts and being familiar with evolving vocabulary (taxonomies, metadata, meta tags and filtering, etc.).
- *Knowledge editors*: repackaging knowledge into the most accessible, appropriate formats.
- *Networkers and knowledge brokers*: with good networks of contacts within and outside the organization.
- *Web designers*: to display and share knowledge in eye-catching ways.
- *Computer programmers*: customizing their instructions and services according to their customers' needs.
- *Knowledge and information disseminators*: rather than custodians of information.
- *Researchers*: both for personal and professional development and for providing up-to-date assistance to users.
- *Knowledge consultants*: providing expert advice beyond the usual operational zone.

- *Knowledge content experts*: keeping up to date with international news in their specialized areas.
- *Metadata specialists*: able to describe and dictate management and preservation strategies for digital information.
- *Knowledge asset managers*: identifying, giving advice on and managing a portfolio of knowledge assets, such as patents, trademarks, copyrights, etc. (Chase, 1998, cited in Jain, 2009).

Some other responsibilities and duties of LIS professionals as knowledge managers, identified by Rooi and Snyman (2006), are to:

- create awareness about the benefits of knowledge sharing;
- encourage teamwork;
- establish platforms which are conducive to informal discussions and interactions (eg, development of communities of practice);
- build and maintain expert and best practice databases;
- become active in the design and development of the organizational intranet and portals;
- take the lead in developing a knowledge-sharing culture in the organization;
- conduct an information and knowledge audit (including identification of information and knowledge needs of the organization and the resources and services currently provided to meet these needs; mapping of information flows within the organization and between an organization and its external environment; analysis of gaps, duplications, inefficiencies, and areas of overprovision, which enables identification of where changes are needed);
- develop information and knowledge databases (ie, expert databases or knowledge repositories); and
- to utilize a combination of technologies such as the intranet and groupware for rapid information access and dissemination.

Traditional IM-related skills of LIS professionals, such as organizing, retrieving, repackaging, and utilizing information, are important for effective KM applications. They have the opportunity to play an important role in KM based on their training and experience, which will be developed and used for many years. Riccio (2011) outlined some interesting roles that LIS professionals can perform by transiting and renewing their traditional IM skills, and by linking these with the processes and core operations of the business in order to be successful in KM activities. Some of the roles suggested by Riccio (2011) arise from:

- being flexible to thinking laterally;
- being a team player to thinking about the organization globally, not just their professional function;

- people skills to being persuasive, selling themselves, their skills, and their ideas within the organization;
- creating, recording, and storing information effectively to thinking about how information is used and planning strategically;
- strong communication skills to effectively managing change;
- assessing and evaluating information to creating systems to connect the right people to the right information.

However, there is no evidence in the LIS literature that LIS professionals are well placed to take the advantage of this opportunity to contribute to organizational success by performing these emerging roles; instead graduates of business schools, particularly those with an information systems background, are politically well placed to play significant KM roles (Choo, 1998). The findings of LIC/TFPL research indicate the importance of IM skills in a KM environment, but people employing these skills in a knowledge environment do not necessarily come from the LIS profession (LIC/TFPL, 1999). A Canadian study by Ajiferuke (2003) looked at the role of LIS professionals who are members of the Special Libraries Association. More than 80% of those working in companies that are engaged in KM activities are involved in KM initiatives. More than half of these consider themselves as key members of the team, although very few are in leadership roles.

MAJOR THREATS AND CHALLENGES FOR LIS PROFESSIONALS

The opportunities emerging from the origin of KM have also created some challenges for LIS professionals. The challenges lie in applying competencies used in managing information to the broader picture of managing knowledge (Bishop, 2001). One of the major challenges for LIS professionals is to change their image and status. Rooi and Snyman (2006) emphasize that LIS professionals should think more broadly, contextually, and strategically in order to advance their roles, image, and status in the organization, rather than delivering a support service. They need to gain management skills and business knowledge because a lack thereof is among the main reasons discussed in the literature for the librarian's low status and image in the eyes of employers. This perception will change if librarians equip themselves with professional competencies (ie, lateral thinking skills, strategic planning abilities, marketing capacity, etc.) and obtain a deeper and more complete understanding of how the organization creates, shares, and uses knowledge.

They should align the goals of the library with those of the organization and focus on adding value to services to ensure more time is spent turning information into knowledge and less on seeking information.

LIS professionals must understand and express the value of their skills in terms of organizational goals, and transfer them to the organizational environment instead of hiding and protecting them. They must develop an ability to change and adapt their traditional style of work and move from the background to the center of the organization. They also need to develop new services and products to improve information services and achieve organizational objectives. If LIS professionals remain reluctant to make the changes needed in the knowledge environment, and are unable to acquire the new skills required for managing tacit knowledge, they will become irrelevant to their organization and will probably lose out in a competition for employment to people from other fields (Sarrafzadeh, 2005). The major obstacles that prevent LIS professionals from succeeding in KM projects are:

- lack of sufficient skills and competencies;
- reluctance of library professionals to accept changes;
- misunderstanding of KM concepts;
- lack of a knowledge-sharing culture;
- lack of the provisions of incentives or rewards for innovation and sharing of knowledge;
- lack of top management commitment; and
- lack of collaboration and lack of resources (financial, technological, and human).

Misunderstanding of KM concepts among LIS professionals is a major issue, which has been discussed widely in the LIS literature. LIS professionals are still debating whether KM differs from previous concepts and practices or whether it represents a mere relabeling of these preexisting fields and practices. The origins of this dilemma lie in the explicit aim expressed by many KM authors of addressing and managing the transfer of tacit knowledge into explicit knowledge. Its key proposition is that the source of competitive advantage and organizational success lies in tacit knowledge that needs to be converted into explicit knowledge in order to be managed (Schultze and Stabell, 2004; Vasconcelos, 2008). The most common shortcomings of KM initiatives in libraries stem from the confusion surrounding the terms information and knowledge, and how each of these terms relates to the term management (Southon et al., 2002, cited in Gandhi, 2004). Many LIS professionals equate KM with the organization of knowledge (Rowley, 1999, cited in Gandhi, 2004), but there are differences between the two. Jain (2009) suggests the following measures to overcome the challenges faced by LIS professionals:

- *Content development in digital formats*: information professionals must widen the scope of IM, identifying information sources and providing effective, relevant and accessible information services that capitalize on the library and information environment of the 21st century (Rath, 2006, cited in Jain, 2009).
- *Continuing education and training programs*: developing professional skills through refresher courses, conferences, workshops, seminars, etc.
- *Financial support*: developing appropriate infrastructure/resources.
- Intellectual capital management.
- Technological—trauma and infrastructure.
- Change management.
- Capture of tacit knowledge.
- Introduction of multidisciplinary growth of subjects.
- *Need-based curriculum*: an education curriculum needs to be conceived in relation to market needs and employer perceptions about the competencies of professionals (Rehman, 2008, cited in Jain, 2009).
- Balancing both tradition and technology while designing curricula.
- The ability to adopt a just-in-time rather than just in-case approach (Jones, 2008, cited in Jain, 2009).
- Creating innovations in teaching, learning, and research methods to improve the transfer of knowledge.

KM COMPETENCIES

There is widespread recognition in the LIS literature that LIS professionals lack adequate exposure and knowledge of the essence of KM, and thus find it difficult to actively contribute in any meaningful way to the ongoing debate as well as to the advancement of KM. They have difficulty understanding the key concepts and the distinct dimensions of KM. By and large, they lack the necessary expertise to engage in the exploration and practice of KM. Since the focus of KM is on human as well as organizational issues, different types of skills and competencies are needed for library practitioners to work in a KM environment. Some authors have identified the competencies that LIS professionals need to be successful in KM practice. Investigating the necessary KM skills for effective integration and use of internal knowledge, Abell and Oxbrow (2001) observed that the LIS sector needs to develop a range of interpersonal and business skills in its staff to add value to a knowledge-based environment. Koenig (1999) highlights the importance of both LIS traditional skills in the information environment with skills in indexing, cataloging, authority control, and database management for the organization and structuring of information and knowledge, as well as additional skills in the business environment with managerial, leadership and interpersonal skills for leveraging intellectual assets throughout an organization, fostering innovation and change, and developing an organizational culture of knowledge sharing. Rooi and Snyman (2006) argue that librarians have the opportunity to play an important role in KM on the basis of their training and experience developed and used over many years. However, they need to extend and renew these skills and link them with the processes and core operations of the business in order to be successful in the practice of KM. Morris (2001) also points out that LIS professionals already possess the essential theoretical and practical skills to work with KM. They have opportunities to use these skills in creative and imaginative ways to influence information strategies at boardroom level and in corporate decision-making, but they have to acquire other skills related to management, business, and information and communication technology to take advantage of their emerging roles in the knowledge economy. Some researchers (Siddike and Islam, 2011; Skyrme, 1998; Todd and Southon, 2001) have identified the need for different types of competencies for LIS professionals involved in KM practice. Based on these findings, they proposed several types of competencies for the successful application of KM practice in libraries, which may be grouped into the following broad categories:

- people-centered skills (communication, facilitation, coaching, mentoring, networking, negotiating, consensus-building, and team-working skills);
- skills associated with the management of an organization as a whole (cultural, leadership, strategic, and restructuring skills);
- information processing and management skills (developing knowledge taxonomies, organizing knowledge resources on websites and portals, and understanding the information and knowledge needs of users);
- skills related to the use and application of IT.

(For a detailed discussion on KM competencies, see Chapter 7.)

MAJOR OUTCOMES

- The concept of KM emerged in the business sector, but now it is being used in public sector organizations including academic institutions and their libraries.

- Libraries are having explicit as well as tacit knowledge embedded in working processes and experienced employees.
- Management of knowledge helps an organization to improve its quality of service.
- The perceptions of KM among LIS professionals are varied; they mostly view KM as the management of recorded knowledge, rather than sharing and using the tacit knowledge of their employees.
- LIS professionals have positive attitudes to the application of KM in libraries and see it as the best method of improving library functions and services.
- The skills of LIS professionals in indexing, cataloging, authority control, and database management may be considered relevant for KM, but they need some additional skills in the business environment as regards managerial, leadership, and interpersonal skills.
- KM offers potential opportunities for LIS professionals, including personal career development and enhancement of their position and status within their parent organizations. However, if LIS professionals remain reluctant to change their mindset and gain new skills, they will become irrelevant to their organization and will probably lose out to people from other fields in the competition for employment.

SUMMARY

Though the concept of KM emerged in the business sector, its practices are now being used in the domain of nonprofit and public sector organizations, including academic institutions and libraries. Recently, LIS professionals have started to acknowledge the importance of KM. A commonly held view is that a library is a knowledge-based organization where the organization and maintenance of recorded knowledge is a practice as old as civilization itself.

In spite of having narrow perceptions of KM, there is a developing interest in KM in the LIS community. This conclusion may be drawn on the basis of three major sets of perceptions that emerge from a review of literature. First, the LIS community can and should enter into KM roles through the application of their traditional skills related to IM. Second, there are potential benefits for LIS professionals from being involved in KM, including personal career development and enhancement of their position and status within their parent organizations. Finally, KM offers potential benefits for the development of libraries. However, the success of KM initiatives requires additional skills and competencies among LIS professionals which they currently lack. They must gain organizational political understanding, understanding of business practices, and leadership skills to succeed in KM.

REFERENCES

Abell, A., Oxbrow, N., 2001. Competing With Knowledge: The Information Professionals in the KM Age. Library Association Publishing, London.

Ajiferuke, I., 2003. Role of information professionals in KM programs: empirical evidence from Canada. Inform. Sci. J. 6, 247–257.

Becerra-Fernandez, I., Sabherwal, R., 2006. ICT and knowledge management systems. In: Schwartz, D. (Ed.), Encyclopaedia of Knowledge Management. Idea Group, Harrisburg, PA, pp. 230–236.

Bishop, K., 2001. Information Service Professionals in Knowledge Based Organizations in Australia: What Will We Manage? University of Technology, Sydney. p. 65.

Blair, D.C., 2002. Knowledge management: hype, hope, or help? J. Am. Soc. Inf. Sci. Technol. 50 (12), 1019–1028.

Broadbent, M., 1998. The phenomenon of knowledge management: what does it mean to the information profession? Inf. Outlook 2 (5), 23–34.

Chase, R.L., 1998. Knowledge navigators. Available at: http://www.sla.org/pubs/serial/io/1998/sep98/chase1.html (accessed 12.12.15).

Choo, C.W., 1998. The Knowing Organization: How Organizations Use Information to Construct Meaning, Create Knowledge, and Make Decisions. Oxford University Press, New York.

Corrall, S., 1998. Knowledge management: are we in the knowledge management business? Ariadne 18. Available at: http://www.ariadne.ac.uk/issue18/knowledge-mgt/ (accessed 12.07.15).

Drucker, P.F., 1993. The Post-Capitalist Society. Butterworth Heinemann, Oxford.

Ferguson, S., 2004. The knowledge management myth: will the real knowledge managers please step forward? Available at: http://conferences.alia.org.au/alia2004/pdfs/ferguson.s.paper.pdf (accessed 12.01.16).

Gandhi, S., 2004. Knowledge management and reference services. J. Acad. Libr. 30 (5), 368–381.

Hayes, H., 2004. The role of libraries in the knowledge economy. Serials 17 (3), 231–238.

IFLA, 2009. Knowledge management section. Knowl. Manag. Newslett. 4. Available at: http://archive.ifla.org/VII/s47/pub/KM-Newsletter4.pdf (accessed 15.02.15).

IFLA, 2012. KM section brochure. Available at: http://www.ifla.org/files/assets/km/publications/KM%20brochure%202012.pdf (accessed 15.02.15).

Jain, P., 2007. An empirical study of knowledge management in academic libraries in East and Southern Africa. Libr. Rev. 56 (5), 377–392.

Jain, P., 2009. Knowledge management for 21st century information professionals. J. Knowl. Manag. Pract. 10 (2). Available at: http://www.tlainc.com/articl193.htm.

Jashapara, A., 2005. The emerging discourse of knowledge management: a new dawn for information science research? J. Inf. Sci. 31 (2), 136–148.

Jones, D., 2008. Knowledge Management From the Information Professional Perspectives: Identifying Partners in Your Organisations. Available at: http://factiva.com/infopro/resource8.asp?node=right1 (accessed 16.06.15).

Kebede, G., 2010. Knowledge management: an information science perspective. Int. J. Inf. Manag. 30, 416–424.

Koenig, M.E.D., 1999. Education for knowledge management. Inf. Serv. Use 19 (1), 17–32.

Lastres, S.A., 2011. Knowledge management in changing world. Available at: http://www.futureready365.sla.org/02/28/knowledge-management-in-a-changing-world/ (accessed 15.03.15).

LIC/TFPL, 1999. Skills for knowledge management: a briefing TFPL. Available at: http://www.lic.gov.uk/publications/executivesummaries/k mskills.html (accessed 15.03.15).

Malhan, I.V., Rao, S., 2005. From library management to knowledge management: a conceptual change. J. Inform. Knowl. Manag. 4 (4), 269–277.

Martin, B., 2008. Knowledge management. Annu. Rev. Inform. Sci. Technol. 42 (1), 369–424.

Morris, A., 2001. Knowledge management: opportunities for LIS graduates. In: World Library and Information Congress: 67th IFLA Council and General Conference, Boston, pp. 16–25.

Nonaka, I., Takeuchi, H., 1995. The Knowledge-Creating Company: How Japanese Companies Create the Dynamics of Innovations. Oxford University Press, New York, NY.

Oluic-Vukovic, V., 2001. From information to knowledge: some reflections on the origin of the current shifting towards knowledge processing and further perspective. J. Am. Soc. Inf. Sci. Technol. 52 (1), 54–61.

Onyancha, O.B., Ochalla, D.N., 2009. Conceptualizing 'knowledge management' in the context of library and information science using the core/periphery model. S. Afr. J. Inf. Manag. 11 (4), 1–15. Available at: http://www.sajim.co.za/index.php/SAJIM/article/view/412/402 (accessed 19.11.14).

Owen, J.M., 1999. Knowledge management and the information professional. Inf. Serv. Use 19 (1), 7–16.

Prusak, L., 2001. Where did knowledge management come from? Syst. J. 40 (4), 1002–1007.

Ralph, L.L., Ellis, T.J., 2009. An investigation of a knowledge management solution for the improvement of reference services. J. Inf. Inf. Technol. Org. 4, 17–38.

Rath, P., 2006. Preparing library and information professionals for the 21st century: issues and challenges for library and information science educators in India. Available at: http://dlist.sir.arizona.edu/1358/01/06.Pravakar%5FRath%5Fpp35-40%5F.pdf (accessed 31.01.15).

Rehman, S.U., 2008. Analysing corporate job market for developing information and knowledge professionals: the case of developing nation. Malays. J. Libr. Inf. Sci. 13 (1), 45–58.

Riccio, H.M., 2011. Librarians knowledge management: everything old is new again. AALL Spectr. 15 (7), 24–26.

Rooi, H.V., Snyman, R., 2006. A content analysis of literature regarding knowledge management opportunities for librarians. Aslib Proc. 58 (3), 261–271.

Rowley, J., 1999. Owners of the knowledge. Libr. Assoc. Rec. 101 (8), 475.

Sarrafzadeh, M., 2005. The implications of knowledge management for the library and information professions. Act KM Online J. Knowl. Manag. 2 (1), 92–102. http://www.actkm.org/actkm journal_vol2iss1.php (accessed 16.05.15).

Sarrafzadeh, M., 2008. The Implications of Knowledge Management for the Library and Information Professions. Ph.D. Dissertation, RMIT University. Available at: https://researchbank.rmit.edu.au/eserv/rmit:13384/Sarrafzadeh.pdf (accessed 15.02.15).

Sarrafzadeh, M., Martin, B., Hazeri, A., 2006. LIS professionals and knowledge management: some recent perspectives. Libr. Manag. 27 (9), 621–635.

Sarrafzadeh, M., Martin, B., Hazeri, A., 2010. Knowledge management and its potential applicability for libraries. Libr. Manag. 31 (3), 198–212.

Schultze, U., Stabell, C., 2004. Knowing what you don't know? Discourses and contradictions in knowledge management research. J. Manag. Stud. 41 (4), 549–573.

Siddike, M.A.K., Islam, M.S., 2011. Exploring the competencies of information professionals for knowledge management in the information institutions of Bangladesh. Int. Inf. Libr. Rev. 43, 130–136.

Skyrme, D.J., 1998. Fad or fundamental: making knowledge work for you. Available at: http://www.skyrme.com/ppt/iis40/iis40.ppt#260,5,LifeCycleofaFad (accessed 15.01.15).

Southon, G., Todd, S., Seneque, M., 2002. Knowledge management in three organizations. J. Am. Soc. Inf. Sci. Technol. 53 (12), 1049–1059.
Srikantaiah, T.K., 2000. Knowledge management: a faceted overview. In: Srikantaiah, T.K., Koenig, M.E.D. (Eds.), Knowledge Management for the Information Professionals. Information Today, Medford, NJ, p. 11.
Sydänmaanlakka, P., 2002. An Intelligent Organization. Integrating Performance, Competence and Knowledge Management. Capstone, Oxford.
Teng, S., Hawamdeh, S., 2002. Knowledge management in public libraries. Aslib Proc. 54 (3), 188–197.
Todd, R.J., Southon, G., 2001. Educating for a knowledge management future: perceptions of library and information professionals. Aust. Libr. J. 50 (4), 313–326.
Townley, C.T., 2001. Knowledge management and academic libraries. Coll. Res. Libr. 62 (1), 44–55.
Vasconcelos, A.C., 2008. Dilemmas in knowledge management. Libr. Manag. 29 (4–5), 422–443.
Wagner-Dobler, R., 2004. Tacit knowledge, knowledge management, library science no bridge between. IFLA Publ. 108, 39–46.
White, T., 2004. Knowledge management in an academic library: based on the case study KM within OULS. In: World Library and Information Congress: 70th IFLA General Conference and Council, August 22–27, Buenos Aires.
Wijetunge, P., 2002. Adoption of knowledge management by the Sri Lankan University librarians in the light of the National Policy on University Education. Int. J. Educ. Dev. 22, 85–94.
Wilson, T.D., 2002. The nonsense of knowledge management. Inf. Res. 8 (1), 144. http://InformationR.net/ir/8-1/paper144.html (accessed 18.05.15).

CHAPTER 4
Knowledge Management Approaches

INTRODUCTION

There are different perspectives on knowledge. For example, knowledge may be tacit or explicit, it may be a process or an object, and/or it may reside in individuals or on computers, the Internet or the web. But the concept of KM is based on the idea that an organization's most valuable resource is the knowledge of its people. Today, knowledge is recognized as the most valuable and competitive resource of an organization. However, the role of knowledge as a source of economic and social growth is not new, and back in the late 19th century Marshall stated:

> *Capital consists in a great part of knowledge and organisation ... Knowledge is our most powerful engine of production.*
>
> ***(Marshall, 1890, The Principles of Economics, quoted in Quintas, 2002)***

Since intellectual capital is one of the most important sources of competence for an organization, it would be unwise to assume that the concept of KM is confined to the management of only human resources or people. The field of KM, according to Baskerville and Dulipovici (2006, p. 83), is more pervasive. It is:

> *building on theoretical foundations from information economics, strategic management, organizational culture, organizational behaviour, organizational structure, artificial intelligence, quality management and organizational performance measurement.*

The debate on KM started in the literature around the mid-1990s (Scarbrough and Swan, 2001). Wilson (2002a,b) considers KM as akin to information management, while Scarbrough and Swan (2001) try to establish its relationship to research traditions on the learning organization. The emergence of KM has raised an interesting debate on whether it is related to preexisting disciplines and schools of thought or a legitimate and distinct field. According to Kebede (2010, p. 416), it is:

> *[…] one of the emerging topics of academic and professional discourse in many fields of knowledge, including cognitive sciences, sociology, management science, information science (IS), knowledge engineering, artificial intelligence, and economics.*

Thus many disciplines are taking an interest in KM, and each one has its own approach for managing knowledge. There is a difference between the concerns, referents, and discourses of KM approaches, and as such there is no single approach to KM. According to Lloria (2008, p. 78):

> *KM is gradually taking on a direction of its own, and includes information and knowledge-creating systems, as well as strategic management and innovation.*

The approaches to KM covered in the professional literature originated mainly in Japan, Europe, and the United States. These approaches may be categorized as intellectual theories and knowledge creation theories. Lloria (2008), after analyzing the KM literature, categorized different approaches to KM into three schools of thought: the economic or commercial school, the techno-centric school, and the behavioral school. These categories closely resemble the categories proposed by McAdam and McCreedy (1999), who group KM approaches in accordance with the knowledge model, the intellectual model, and the socially constructed model. These categories may be considered as a way of organizing different KM practices. Library and information science (LIS) professionals must be aware of these approaches as they seek to use some of those practices to benefit library situations. Such benefits include the spirit of collaboration, knowledge sharing, and the institutional cultural changes that can occur from implementing KM practices. In this chapter, different approaches of KM are discussed.

INTELLECTUAL CAPITAL APPROACH

In the mid-1990s, there was an increasing awareness in the business community that knowledge was an important organizational resource that needs to be nurtured, sustained, and accounted for, if possible. The economic school of thought sees knowledge as intellectual capital. Intellectual capital is defined by Stewart (1997) as "intellectual material-knowledge, information, intellectual property, and experience—that can be put to use for creating wealth." Intellectual capital includes human capital, innovation capital, and structural capital, of which human capital is recognized as the major component of intellectual capital. It is the combination of knowledge, skills, innovation, and ability of an organization's individual employees to meet the task. Human knowledge is a kind of tacit knowledge which is embedded in the minds of employees in the form of their competence and commitment.

An intellectual perspective of KM outlined the importance of both the production and management of material wealth which, according to Vasconcelos (2008), is based on measuring the exploitation of knowledge as an economic resource. The economic school of thought believes that organizational effectiveness is dependent on the creation and utilization of intellectual capital.

The fundamental element in the implementation of KM is the identification of intellectual capital assets in the organization. Intellectual capital is defined as "knowledge that produces or creates value. It is an organization's source of competitive advantage and it is an individual's most valuable competitive asset" (Amidon, 1997, cited in Bedford et al., 2015, p. 82). Intellectual capital in an organization includes knowledge, brainpower, know-how, and processes of employees, as well as their ability to continuously improve those processes. Kostagiolas and Asonitis (2009) classified intellectual capital into three categories: (i) human capital; (ii) organizational (or structural) capital; and (iii) relational capital.

Human capital consists of knowledge, skill, innovation, and the ability of the organization's individual employees to meet the task at hand. It incorporates organizational values, culture, and philosophy. Human capital is not owned by the organization as it is lost when employees leave the organization. It includes the staff's competences, skills, knowledge, personal networks, etc. (Roos et al., 2005).

Organizational (or structural) capital consists of brands and intellectual property, patents, trademarks, computer software, automation systems and certain management techniques, organizational routines, procedures, etc., and it is embodied in organizational structure and processes. It remains with the organization even employees leave the organization.

Relational capital is concerned with the external relationships that an organization develops. It includes customers, potential customers, partners, suppliers, investors, creditors, etc. (Roos et al., 2005).

The intellectual capital assets of libraries can also be included in the above-mentioned categories, that is, human capital, organizational (or structural) capital, and relational capital. Intellectual capital assets of the libraries are shown in Table 4.1.

Table 4.1 Intellectual capital assets of libraries

Categories of intellectual capital	Different types of intellectual capital
Human capital	Staff training and mentoring Skills and competences of library employees Innovativeness, creativity, and collaborative attitudes Team development Self-motivation Flexibility, ability to change Experience
Structural capital	Library systems, including library collections and infrastructure Library in-house databases IT literacy Leadership of the academic library Flexible service practices General culture of the library Innovations; patents and trademarks of information products and services Management systems (business plans, quality certification) Library automation systems Web-based services
Relational capital	Orientation and user training programs Collaboration between library staff and library users Collaboration between academics and subject specialists Participation in information networks Trust and cooperation between staff Agreements with authorities Professional association reputations of individuals

TECHNO-CENTRIC APPROACH

The focus of the techno-centric school of thought is on technology for controlling and protecting information and knowledge. Rowley (2003) refers to it as the "information processing model" where the focus is on managing knowledge and the capture and codification of information through information technologies. In any KM system, three principal technology infrastructures are needed for organizing content, searching information once organized, and locating the appropriate expertise (Uriarte, 2008).

The value of information technology (IT) in KM has been recognized by several scholars. In fact, IT provides a platform for the flow of explicit knowledge as well as tacit knowledge. Alavi and Leidner (1999) consider

IT as one of the key enablers of successful KM initiatives, and its role is to solve problems and make people more efficient than those who do not use IT in their activities. It involves the use of information technologies, such as intranets, data warehousing, knowledge repositories, decision support tools and groupware, to enhance the quality and speed of knowledge capture and distribution in the organization (Ruggles, 1998). IT can also enable rapid search, access and retrieval of the information which has been captured and retained, and can support collaboration and communication between the different employees of an organization to share and use tacit knowledge.

Libraries use IT for managing different types of knowledge. With the help of IT, libraries can create knowledge repositories, which store both knowledge and information, often in documentary form. Use of IT in libraries improves knowledge access and transfer. Technologies such as video-conferencing systems, document scanning and sharing tools and telecommunications networks, intranet, advanced web applications, and social media are being used in libraries to improve knowledge access and transfer. The different types of technologies required for organizing content, searching information, and locating expertise are illustrated in Table 4.2.

Table 4.2 Techno-centric approach to knowledge management

Knowledge repository	Internet, intranet, HTML, XML, metadata, taxonomies Full-text search engines Document management system Multimedia repositories
Communities of practice	E-mail Phone calls/teleconferencing Video-conferencing Directory of expertise Social networks
E-learning	Learning management systems E-learning portals Web-based training Electronic performance support systems
Artificial intelligence	Databases Information retrieval system Data-mining tools Decision support tools Enterprise portals Knowledge discovery tools

Modified from Uriarte, F.A., 2008. Introduction to Knowledge Management, ASEAN Foundation, Jakarta, Indonesia.

Reference librarians have been using old information tools like card files of frequently asked questions to capture tacit knowledge for a long time. However, with the recent developments in IT, these practices have been replaced by the use of common knowledge databases, web-based ready-reference databases, and the knowledge base of question point. Recently, intranets and advanced web applications or social networking have also provided an excellent platform for libraries to share, access, and transfer knowledge within or outside libraries. Increasingly, libraries are using blogs, wikis, RSS, social media, and other web applications for knowledge-sharing and transfer purposes.

HUMAN-CENTRIC APPROACH

A human-centric approach to KM implies the way that humans react to the environment. This approach mainly focuses on the management of people who are the ultimate source of knowledge. Since a great amount of knowledge in an organization is tacit in nature, which is embedded in human skills, expertise and know-how of people; capitalizing on these assets is essential in making KM efforts successful. IT is not suitable for managing this type of knowledge (Davenport and Prusak, 1998). Thus the primary concern of this school is tacit knowledge and its transfer among people. This may be achieved by facilitating direct interactions between people and by connecting people with each other (Hansen et al., 1999). However, it requires investment in building networks of people where knowledge is shared not only face to face, but over the telephone, e-mail or via video-conferencing, intranet, the Internet, or social media. Steve Denning defines this approach to KM as the connecting dimension. He states that:

> *IT involves linking people who need to know with those who do know, and so developing new capabilities for nurturing knowledge and acting knowledgeably. Connecting is necessary because knowledge is embodied in people, and in the relationships within and between organizations. Information becomes knowledge as it is interpreted and made concrete in the light of the individual's understandings of the particular context. For example, help desks and advisory services (small teams of experts to whom one can call to obtain specific know-how or help in solving a problem) can be very effective in the short term in connecting people and getting quick answers to questions.*
>
> ***(Denning, 2001, para 2)***

The human-centric school of thought outlined a kind of community of practice model, which support continuous learning and informal information exchange enhanced by the availability of knowledge retained and accessible from within as well as outside an organization. It also recognizes the perceived usefulness of the individual contributions and teamwork (Kulkarni et al., 2006). This approach places the emphasis on building communities. According to Lloria (2008), "the community is recognized as a fundamental context for sharing knowledge with trust as its enabler" (p. 82).

It is about the process—how an organization can maximize the abilities of its personnel. It requires assessing, changing, and improving human skills and behavior through training and professional development. It also requires an investment in people and focus on recruitment, the office environment, and corporate culture built on trust of management, thus contributing to the retention of people and their skills or expertise.

Lee (2005) viewed this approach to KM from a human resources management point of view, and argues that libraries can improve KM practices in all of the key areas of library services through proper human resources management. He states that:

> *Libraries may encourage the transfer of knowledge and experience from experienced staff to new staff members. A mentoring system should be in place to help newcomers to learn from experienced library staff. Informal seminars and brown-bag sessions where staff can interact and exchange "lessons learned", "best practices" and other specific experience and knowledge should be scheduled at regular intervals and at convenient times. Special interest groups and chat rooms can be created through intranet. Since many valuable experiences have been accumulated over time, libraries should pay attention to favorable working conditions and environment, which will contribute to better staff retention.*

KNOWLEDGE CREATION AND CONVERSION APPROACH

This approach is based on the knowledge creation and conversion model of Nonaka and Takeuchi (1995). They proposed a knowledge creation and conversion model, popularly known as the SECI (socialization, externalization combination, internalization) model. The four modes of knowledge conversion interact in the spiral of knowledge creation. Through these modes, knowledge is converted from one form of knowledge (tacit or explicit) to another (tacit or explicit), as shown in Fig. 4.1.

From the description of the SECI model of Nonaka and Takeuchi, it appears that tacit and explicit knowledge are two diverse concepts. In fact, according to Tredinnick (2006), the concepts of tacit and explicit knowledge themselves suggest that the transformation of knowledge into information is simply a matter of codification, and librarians possess the requisite skills to codify information.

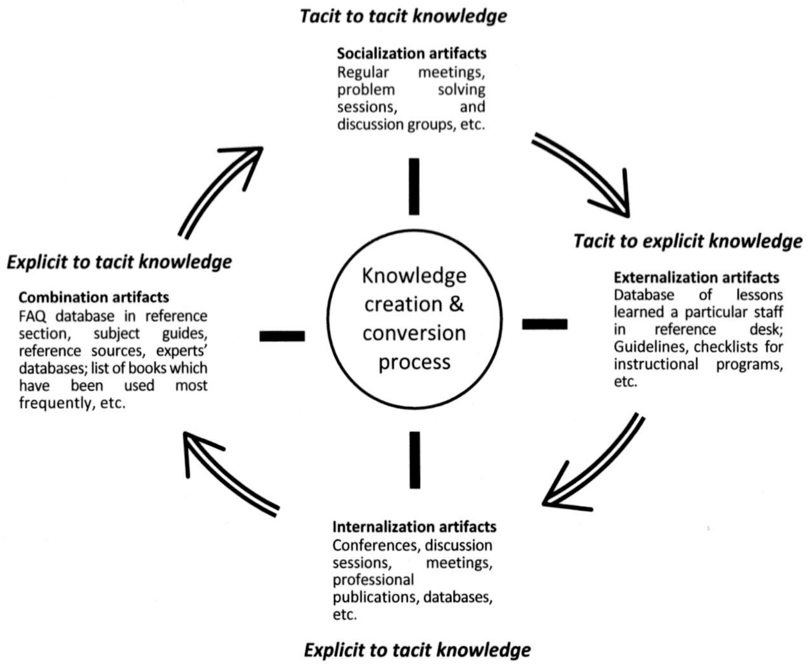

Fig. 4.1 Knowledge creation and conversion process.

The SECI model of Nonaka and Takeuchi focuses on the important issues of how knowledge may be created and transformed through organizational sharing, and is useful for identifying and evaluating certain key activities in the management of knowledge. Like many other business organizations, academic libraries may be regarded as a system of integrated activities and business processes that work together collaboratively in order to achieve overall organizational goals. Academic libraries are no longer just places to get information, they are also where people can exchange information and experiences, learning and creating new knowledge, and their essence is to provide knowledge and learning.

The first step of the KM process is the conversion of tacit knowledge into tacit knowledge through "socialization." In an academic library context, communication between librarians is a social process for sharing knowledge and learning from each other. As a result of continuous interactions among librarians and other professional groups, their knowledge can be transferred from one librarian to another through regular formal/informal meetings, problem-solving sessions, forums, discussion groups, and so on. Information and communication technologies, particularly telephone, e-mail, online discussion forums, social media, as well as internal or external professional gatherings, networking, and social artifacts, can also facilitate such interactions (Daneshgar and Parirokh, 2007).

The second step in the KM process is called "externalization," which is based on the conversion of tacit knowledge into explicit knowledge. In this process, tacit knowledge is codified, sorted, categorized, and held in a database or document in order to be accessed and reused by others. Academic libraries are also expected to create, gather, store, and disseminate knowledge to be reused by other employees of the library. Databases of lessons learned, best practices of particular staff at a reference desk, and results of a problem-solving or brainstorming meeting which is a combination of ideas exchanged in face-to-face interactions in socialization mode that are converted into guidelines and checklists for future use are some examples of converting tacit knowledge into explicit knowledge in a library.

The third step is known as "combination" and refers to the conversion of explicit knowledge to explicit knowledge. Davenport and Prusak (1998) have formally recognized that libraries can play a critical role in creating explicit knowledge through various activities such as content management, organization of knowledge, and evaluating the validity and reliability of information obtained from unfamiliar sources. Further, subject guides, lists of reference sources, and experts' databases (a database that consists of details from experts that agreed to be contacted) are some examples of explicit knowledge that can be created in the externalization mode but need to be updated constantly.

The fourth step is "internalization," which is conversion of explicit knowledge into tacit knowledge through comparing and combining the acquired (explicit) knowledge with their personal knowledge base. In this case, previous knowledge will be corrected or modified and new knowledge is created within the learners' minds. Conferences, discussion sessions, meetings, and professional publications are some examples that provide opportunities for librarians to analyze and assess their knowledge and increase their thinking abilities, and to create new knowledge.

All four steps are crucial in the creation of new knowledge, as this in turn will result in libraries providing appropriate and timely services to their users. Jantz (2001) believes if academic libraries and librarians create, use, and share their organizational knowledge, it will certainly improve their operations and services. The process of knowledge creation and conversion in academic libraries is shown in Fig. 4.1.

CODIFICATION APPROACH

KM approaches are also characterized in terms of "codification" and "personalization."

The codification approach to KM is concerned with the extraction of knowledge from the person who owned it, storing it in databases, and promoting its subsequent reuse by anyone who needs it (Kumar and Ganesh, 2011). The codification of knowledge is dependent on the use of information technologies, such as intranets, data warehousing, knowledge repositories, decision support tools, and groupware (Ruggles, 1998), to enhance the quality and speed of knowledge creation, capture, and distribution within the organization.

The purpose of the codification approach to KM is to articulate tacit knowledge (make it explicit). Once tacit knowledge is converted to explicit knowledge, the organization is in less danger of losing its knowledge capital when employees leave the organization (Davenport and Prusak, 1998). Codification of tacit knowledge is not simply to facilitate retrieval of information, but helps to reuse knowledge in new ways that entail reflection, criticism, learning, and ultimately the creation of new knowledge that had not previously existed (Choo, 2000).

Over the last three decades a number of libraries in the world have converted their card-based ready-reference files to electronic formats using database management software. Some of them have experimented with using web-based technologies to codify organizational knowledge in reference services (Jantz, 2001). Libraries are using knowledge databases, web-based ready-reference databases, and the knowledge base of question point to codify organizational knowledge in reference services.

PERSONALIZATION APPROACH

Scholars who support the personalization approach to KM believe that a great deal of organizational knowledge is tacit in nature and that use of IT alone is not suitable for capturing and sharing this type of knowledge. Instead of using IT as a medium of codification of knowledge, the primary focus of the personalization approach is on building networks of people through socialization. Through this process, common unarticulated beliefs and embodied skills of one person are shared and transmitted to another person, and it becomes part of the other person's tacit knowledge base. This may happen by facilitating direct interactions between people, by connecting people with each other (Hansen et al., 1999). This approach to KM requires investment in building networks of people, where knowledge is shared not only face to face, but also over the telephone, by e-mail, and via video-conferencing. Corporate yellow pages (a platform for providing information about which expertise resides in whom), communities of practice, storytelling, and setting up shared physical and virtual spaces that inspire constructive interactions (Nonaka and Konno, 1998) are some other practices belonging to the personalization approach to KM.

Sarrafzadeh et al. (2010) stated that librarians can use the personalization approach for managing tacit knowledge by (i) keeping communities of practice alive and (ii) providing easy access to human resources.

Keeping Communities of Practice Alive

The librarian's role is to keep the community alive by bringing in current awareness materials, and also by stewarding information by recording community activity and archiving it so that it can be preserved for reuse.

Providing Easy Access to Human Resources

KM recognizes that people are the most important assets of organizations. Providing easy access to human resources, including knowledgeable experts, by identifying their area of expertise and experience is an area of activity for LIS professionals. According to Choo (2002), maintaining online and current vitae and résumés of employees in the organization is one way to track who owns what knowledge and how they can be contacted.

OTHER APPROACHES TO KM IN LIBRARIES

The basic goal of KM within libraries is to leverage the available knowledge that may help librarians to carry out their tasks more efficiently and effectively. KM also aims to extend the role of librarians to manage all types of information and tacit knowledge for the benefit of the library. The KM process involves the creation, capturing, sharing, and utilization of knowledge. Different approaches used in libraries for managing knowledge are discussed below.

Organizational Learning/Innovation Approach

Acquisition of knowledge by employees is one of the important steps in the KM implementation process. Knowledge can be acquired and enhanced by providing training or learning opportunities to the staff. Continuous learning through professional training courses or attending workshops and seminars are some of the important methods of acquiring knowledge and developing competencies among employees as regards their involvement in KM practice.

Knowledge Sharing

There is a strong view expressed in the literature that knowledge which is embedded in employees has no value until it is utilized and shared among other employees of an organization. Knowledge in an organization can be shared through the formation of communities of practice, formal or informal meetings, face-to-face interactions, mentoring, apprenticeships, and use of best practices. According to White (2004), KM systems generally fail if there is not a knowledge-sharing culture in place. Sharing of knowledge depends on the strategy of an organization which might best encourage and motivate employees to share their most valuable personally held knowledge (Hariharan, 2005). Gibbert and Krause (2002) argue that knowledge sharing cannot be forced, but can only be encouraged and facilitated. Further, they mention that knowledge sharing can be induced where there are perceived benefits for employees in terms of incentives or rewards.

ICT-Based Data Banks or Knowledge Repositories

IT serves as a powerful enabler and provides effective and efficient tools for all facets of KM applications, including capturing, storing, sharing, and access to knowledge (Gandhi, 2004). ICT also supports the process of knowledge sharing by facilitating people to locate as well as to communicate with each other (Roknuzzaman et al., 2009). Academic libraries have a variety of knowledge sources available inside, as well as outside, the library. Availability and exploitation of both internal and external sources of knowledge are essential for the improvement of work efficiency of the staff, as well as reducing the chance of redundancy. Academic libraries can use ICT for the automation of library functions and services, creation of knowledge repositories, development of databases of best practices, library portals and intranets, which help to locate, capture, store, and share internal knowledge.

Networking and Partnership With Other Libraries

Access to external information and knowledge resources through library networks or partnerships with other libraries, including links to library professional groups and publications, etc., is also recognized as an important method of KM application in academic libraries. Networks such as partnerships with other public or private organizations represent a solution for extended access to knowledge, for more creative uses, and for increased quality of the products and services which libraries offer to their users.

Collaborative Tools

Modern ICT-based collaborative tools, such as blogs, wikis, shared classification systems (tagging), social networks, etc., are being used in libraries to support the process of knowledge capture, storing, and sharing. These tools are also used in libraries to connect library users with libraries and to form relationships between librarians and library users. These tools also allow users and organizations to create accounts for bookmarking online content to help academic libraries with collaboration and networking, organization and sharing of electronic resources, and teaching information literacy. The implications of different approaches to KM in libraries are illustrated in Table 4.3.

Table 4.3 Different approaches to knowledge management in libraries

ICT-based data banks/ knowledge repositories	Creation and access to internal knowledge resource bases (ie, automation of library operations and services, creating knowledge repositories and digital libraries as tools for KM, involving projects, content, policies, etc.) Knowledge-based systems
Organizational learning/ innovation	Providing training and learning opportunities to employees for acquiring new knowledge and developing competencies and innovation (ie, through training programs, participation in communities of practice, formal/informal meetings, e-learning, workshops, seminars, etc.)
Collaborative tools	KM tools, sometimes but not always based on technologies, Web 2.0 collaborative tools (blogs, wikis, social networking, bookmarking, etc.)
Knowledge sharing	Encouraging staff to share knowledge through the provision of rewards/incentives, trust, teamwork, etc.)
Library networks and partnerships	Extending access to external information/ knowledge resources through library networks, or partnerships with other libraries, library portals including links to library professional groups and publications, etc.)

APPROACHES TO MANAGING KNOWLEDGE IN LIBRARIES: A CASE STUDY OF INDIAN ACADEMIC LIBRARIES[1]

The major objective of this case study was to investigate the "current state" of adoption of KM approaches in Indian academic libraries. More specifically, the following questions are identified and addressed in the study:

1. What are the tools and techniques academic libraries use for managing and sharing knowledge?
2. What is the "current state" of adoption of KM strategies in Indian academic libraries?

A descriptive survey method was used to collect data. A questionnaire was designed and distributed to 62 employees of 32 academic libraries (28 central university libraries and seven libraries of Indian institutes of management). The primary respondents were librarians, deputy librarians, and assistant librarians. For the purpose of identifying the most commonly used KM approaches in academic libraries, 14 indicator variables (seven each for codification and personalization) were identified from a review of the literature and retained for analysis. The variables were evaluated using a five-point scale, where 1 was categorized as "doesn't exist or not in use" and 5 denoted "extensively used." The respondents were asked to indicate the extent to which these indicator variables are being used in their libraries. A total of 45 completed questionnaires were received from 15 central university libraries and five libraries of Indian institutes of management. Descriptive statistics were applied for data analysis and the results are presented in Table 4.4.

Analyses of data revealed mean scores of the 14 indicator variables ranging from 4.60 to 1.63, as shown in Table 4.1. The mean score provides an indication of the usage in the academic libraries under study. The table can be analyzed from two perspectives: by the absolute mean score compared to all items and by considering the KM approach that each item represents independently.

A closer inspection of the results shows that, of the 14 indicators, 6 had high mean scores, that is, 3.45. These were Internet (including e-mail and Web 2.0 applications), intranet, search engines/information retrieval systems, phone calls/teleconferencing, document management/content management systems, and web-based training/e-learning.

[1]This section of the chapter is based on an article by Mohammad Nazim and Bhaskar Mukherjee "Managing and sharing knowledge in academic libraries" published in *Journal of Knowledge Management Practice* (2012), Vol. 13, Issue 2. Available online at: http://www.tlainc.com/articl305.htm.

Table 4.4 Utilization of knowledge management tools in libraries

KM technologies, tools, and practices	C/P[a]	Mean	Overall mean[b]
Internet (including e-mail and Web 2.0 applications)	P1	4.60	Used
Intranet	C1	4.50	Used
Search engines/information retrieval system	C2	4.40	Used
Phone calls/teleconferencing	P2	4.35	Used
Document management/content management system	C3	3.75	Used
Web-based training/e-learning	C4	3.45	Used
Multimedia repositories	C6	3.15	Moderately used
Mentoring/tutoring	P4	3.00	Moderately used
Working groups/communities of practice	P3	2.85	Moderately used
Benchmarking/best practices	C5	2.80	Moderately used
Video-conferencing	P5	2.65	Moderately used
Data mining/knowledge discovery tools	C7	2.35	Partially used
Expertise locator/directory of expertise	P6	2.30	Partially used
Storytelling	P7	1.63	Partially used

[a] C, codification; P, personalization.

[b] For the purpose of marking the overall perceptions of respondents, the following scoring system designed by Sarrafzadeh et al. (2010) was used: mean 1–1.44 = not used; mean 1.45–2.44 = partially used; mean 2.45–3.44 = moderately used; mean 3.45–4.44 = used; mean 4.55–5 = extensively used.

Of the 7 indicator variables investigated for identifying the level of use of the codification approach, Intranet scored the highest (mean 4.50), followed by search engines/information retrieval systems (mean 4.40), document/content management systems (mean 3.75), and web-based training/e-learning (mean 3.45). The other three indicator variables had means <3.45, indicating that they were being used moderately or partially. The values are: Multimedia repositories (mean 3.15), benchmarking/best practices (mean 2.80), and data mining/knowledge discovery tools (mean 2.35).

Regarding the use of the personalization approach of KM, the Internet (including e-mail and Web 2.0) was found to be the most utilized tool (mean 4.60), followed by phone calls/teleconferencing (mean 4.35) and mentoring/tutoring (mean 3.0). Other practices related to the personalization approach of KM in the libraries surveyed were working groups/communities of practice (mean 2.85), video-conferencing (mean 2.65), expertise locator/directory of expertise (mean 2.30), and storytelling (mean 1.63).

A question that has attracted interest in the literature is: How must a given organization balance the two approaches of KM for maximum advantage? Some scholars strongly favor a biased approach, while others suggest using both approaches simultaneously and giving them equal importance. Hansen et al. (1999) proposed a 20:80 split between these two approaches, that is, an organization must adopt either 80% codification and 20% personalization or vice versa to effectively manage its knowledge. Jasimuddin et al. (2005) argued that a predominance of either approach is undesirable; they need to be integrated such that the benefits of both tacit and explicit knowledge can be gained. In order to identify which KM approach is predominant in academic libraries, the mean scores of the indicator variables of both codification and personalization approaches were calculated and compared. The analysis reveals (Table 4.5) that both approaches are utilized in a balanced manner. However, the codification approach is slightly dominant over personalization, with a minor difference between their mean scores, that is, 0.33.

Table 4.5 Knowledge management approaches in libraries: codification versus personalization

KM strategies	Mean
Codification	3.48
Personalization	3.05
Difference in mean	0.33

SUMMARY

As discussed above, different approaches to KM involve quite different emphases and practices, and one might naturally be led to ask, "Which approach is right?" Many of the debates on KM have centered on notions of knowledge vis-à-vis information, on ideas about the interrelationships between tacit and explicit knowledge, and on whether they can or cannot be managed. We have discussed different approaches for effectively managing both explicit and tacit knowledge in libraries. If the respective advantages of each approach can be combined, an organization would be able to develop and apply new knowledge more quickly and more extensively than organizations that do not try to manage knowledge or that use only a single approach. Thus organizations must devise and implement a hybrid KM approach that synthesizes the right combination and balance for the management of both tacit and explicit knowledge.

It appears from the case study findings that the type of approaches used in academic libraries involve both codification and personalization, with a slight dominance of codification over personalization. However, some elements of both codification and personalization approaches were not being used by these libraries. Data mining, knowledge discovery tools, benchmarking, best practices, working groups, communities of practice, video-conferencing, directory of expertise, and storytelling were recognized as important tools and practices in KM, but they were not being used to a great extent in the academic libraries surveyed. The Internet, intranets, telephone calls/teleconferencing, search engines, and document management/content management systems are the most frequently used tools and practices in academic libraries. Thus libraries are using only those tools and practices which are easily accessible and which librarians are aware of.

REFERENCES

Alavi, M., Leidner, D., 1999. Knowledge Management Systems: Issues, Challenges and Benefits. article 7. Available at: Communications of the Association for Information Systems, vol. 1. http://cais-isworld.org/articles/1-7.default.asp?View=pdf&x=34&y=11 (accessed 14.06.15).

Amidon, D.M., 1997. Innovation Strategy for the Knowledge Economy: The Ken Awakening. Butterworth-Heinemann, Boston, MA.

Baskerville, R., Dulipovici, A., 2006. The theoretical foundations of knowledge management. Knowl. Manag. Res. Pract. 4 (2), 83–105.

Bedford, D.A.D., Donley, J.K., Lensenmayer, N., 2015. The role of librarians in a knowledge society: valuing our intellectual capital assets. In: Current Issues in Libraries, Information Science and Related Fields. Advances in Librarianship, vol. 39. pp. 81–113. Published online: 15 June 2015 http://dx.doi.org/10.1108/S0065-283020150000039011 (accessed 15.12.15).

Choo, C.W., 2000. Working with knowledge: how informational professionals help organisations manage what they know. Libr. Manag. 21 (8), 395–403.
Choo, C.W., 2002. Information management, knowledge management and information professional. In: Information Management for the Intelligent Organization: The Art of Scanning the Environment. Information Today, Medford, NJ, pp. 257–279.
Daneshgar, F., Parirokh, M., 2007. A knowledge schema for organizational learning in academic libraries. Knowl. Manag. Res. Pract. 5, 22–33.
Davenport, T.H., Prusak, L., 1998. Working Knowledge: How Organizations Manage What They Know. Harvard Business School Press, Boston, MA.
Denning, S., 2001. Connecting vs. Collecting Knowledge. Available at: http://www.stevedenning.com/Knowledge-Management/connecting-vs-collecting.aspx (accessed 23.11.15).
Gandhi, S., 2004. Knowledge management and reference services. J. Acad. Librariansh. 30 (5), 368–381.
Gibbert, M., Krause, H., 2002. Practice exchange in a best practice marketplace. In: Davenport, T., Probst, G. (Eds.), Knowledge Management Casebook: Best Practices. Publicis MCD, Berlin, pp. 68–84.
Hansen, M.T., Nohria, N., Tierney, T., 1999. What is your strategy for managing knowledge? Harv. Bus. Rev. 77 (2), 106–116.
Hariharan, A., 2005. Critical success factors for knowledge management. Knowl. Manag. Rev. 8 (2), 16–19.
Jantz, R., 2001. Knowledge management in academic libraries: special tools and processes to support information professionals. Ref. Serv. Rev. 29 (1), 33–39.
Jasimuddin, S.M., Klein, J.H., Connell, C., 2005. The paradox of using tacit and explicit knowledge: strategies to face dilemmas. Manag. Decis. 43 (1), 102–112.
Kebede, G., 2010. Knowledge management: an information science perspective. Int. J. Inf. Manag. 30, 416–424.
Kostagiolas, P., Asonitis, S., 2009. Intangible assets for academic libraries. Libr. Manag. 30 (6/7), 419–429.
Kulkarni, U., Ravindran, S., Freeze, R., 2006. A knowledge management success model: theoretical development and empirical validation. J. Manag. Inf. Syst. 23 (3), 309–347.
Kumar, J.A., Ganesh, L.S., 2011. Balancing knowledge strategy: codification and personalization during product development. J. Knowl. Manag. 15 (1), 118–135.
Lee, H.W., 2005. Knowledge management and the role of libraries. Chin. Librariansh. Int. Electron. J. 19. Available at: http://www.white-clouds.com/iclc/cliej/cl19.htm (accessed 26.05.15).
Lloria, M.B., 2008. A review of the main approaches to knowledge management. Knowl. Manag. Res. Pract. 6 (1), 77–89.
Marshall, A., 1890. Principles of Economics. Macmillan, London.
McAdam, R., McCreedy, S., 1999. The process of knowledge management within organizations: a critical assessment of both theory and practice. Knowl. Process. Manag. 6 (2), 101–113.
Nonaka, I., Konno, N., 1998. The concept of "*Ba*": building a foundation for knowledge creation. Calif. Manag. Rev. 40 (3), 40–50.
Nonaka, I., Takeuchi, H., 1995. The Knowledge-Creating Company: How Japanese Companies Create the Dynamics of Innovations. Oxford University Press, New York, NY.
Quintas, P., 2002. Managing Knowledge in a New Century, Managing Knowledge: An Essential Reader. Sage and Oxford University Press, London.
Roknuzzaman, M., Kanai, H., Umemoto, K., 2009. Integration of knowledge management process into digital library system: a theoretical perspective. Libr. Rev. 58 (5), 372–386.
Roos, G., Pike, S., Fernström, L., 2005. Managing Intellectual Capital in Practice. Butterworth-Heinemann, Elsevier, Oxford.

Rowley, J., 2003. Knowledge management—the new librarianship? From custodians of history to gatekeepers to the future. Libr. Manag. 24 (8/9), 433–440.
Ruggles, R., 1998. The state of the notion: knowledge management in practice. Calif. Manag. Rev. 40 (3), 80–89.
Sarrafzadeh, M., Martin, B., Hazeri, A., 2010. Knowledge management and its potential applicability for libraries. Libr. Manag. 31 (3), 198–212.
Scarbrough, H., Swan, J., 2001. Explaining the diffusion of knowledge management: the role of fashion. Br. J. Manag. 12, 3–12.
Stewart, T.A., 1997. Intellectual Capital: The New Wealth of Organizations. Doubleday, New York, NY.
Tredinnick, L., 2006. Web 2.0 and business: a pointer to the intranets of the future? Bus. Inf. Rev. 23 (4), 228–234.
Uriarte, F.A., 2008. Introduction to Knowledge Management. ASEAN Foundation, Jakarta, Indonesia.
Vasconcelos, A.C., 2008. Dilemmas in knowledge management. Libr. Manag. 29 (4/5), 422–443.
White, T., 2004. Knowledge management in an academic library: based on the case study KM within OULS. In: World Library and Information Congress: 70th IFLA General Conference and Council, August 22–27, Buenos Aires.
Wilson, T.D., 2002a. The non sense of knowledge management. Inf. Res. 8 (1). Available at: http://informationr.net/ir/8-1/paper141.html (accessed 12.12.15).
Wilson, T.D., 2002b. Information management. In: Feather, J., Sturges, P. (Eds.), International Encyclopaedia of Information and Library Science. second ed. Routledge, London.

CHAPTER 5

Knowledge Management Strategy

INTRODUCTION

Today, knowledge is recognized as a critical resource for sustaining competitive advantage, learning new skills, solving problems, and developing competencies. Knowledge management (KM) has become an important issue within all kinds of organizations. Organizations implement KM to optimize various types of knowledge resources and maximize their strategic value. If done properly, it can provide tremendous value-added benefits to an organization (Liebowitz, 2001).

KM is viewed as a planned and structured approach to manage the creation, sharing, harvesting, and leveraging of knowledge as an organizational asset, and to enhance an organization's ability, speed, and effectiveness in delivering products or services for the benefit of clients, in line with its business strategy (Du Plessis and Boon, 2004). The success of KM initiatives in an organization depends on creation, sharing, and proper use of knowledge (Gandhi, 2004), because creation transfer and use of knowledge within an organization reduce the chances of duplication, improve productivity, and save significant costs, while lack of transfer and use can lead to information overload and confusion, as well as wasted manpower (Clarke, 2004).

KM in libraries is not a new idea; it has a long history in library practice in the sense of managing recorded or codified knowledge. Librarians have been managing knowledge for hundreds of years, but their role has always been to identify and organize information, share information resources, and connect people to the information they need. The fundamental shift in organizational strategy is due precisely to the realization that knowledge and information are not the same. Information is relatively easy to identify, store and transfer, but it is not the same for knowledge. In this context, the earlier roles of librarians were confined to the management of information. Although information management is an important pillar of KM, KM encompasses broader issues and, in particular, creation of processes and behaviors that allows transformation of information into organizational knowledge. Additionally, KM includes a knowledge component that requires several organizational initiatives, including "the care, feeding and training of experts" (Blair, 2002; quoted in Sinotte, 2004, p. 193). This, according to Sinotte (2004), includes both learning and sharing as fundamental processes that are essential in order to utilize existing knowledge and create new knowledge (p. 193). This chapter explains different types of knowledge assets of an academic library and outlines a KM strategy for managing knowledge assets in academic libraries.

CATEGORIES OF KNOWLEDGE ASSETS IN A LIBRARY

One of the important functions of KM is to identify the different types of knowledge in an organization and to develop a strategy to apply that knowledge into practice to maximize its strategic value. Over the centuries many attempts have been made to classify knowledge. However, different fields have focused on different dimensions of knowledge. This has resulted in numerous classifications and distinctions based on philosophy and even religion (Frost, 2010). The literature includes numerous typologies of knowledge, including: scientific and practical knowledge (Hayek, 1945); objective knowledge and knowledge based on experiences (Penrose, 1959); declarative and procedural knowledge (Winter, 1987); incorporated, migratory, embedded, and codified knowledge (Zuboff, 1988; Badaracco, 1991; Blacker, 1993); tacit, explicit, and cultural knowledge (Choo, 2000); personal, proprietary, public knowledge, and common sense (Boisot, 1998); and core, advanced, and innovative knowledge (Zack, 1999).

One of the most cited theories of knowledge classification in the KM literature is one that distinguishes knowledge either as tacit or explicit. The concept of tacit and explicit knowledge was first introduced by Michael Polanyi in 1962, and was later adopted and elaborated by Nonaka (1991) and Nonaka and Takeuchi (1995). One of the fundamental steps in KM is to define and identify what are the key knowledge assets that need to be managed in an organization. In order to manage knowledge, it is essential to understand the nature of different types of knowledge assets in an academic library. Knowledge in academic libraries may me classified into four categories: tacit knowledge, explicit knowledge, procedural knowledge, and cultural knowledge.

Tacit Knowledge

Michael Polanyi described tacit knowledge as knowing more than we can tell, or knowing how to do something without thinking about it, like riding a bicycle (Polanyi, 1967, quoted in Smith, 2001). According to Smith (2001), it is "practical, action-oriented knowledge or 'know-how' based on practice, acquired by personal experience, seldom expressed openly, often resembles intuition" (p. 314). So tacit knowledge is a kind of personal knowledge that is learned by members of an organization through experience and learning by doing, and is used to perform their work. It contains mental models, perceptions, insights, assumptions, personal beliefs, subjective insights, intuitions, instinct, and values. Since tacit knowledge is embedded in the minds of individuals in the form of their experience and competence, it is very difficult (not impossible) to codify and transfer to others. In the words of Nonaka (1991), "tacit knowledge is highly personal. It is hard to formalize and, therefore, difficult to communicate to others" (p. 98). Tacit knowledge can sometimes be communicated through a shared understanding between individuals. In other cases, tacit knowledge must be converted into explicit knowledge (ie, words, models, or numbers that can be understood) before sharing or communicating it to others (Becerra-Fernandez and Sabherwal, 2006). There are two dimensions of tacit knowledge as described by Smith (2001), the technical dimension and the cognitive dimension:

1. The technical dimension of tacit knowledge encompasses the kind of informal and personal skills often captured in terms of "know-how". This know-how is demonstrated when people master a specific body of knowledge or use skills like those gradually developed by master craftsmen. A craftsman develops a wealth of expertise after years of experience. But he often has difficulty articulating the technical or scientific principles of his or her craft. Thus highly subjective and personal insights, intuitions, hunches, and inspirations derived from a person's experience fall within the technical dimension of tacit knowledge.
2. The cognitive dimension of tacit knowledge consists of beliefs, perceptions, ideals, values, emotions, and implicit mental models so ingrained they are taken for granted (Sternberg, 1997). Cognitive tacit knowledge is deeply embedded in the human brain and therefore cannot be articulated very easily. Although not completely expressible in words or symbols, it may be communicated or revealed to others through rich modes of discourse that include the use of metaphors, analogies, demonstrations, mentoring, and stories.

Wijetunge (2002) classified the tacit knowledge of a university into two categories: internal tacit knowledge and external tacit knowledge. Internal tacit knowledge consists of senior and experienced employees with a sound knowledge of work procedures, rules and regulations, etc. and the unarticulated knowledge of the librarians themselves. External tacit knowledge consists of personnel external to the university with expert knowledge, that is, service personnel, subject experts, and any other person who provides expertise to university libraries.

Bedford et al. (2015) discuss a library's tacit knowledge that takes the form of intellectual assets, which they define as "an aggregation of the intellectual capital of all of its employees." It consists of answers to questions, knowledge of sources, knowledge of subject domains, knowledge of information behaviors, knowledge of the publishing industry, foresight, etc.

Explicit Knowledge

Explicit knowledge is defined by Choo (2000) as "knowledge that is expressed formally using a system of symbols, and can therefore be easily communicated or diffused." It is codified and digitized in books, documents, reports, spreadsheets, white papers, memos, training courses, and the like. Unlike tacit knowledge, explicit knowledge is formal and systematic, and therefore it can easily be retrieved, communicated, and shared through print, electronic, and other formal means. It is a type of academic knowledge that may be acquired through formal education or structured study. Since explicit knowledge is formal and systematic, it is described in formal languages, like manuals, mechanical expressions, copyright, and patents; it is codified and stored in documents, databases, and web pages; and it is retrieved with the help of high-quality, reliable, fast information retrieval systems. However, the process of sharing explicit knowledge requires monetary investment for the development of an information technology infrastructure.

Choo (2000) distinguishes explicit knowledge either as object-based or rule-based. Object-based knowledge is found in artifacts such as products, patents, software code, computer databases, technical drawings, tools, prototypes, photographs, voice recordings, films, and so on. Object-based knowledge is represented by strings of symbols (words, numbers, formulas), or is embodied in physical entities (equipment, models, substances).

Rule-based knowledge is codified into rules, routines, or operating procedures. A substantial part of an organization's operational knowledge about how to do things is contained in its rules, routines, and procedures.

An organization's explicit knowledge also takes the form of intellectual assets which, according to Patrick Sullivan, are "the codified, tangible, or physical descriptions of specific knowledge to which the company can assert ownership rights. Any piece of knowledge that becomes defined usually by being written down or entered into a computer qualifies as an intellectual asset and can be protected. Intellectual assets are the source of innovation that the firm commercializes" (Sullivan, 1998, p. 23, cited in Choo, 2000).

Explicit knowledge codified as intellectual assets is valuable to an organization because it adds to the organization's observable and tradeable stocks of knowledge (Choo, 2000). After codification, explicit knowledge assets can be reused to solve many similar types of problems or connect people with valuable, reusable knowledge. Once explicit knowledge is codified, it remains with the organization even after its inventors or authors leave the organization. Explicit knowledge serves three important purposes in an organization, as explained by Choo (2000):

- it encodes past learning in artifacts and rules;
- it facilitates coordination between disparate activities and functions in the organization; and
- it signifies technical skill and procedural rationality, and so helps the organization to present a self-image of competence, legitimacy, and accountability.

Bedford et al. (2015) observed that "explicit and encoded resources that libraries manage fall into the explicit knowledge category in the intellectual capital profile of their authors or creators" (p. 83). A library's explicit knowledge includes collection development policies, collection guides, conference proceedings, formal educational credentials, frequently asked questions, information standards, presentations, professional publications, reading lists, webinars, and workshops. Wijetunge (2002) identified two types of explicit knowledge in an academic institution: internal explicit knowledge and external explicit knowledge. Internal explicit knowledge consists of reports, guidelines, theses, databases, minutes of meetings, and any other type of tangible knowledge containers generated within the university. External explicit knowledge encompasses tangible material in the form of books, journals, reports, CD-ROMs, and any other media produced outside the university.

Procedural Knowledge

Procedural knowledge is defined as "an understanding of how to do a task or carry out a procedure" (Awad and Ghaziri, 2004, p. 68). It consists of step-by-step procedures for handling various tasks or explaining various occurrences. Procedural knowledge is contained in the application of a procedure and it is reflected in manual, cognitive, and mental skills. Procedural knowledge usually involves psychomotor skills such as holding on to a handrail while riding an escalator. However, some procedural knowledge is not psychomotor. Examples of procedural knowledge in the context of a library include acquisitions and selection knowledge, budgeting knowledge, cataloging knowledge, circulation knowledge, facilities management knowledge, information-finding strategies, knowledge of information sources, literacy training knowledge, personnel management knowledge, etc.

Cultural Knowledge

Davenport and Prusak (2000) emphasized that, for a KM system to be successful, it is critical to have a knowledge-oriented culture; that is, a culture that encourages and rewards knowledge sharing. The cultural knowledge of an organization consists of the beliefs that are held to be true based on experience, observation, and reflection about itself and its environment (Choo, 2000). An organization, over time, develops shared beliefs about the nature of its main business, core capabilities, markets, competitors, and so on. These beliefs are used as criteria for judging and selecting alternatives and new ideas, and for evaluating projects and proposals. Cultural knowledge is used in an organization to answer questions such as "What kind of an organization are we?," "What knowledge would be valuable to the organization?," and "What knowledge would be worth pursuing?" The answers in turn depend on shared assumptions and beliefs about what business the organization is in, what its core competencies are, and how it wants to grow over time (Choo, 2000).

Leonard (1995) describes how organizations supply and sustain values and norms that "determine what kinds of knowledge are sought and nurtured, what kinds of knowledge-building activities are tolerated and encouraged" (cited in Choo, 2000). Although cultural knowledge is not written down (but is conveyed in stories, histories, and reward or evaluation systems), it remains with the organization through employee changes and staff turnover. Cultural knowledge in a library includes collaborative, community-oriented, fair rewards and recognitions, service orientation and attitude, learning culture, mentoring and coaching culture, open-mindedness, being open to different types of learning experiences, being open to experimentation, and a strong community culture (Bedford et al., 2015).

To make KM efforts successful, it is important to differentiate between information and knowledge. Gandhi (2004, p. 371) emphasizes that:

> *Not all information is knowledge. Information cannot become knowledge until it is analyzed and acted upon, and it will only be acted upon in the right organizational culture. While most organizations and employees suffer from information overload, they do not suffer from knowledge overload. On the contrary, there is a dearth of*

knowledge. One of the biggest challenges of KM lies in being able to make sense of the mountains of information, sifting out valuable information, and sharing it.

Academic libraries have different types of knowledge: tacit, explicit, procedural, and cultural. In libraries, tacit knowledge resides in senior and experienced employees with a sound knowledge of information resources, work procedures, rules and regulations, etc. and the unarticulated knowledge contained in the librarians themselves. Explicit knowledge is either created within the organization, including reports, memos, guidelines, theses, minutes of meetings, etc., or acquired from external sources, including books, journal articles databases, external reports, government information, etc. Procedural knowledge includes the knowledge of various library processes and functions (eg, knowledge of acquisition and technical processes, etc.). Cultural knowledge includes "the shared assumptions and beliefs that are used to describe and explain reality, as well as the criteria and expectations that are used to assign value and significance to new information" (Choo, 2000). Examples of different types of knowledge assets of libraries are shown in Table 5.1.

All categories of knowledge are considered as the key knowledge assets of an academic library which should be managed properly. KM provides academic libraries with an enormous opportunity to improve their effectiveness, both for themselves and their parent institutions. Librarians in academic libraries can adopt KM practice as a way to expand the library's role in areas such as administration or support services, where libraries have had little impact in the past. IT serves as a tool to help with capturing, organizing, sharing, and applying knowledge. An open favorable culture that encourages sharing of ideas and best practices and the transfer of knowledge is a critical enabler of KM.

STRATEGY TO MANAGE KNOWLEDGE IN LIBRARIES

One of the important objectives of KM is to turn an organization into a learning and sharing organization by linking people together and creating a flow of knowledge generated by people in different units. Thus the purpose is innovation and reuse. Innovation is closely linked to the generation of new knowledge or new linkages between existing knowledge, while reuse forms the basis for organizational learning and should be viewed more as a dissemination of innovation (Dalkir, 2005). A KM strategy is a general, issue-based approach to defining operational strategy and objectives with specialized KM principles and approaches (Srikantaiah and Koenig, 2000).

Table 5.1 Knowledge assets of libraries

Types of knowledge	Examples of different types of knowledge
Tacit knowledge	Answers to questions
	Knowledge of library collections
	Knowledge of subject domains
	Knowledge of information behaviors
	Knowledge of scholarly publishing models
Explicit knowledge	Collection development policies
	Collection guides
	Conference proceedings
	Formal educational credentials
	Frequently asked questions
	Information standards
	Professional publications
	Reading lists
	Webinars and workshops
Procedural knowledge	Acquisitions and selection knowledge
	Budgeting knowledge
	Cataloging knowledge
	Circulation knowledge
	Facilities management knowledge
	Information-finding strategies
	Knowledge of information sources
	Literacy training knowledge
	Management knowledge
	Program planning knowledge
	Reference service knowledge
	Knowledge of search strategy formulation
	Storytelling knowledge
	System design knowledge
Cultural knowledge	Collaborative, community-oriented, fair rewards and recognitions
	Service orientation and attitude
	Learning culture
	Mentoring and coaching culture
	Open-mindedness
	Different types of learning and experimentation experiences
	Strong community culture

Courtesy Bedford, D.A.D., Donley, J.K., Lensenmayer, N., 2015. The role of librarians in a knowledge society: valuing our intellectual capital assets. In: Current Issues in Libraries, Information Science and Related Fields. Advances in Librarianship, vol. 39, pp. 81–113. Published online: 15 June 2015 http://dx.doi.org/10.1108/S0065-283020150000039011 (accessed 15.12.15).

The objective is to identify how the organization can best leverage its knowledge resources to develop innovative products and services and to gain a competitive advantage over its competitors. One of the important steps in KM implementation is to define a KM strategy. Once the KM strategy is clearly defined, other options like baselining and technology may be explored. KM strategy helps an organization to develop a road map that can be used to identify and prioritize KM initiatives, tools, and approaches in such a way as to support its long-term business objectives. A KM strategy, according to Dalkir (2005), helps to address the following questions: (i) Which KM approach, or set of KM approaches, will bring the most value to the organization? (ii) How can the organization prioritize alternatives when any one or several of the alternatives are appealing and resources are limited?

Academic libraries have long been described as the heart of their universities because of the strategic position they occupy. They were established to support the mission of the universities by providing resources to aid teaching, learning, and research. The environment in which academic libraries operate today and the way people search and access information has changed due to the rapid developments in information and communication technologies (ICT). Development of the Internet, the World Wide Web, user-friendly databases, and search engines has not only made a profound impact on the structure and functioning of academic libraries, but also has challenged the status of academic libraries as the only provider of information. This is because of the alternatives, such as Google Scholar, that are available for people to locate and access scholarly literature from commercial publishers. Technological changes, along with external pressure of market forces, have forced academic libraries to transform their structures and implement new managerial processes. These changes help them become more flexible and thereby stimulate innovation and performance to survive in the face of competition from emerging groups of information suppliers and ever increasing levels of user expectations (Sarrafzadeh et al., 2010). KM is one of these processes, and has been recognized worldwide as a very useful solution for the survival and success of academic libraries (Porumbeanu, 2010).

KM strategies are broadly classified as (i) codification and (ii) personalization. The major difference between these two strategies is that they emphasize different aspects of KM; that is, one strategy focuses on knowledge transfer and sharing, and the other on processes and technology. A codification strategy is described as extracting explicit knowledge from the person who developed it, storing it in databases, and promoting its subsequent reuse by anyone who needs it (Kumar and Ganesh, 2011). The success of a codification strategy for managing knowledge in an organization depends on the use of information technologies, such as intranets, knowledge repositories, document management systems, information retrieval systems, data mining or knowledge discovery tools, etc., to enhance the quality and speed of knowledge capture, storage, organization, retrieval, and transfer.

It is also believed that a great deal of organizational knowledge is tacit in nature and the use of information technology alone is not sufficient to share and use this type of knowledge. Therefore the emphasis of a personalization strategy is on tacit knowledge and its transfer and sharing among employees. This may be facilitated by direct interactions between people by connecting them with each other (Hansen et al., 1999). However, the use of this strategy requires investment in building networks of people, where knowledge is shared not only face to face, but also virtually over the telephone, by e-mail, and via video-conferencing. Use of the Internet (e-mail, social networking, etc.), teleconferencing and video-conferencing, communities of practice, storytelling or mentoring, and setting up shared physical and virtual spaces are some of the common practices related to this strategy.

KEY COMPONENTS OF KM STRATEGY

KM strategy has three critical components: people, processes, and information technology. Each of these components plays a significant role in KM and can have a tremendous impact on its success or failure. The state of knowledge maturity can be measured by systematically addressing these three basic pillars of KM, as they are recognized as the key foundation areas of KM:

- *People*: people and culture—these address the "mindset" and relate to attributes of assessing people and culture.
- *KM process*: process and strategy—these facilitate and guide the efforts of the people to capture and use the knowledge in the organization to achieve business benefits.
- *Information technology*: information technology infrastructure—this is an enabler that helps people harness the maximum out of KM initiatives.

People and Culture

One of the most important enablers of KM is an open and favorable culture that encourages people to interact with each other, share ideas, experiences and viewpoints, and be heard without fear of reprisals. The absence of a favorable culture that encourages collaboration, trust, knowledge sharing, listening, learning, and creativity can be a major barrier in developing and implementing a successful KM project. KM has two parts: first, management of knowledge and information; and second, the management of individuals who possess specific expertise, abilities, or knowledge. These two parts are integrated with the help of specific processes and technology to facilitate KM. The ultimate goal of KM is to manage explicit and tacit knowledge within an organization. Explicit knowledge in an organization can easily be identified, acquired, organized, stored, and transferred. To manage explicit knowledge, organizations must:

- generate, create, or acquire knowledge;
- codify and organize knowledge to facilitate easy access;
- make knowledge available to others through communication or publications;
- facilitate access to, and retrieval of, knowledge; and
- use and apply knowledge to solve problems, support decisions, improve performance, coach, and analyze situations and processes to support business activities (Sahasrabudhe, 2000, cited in Gandhi, 2004).

As discussed above, the most valuable knowledge of an organization resides in the minds of its workers, which is usually known as tacit knowledge or the intellectual assets of an organization. Organizations face difficulties in transferring and utilizing this type of knowledge. To make use of this knowledge, it must either be converted into an explicit form or shared with others. Different techniques are used for the codification or articulation of tacit knowledge. Knowledge may be shared either face to face or remotely with the help of ICT. Communities of practice, apprenticeship, mentoring, tutoring, formal and informal meetings, conferences, seminars, workshops, etc. are some of the methods of sharing knowledge face to face. Telephones, video-conferencing, e-mail, intranets, and social networking are some important ICT-based tools used to share knowledge virtually. Gandhi (2004) mentioned that "tacit knowledge can be managed in two ways. It can be converted to explicit knowledge, through written communications, interviews, and oral histories. Organizations can also create knowledge communities or communities of practice to transfer tacit knowledge through face-to-face interaction, verbal communication and dialog, hands-on instruction, interactive problem solving, networking, coaching, mentoring, training, and professional development opportunities" (p. 371).

The success of an organization depends largely on its culture, which in turn influences the employees' attitudes and behaviors. In the context of a discussion on the strategy of KM implementation, the change of culture at organizational level is extremely important. The existence of a favorable environment for communication, collaboration, knowledge sharing and transfer, as well as easy identification of the organization's knowledge assets, is essential in making KM initiatives successful. If libraries and other information services are to survive in the contemporary information marketplace, the creation of a culture oriented towards performance, which appreciates and encourages communication, collaboration and that rewards creativity and new ideas is essential. This also has to be a culture oriented towards people, employees and users, one which meets their information needs and one of permanent change, oriented towards learning and continuous professional training, and one that stimulates knowledge sharing and development. Thus a knowledge and learning-oriented culture would facilitate the implementation and development of KM systems, which are extremely important for organizations such as libraries.

KM Processes

KM provides an opportunity for libraries to leverage the available knowledge that may help librarians to carry out their tasks more efficiently and effectively (Maponya, 2004). The KM process, according to Roknuzzaman et al. (2009), consists of the following steps:

- identification of knowledge needs;
- the assessment of existing knowledge resources and services;
- acquisition of new knowledge in order to accomplish the knowledge needs;
- integration of new knowledge and services;
- modification of the existing system;
- replacing outdated knowledge;
- evaluation of knowledge;
- continuous improvement; and
- providing knowledge in the best possible way to all members of the community.

Thus the process of KM implementation involves identification, acquisition, capture, codification, storage, sharing, and application of knowledge. These processes are facilitated by the application of IT. Additionally, an open and favorable culture is required to encourage people to share their knowledge and best practices with other people in the organization. The process of KM implementation is a dynamic and cyclical process that motivates employees to continuously engage in acquiring new knowledge, creating new information and knowledge on the basis of acquired knowledge, sharing knowledge with other employees in the organization, and applying new knowledge to improve the overall performance of the organization in terms of developing innovative products and services. But three things are essential to make KM initiatives successful. First, people must have the knowledge and willingness to acquire new knowledge; second, they must use and apply that knowledge in working practice; and third, they must have the ability to know when to apply or use that knowledge (Gandhi, 2004). The knowledge processes introduced above are briefly described below.

Knowledge Identification and Acquisition

The first step in the KM process is the identification of existing knowledge which is valuable, reliable, and useful to the organization. According to Gandhi (2004), the following types of knowledge may be useful for librarians in libraries:

- knowledge of a specific job or task, for example, how to do reference work;
- a list of subject- or task-level experts who have the best qualifications, the latest training, or the expertise to best perform certain jobs/tasks;
- a list of experts who can solve particular types of problems that have the potential to reoccur;
- knowledge of historical precedents—have certain processes been tried before and what was their outcome;
- knowledge of users and competitors; and
- knowledge about creating successful project teams—knowing who has the skill sets for similar projects and who has worked together successfully in the past.

For the mapping and inventory of existing knowledge resources, libraries need to carry out a knowledge audit. With the help of a knowledge audit, libraries can easily measure the gap between available knowledge and required knowledge. This gap can be filled by acquiring new knowledge in the organization.

If the required level of knowledge is not available, then it has to be acquired. Since the success of KM depends on the availability of knowledge in the organization, staffs that are recruited must have knowledge of work processes. They are also expected to acquire knowledge continuously from different sources to keep them updated. According to Maponya (2004), knowledge in libraries can be acquired through:

- establishing knowledge links or networking with other libraries and with institutions of all kinds;
- attending training programs, conferences, seminars, and workshops;

- subscribing to listservs and online or virtual communities of practice; and
- buying knowledge products or resources in the form of manuals, blueprints, reports, and research reports.

Knowledge in libraries is also acquired through knowledge fairs, learning communities, study mission, tours, advisory boards, job rotation, stories, myths, and task forces, experiments, and observations (Smith, 2001). Other methods of knowledge acquisition in libraries include transfer of knowledge directly from experienced employees to less experienced employees. The process of direct transfer of knowledge from people to people is known as socialization, where skills may be transferred through training, apprenticeship, and mentoring. Additionally, libraries organize training programs, conferences, seminars, methodological workshops, and formal or informal meetings to provide learning opportunities for their employees.

Knowledge is also acquired indirectly by writing down the answers to the following questions:

1. What do you know about your strengths?
2. What are the strengths, weaknesses, values, and ambitions of others with whom you work?
3. How would you approach a similar job differently in the future?

If a library does not possess sufficient levels of knowledge internally, it must therefore be acquired from external sources if it is useful to the goals of the library. The library as an organization must look outside its own boundaries to outsource or acquire new knowledge. Knowledge, particularly tacit knowledge, can be acquired through external sources by collecting and compiling information about knowledgeable human resources. One of the best methods is to maintain résumés online and keep these résumés updated. These résumés must show the unique expertise of people so that they may be consulted. Choo (2000) suggests compiling an expert directory for providing quick access to expertise. This can be done by maintaining electronic yellow pages. The electronic yellow pages must be organized properly to find relevant experts. They should include complete contact details so that when an expert is located, he or she may be contacted for assistance. A link should be provided in the yellow page for sending e-mails or viewing personal home pages.

Knowledge Capture and Codification

According to Gandhi (2004), knowledge capture "involves the key inputs and outputs of knowledge. Key inputs may include specific data and information, verbal or written communications, and other shared explicit and tacit knowledge such as best practices. Key outputs may be [in the form of] internal documents, reports, research papers, procedures, internal benchmarks, and best practices" (p. 373). Knowledge capture is important for the success and development of a knowledge-based organization. Much of the knowledge in an organization resides in the heads of the people, and if it is not captured and stored, it is more likely to be lost when an employee leaves the organization. Therefore it is essential to identify the expertise and the skills of staff and capture it to avoid a collective loss of organizational memory.

Libraries need to develop systems to identify people's expertise so that it may be captured, shared, and reused in the future. Formal processes of capturing knowledge include collating internal profiles of librarians and also standardizing routine information-update reports. Additionally, libraries can capture the most commonly received enquiries at the reference desk and place them within easy reach to better serve users in the shortest time possible. It is important to create databases of frequently asked questions to enable librarians to not only provide an in-depth customized reference service but also to become knowledgeable about handling different enquiries (Maponya, 2004).

Since tacit knowledge is intuitive and practice-based, it cannot easily be passed on to others. To make the best use of tacit knowledge, it must be codified into an explicit form. Once tacit knowledge is codified and converted to explicit knowledge, it may easily be stored, organized, combined, accessed, shared, and manipulated in different contexts. The codification of knowledge provides several benefits to libraries:

- Codification enables libraries to secure knowledge. A library is in less danger of losing its intellectual assets, even when its employees retire or leave the organization.
- Codification enables fast access and retrieval of knowledge.
- Codification facilitates sharing, reuse, reflection, and ongoing learning.

The processes of codification and representation of knowledge for access and reuse are not new to Library & Information Science (LIS) professionals, as they are involved in many stages of the knowledge processing cycle. Gandhi (2004) outlined the following steps in the codification and representation of knowledge:

1. Identifying, acquiring, or extracting valuable knowledge from documents, discussions, or interviews, usually accomplished with the help of subject matter experts.
2. Refining, writing up, and editing "raw knowledge" (such as project files, presentations, e-mail messages), and turning it into "processed knowledge" (such as lessons learned, best practices, case studies).

3. Organizing the processed knowledge and making it accessible by adding index terms, subject headings, cross-reference links, and metadata.
4. Packaging, publishing, and disseminating knowledge through a variety of channels, including intranet web pages, CD-ROMs, subject-oriented pathfinders, and "knowledge portals" that are focused on particular business needs or issues.
5. Designing and managing the overall information architecture consisting of a set of well-defined standards and schemes for organizing, classifying, publishing, and navigating the organization's intellectual content.

Knowledge Organization and Retrieval

Knowledge organization and retrieval refers to the processes of "knowledge structuring and storing that make it more formalized and accessible" (Massa and Testa, 2009, p. 130). These processes focus on developing systems to systematically capture, record, organize, and store the key inputs and outputs of knowledge, and to find, collect, and organize internal knowledge and best practices (Gandhi, 2004).

Librarians have experience of knowledge organization. They have already using library classification schemes, cataloging codes, lists of subject headings, thesauruses, and metadata sets for creating surrogates of documents. This experience may be utilized by librarians in the development and use of knowledge taxonomies, knowledge mapping, electronic yellow pages, data mining, and data warehousing to manage both tacit and explicit knowledge. Librarians also have the expertise to achieve file management, create databases and archives to enable knowledge sharing for all of this material and to make it available to a wider audience. The experience of librarians in the organization of knowledge via metadata, understanding user needs, knowledge of integrated and federated searching, and professional skills must extend beyond commercial information (Roknuzzaman et al., 2009).

In a university, faculty members and researchers produce thousands of research papers, books, theses, conference papers, reports, and working papers. Much of this material is not published commercially in books or journals. "Learning objects" are produced for use in teaching and they are not easy to locate outside the course for which they have been developed. Much of this material is created in digital form and this might be captured using web-based digital submission systems. Librarians have already realized the need to create institutional repositories (IRs) for capturing, organizing, archiving, and providing access to knowledge generated within a university. IRs are created for members of the university to store scholarly output so that it can be managed well and retrieved easily.

Once knowledge is organized, it can be stored in knowledge repositories for preservation as well as multiple uses. For the purpose of knowledge retrieval distribution and sharing, a number of knowledge discovery tools and techniques are used to facilitate the retrieval process. Web-scale discovery tools, data mining, browsing, and searching are some of the popular tools used for knowledge discovery and retrieval. Since explicit knowledge can simply be converted into digital form, it can easily be kept in digital files and databases. However, organizing and storing tacit knowledge is still a challenge for LIS professionals. Since tacit knowledge is hard to articulate, it might need to be packaged in a more indirect form, like a storytelling video. Agent-based retrieval systems may be used to capture the interests and or knowledge of library staff and users.

Knowledge Transfer and Sharing

Knowledge transfer is described by Massa and Testa (2009) as "the processes of transferring, disseminating and distributing knowledge in order to make it available to those who need it" (p. 130). The transfer of knowledge encompasses activities and processes associated with the flow of artifacts from one agent to another. Sharing of knowledge is described by Van den Hoof and De Ridder (2004) as the process whereby individuals mutually exchange explicit and tacit knowledge and jointly create new knowledge. Explicit knowledge can easily be captured, stored in databases, retrieved, and distributed across the organization. However, valuable knowledge exists in people; it is more difficult to share this information. Providing access to this know-how to other organizational members eliminates duplication of efforts and forms the basis for problem solving and decision-making.

Transfer of knowledge enables library staff to put this knowledge into practice and share it with their colleagues. Then it may be collectively applied, utilized, and used to attain the library's ultimate goals of satisfying users' needs, developing research activities, creating new knowledge, promoting library functions, and building up a knowledge culture. The competitiveness, quality of products and services, and overall performance of the library largely depend on the dissemination or transfer of knowledge. Knowledge sharing among employees of the library gives way to sharing of ideas and knowledge. This is a very effective means of knowledge creation, especially in the case of tacit knowledge. The more the employees interact, the more tacit knowledge is created. Effective knowledge-sharing practices enable libraries to reuse and regenerate knowledge at individual and organizational levels. Knowledge in the library can be transferred and shared in the form of a number knowledge-based services and products, including e-mail, electronic publications, presentations, websites, online discussion forums, video-conferencing and collaboration tools, virtual classrooms, corporate intranets, web portals, blogs, knowledge banks, etc. (Roknuzzaman et al., 2009).

Knowledge Use and Application

Knowledge application is defined "as the process of incorporating knowledge into an organization's products, services and practices to derive value from it" (Massa and Testa, 2009, p. 130). The life cycle of KM begins with the acquisition of knowledge and ends with the application of this acquired knowledge in practice. Employees use and apply this knowledge to improve performance and generate new knowledge in the process. The application of knowledge is the ultimate goal of the whole knowledge process. Knowledge is used and applied for taking decisions and solving problems. In the library context, the acquired knowledge may be used and applied for responding to the answers of reference questions, taking decisions about the best reference sources to consult to answer a particular question, developing need-based collections, planning and redesigning innovative library services, avoiding redundancy, etc.

Information Technology

KM initiatives have the best chance of success when the organization's information technology infrastructure is already in place, is robust and diversified enough to suit differing needs of staff, enabling staff to coordinate. IT applications facilitate and improve the process of collection, organization, storage, and dissemination of knowledge. Organizations use IT-based systems, such as relational database management systems, document management systems, the Internet, intranets, search engines, workflow tools, performance support systems, decision support systems, data mining, data warehousing, e-mail, video-conferencing, bulletin boards, news groups, and discussion boards. These systems provide a number of possible solutions for capturing, organizing, and sharing recorded human knowledge. Thus information technology is vital in enabling and facilitating many KM processes and initiatives. With the proper use of information technology, organizations can extract and organize knowledge, make it accessible to employees, and even speed up the knowledge transfer process.

IT supports KM initiatives in academic libraries in two ways: by providing the means to acquire, organize, store, retrieve and disseminate knowledge (Sabashini et al., 2012), and by connecting library users with librarians and library services through the use of web-based ICT tools to communicate with library users and share information and knowledge (Jain, 2007; Yuan et al., 2013). The most common applications of IT-based tools in academic libraries include:

- communication tools such as e-mail, instance messaging, telephones, teleconferencing, intranets, video-conferencing, etc.;
- long-standing tools such as databases, institutional archives, etc.; and
- social media tools such as wikis, blogs, online communities, and social networking sites.

Some examples of ICT that can enhance or support KM initiatives are listed below:

- video-conferencing/telephone
- groupware; an example is Lotus notes
- intranets/Internet
- portals
- expertise location
- electronic bulletin boards
- knowledge directories
- databases
- electronic mails
- intelligent search engines
- blogs/Facebook/Twitter.

KM MODEL FOR LIBRARIES

Several KM models have been developed for manufacturing and service sector organizations. On the basis of a review of literature and personal observations during the research, a model for the successful implementation of KM is proposed to suit the requirements and conditions of academic libraries. An attempt is made to outline the elements of the proposed model to formulate some basic steps which may be followed as the starting point in the implementation of KM in academic libraries. The proposed model is composed of five elements, as shown in Fig. 5.1.

Knowledge and Expertise

The fundamental element of the proposed model is the requirement of professional competencies. Professional competencies based on activities such as knowledge organization and preservation, information search, retrieval and dissemination, the creation of information products and services

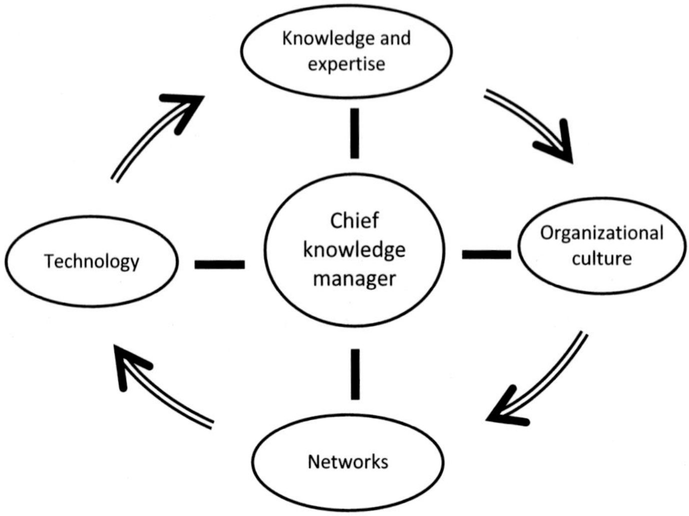

Fig. 5.1 Knowledge management model for libraries.

with added value constitute essential organizational assets of academic libraries. Therefore firstly academic libraries should identify and focus on those few processes which they do best, developing and improving them all the time. Through a variety of mechanisms of organizational learning, academic libraries can create, collect, and use the knowledge necessary for these processes. Based on this knowledge, they can develop new operating procedures and improve the existing ones. Organizational learning is essential for developing professional competencies and it must be fostered and enhanced continuously.

Organizational Culture

The second element of the proposed model is the people, the human resources, and the organizational culture. Organizational culture (including aspects such as communication, organizational learning, knowledge sharing, and communities of practice) is a fundamental element of the KM process. The chances of success in the implementation of KM are almost absent in any kind of organization, including libraries, without the development of a collective culture open to change. For increased efficiency in KM in academic libraries, learning, creativity, and quality should be valued and sought, the acquisition of new skills and knowledge must be an ongoing process, investment in human resources and in the further training of employees should be made. Communities of practice should be encouraged. An online discussion forum may be created, which may help to improve the processes of organizational learning, sharing of knowledge and expertise. Appropriate measures must be taken by librarians so that knowledge sharing takes place, perhaps leading to the establishment of organizational changes to encourage greater use of this forum. A system must be set up for periodic evaluations and rewards to encourage people to contribute their knowledge and to use the knowledge of others.

Information Technology Infrastructure

The third element of the proposed model is technology, which can underpin the process of KM by improving the methods of organizational learning and knowledge sharing. Technology plays a fundamental role in creating a culture and an infrastructure to stimulate and enable access to knowledge and expertise exists in the organization. KM systems based on advanced technologies may collect the relevant knowledge and experience in an organization and may make it available anywhere and any time, thus supporting the process of decisions that are made within the library. KM systems support the processes of identification and codification of knowledge, sharing and distribution of knowledge, and also the processes of creation of new knowledge and integration of this into the organization. With these systems, knowledge can be preserved in the organizational memory for the training of future employees and for helping them in making decisions. Technology-based systems can also connect academic libraries to external sources of knowledge. With the help of these systems, people having expertise in specific areas can be located and a knowledge directory can be created. This knowledge directory can help people: (i) contact specific areas of expertise, (ii) get in touch with those who possess knowledge, and (iii) easily identify experts and share knowledge with them.

Networks

The fourth element of the proposed model is networks, such as the partnerships with other public or private organizations and libraries. Networks and collaboration represent a solution for extended access to knowledge for more creative uses and for increased quality of the processes and services. Academic libraries should be organized in networks, with all the human, information, knowledge, and technology resources they possess. This will provide an opportunity for academic libraries to use human knowledge productively, and thereby make academic libraries more efficient and competitive. Also, as part of a network, academic libraries are able to focus on creating and improving the facilities and infrastructure that encourage and support learning. Through partnerships and networks, academic libraries have more knowledge assets, which ultimately improve overall library functions and services.

Creation of the Position of Knowledge Manager

The last element of the proposed KM model is the creation of the position of knowledge manager in academic libraries. The creation of a knowledge manager position appreciably increases the chances of success in the implementation of KM in academic libraries. Knowledge managers will coordinate the technological infrastructure, human resources, the processes of creation, use and sharing of knowledge, and the cooperative relationships of the organization. They will be responsible for the smooth running of the processes of KM within the academic library, will coordinate the design and implementation of KM programs and systems that will find new sources of knowledge and will identify new ways to use knowledge effectively in the organization.

This model will help academic libraries in the implementation of KM through the:

- identification of the most important processes, products and services of academic libraries, and their evaluation;
- identification of knowledge resources and skills in the organization in order to exploit these resources; and
- identification of potential external partners for collaboration.

The proposed model places the knowledge assets of the organization (which are in the minds of people, in the organization processes, practices, and activities) at organizational level to support the expansion and improvement of the main activities deployed by academic libraries:

- the acquisition, organization, processing, and preservation of documents;
- information search and retrieval;
- information dissemination;
- development of information processes and services;
- provision of information services for users, etc.

SUMMARY

The process of KM implementation starts with the internal analysis of the organization to identify its main activities, operations, and most requested services. The next step in the process of KM implementation is the identification of relevant skills, competences and knowledge, which are the basis of carrying out different operations and providing services. Once the relevant and appropriate skills, competences and knowledge are identified, they must be put into action through the application of appropriate KM tools and techniques. If relevant skills, competences, and knowledge are not available internally in the organization, they must be acquired, developed, and improved through the process of organizational learning. Additionally, an organizational culture, which is open to change and favorable in terms of organizational learning, knowledge sharing cooperation and teamwork, is essential for better communication at organizational level. Finally, a well-defined KM strategy needs to be formulated in order to integrate the essential components of a KM system, that is, people, processes, and information technology. The success or failure of KM implementation largely depends on systematically integrating these three basic pillars of KM, as they are recognized as the key foundation areas of KM. Formulation of a well-planned KM implementation strategy is one of the important steps in the KM implementation process, as it leads the whole organization towards achieving a successful KM implementation and allows it to stay competitive. The KM strategy should be rooted in and guided by an understanding of the nature and types of organizational knowledge, so that it can tell us what works, what matters, what we should trust, where things can go wrong, and how we can fix them.

REFERENCES

Awad, E.M., Ghaziri, H.M., 2004. Knowledge Management. Pearson Education International, Upper Saddle River, NJ.

Badaracco, J.L., 1991. The Knowledge Link: Competitive Advantage Through Strategic Alliances. Harvard Business School Press, Boston, MA.

Becerra-Fernandez, I., Sabherwal, R., 2006. ICT and knowledge management systems. In: Schwartz, D. (Ed.), Encyclopaedia of Knowledge Management. Idea Group Publishing, Harrisburg, PA, pp. 230–236.

Bedford, D.A.D., Donley, J.K., Lensenmayer, N., 2015. The role of librarians in a knowledge society: valuing our intellectual capital assets. In: Current Issues in Libraries, Information Science and Related Fields. Advances in Librarianship, vol. 39, pp. 81–113. Published online: 15 June 2015 http://dx.doi.org/10.1108/S0065-283020150000039011 (accessed 15.12.15).

Blacker, F., 1993. Knowledge and the theory of organizations: organizations as activity systems and the reframing of management. J. Manag. Stud. 30, 863–884.

Blair, D.C., 2002. Knowledge management: hype, hope, or help? J. Am. Soc. Inf. Sci. Technol. 50 (12), 1019–1028.

Boisot, M., 1998. Knowledge Assets: Securing Competitive Advantage in the Information Economy. Oxford University Press, New York, NY.

Choo, C.W., 2000. Working with knowledge: how informational professionals help organisations manage what they know. Libr. Manag. 21 (8), 395–403.

Clarke, R., 2004. KM in the main library of the University of West Indies, Trinidad. Inf. Dev. 20 (1), 30–35.
Dalkir, K., 2005. Knowledge Management in Theory and Practice. Elsevier Butterworth-Heinemann, Burlington, MA.
Davenport, T.H., Prusak, L., 2000. Working Knowledge: How Organizations Manage What They Know. Harvard Business School Press, Boston, MA.
Du Plessis, M., Boon, J.A., 2004. The role of knowledge management in e-business and customer relationship management: South African case study findings. Int. J. Inf. Manag. 24 (1), 73–86.
Frost, A., 2010. The different types of knowledge. Available at: http://www.knowledge-management-tools.net/different-types-of-knowledge.html (accessed 14.12.15).
Gandhi, S., 2004. Knowledge management and reference service. J. Acad. Librariansh. 30 (5), 368–381.
Hansen, M.T., Nohria, N., Tierney, T., 1999. What is your strategy for managing knowledge? Harv. Bus. Rev. 106–116.
Hayek, F.A., 1945. The use of knowledge in society. Am. Econ. Rev. 35, 519–530.
Jain, P., 2007. An empirical study of knowledge management in academic libraries in East and Southern Africa. Libr. Rev. 56 (5), 377–392.
Kumar, J.A., Ganesh, L.S., 2011. Balancing knowledge strategy: codification and personalization during product development. J. Knowl. Manag. 15 (1), 118–135.
Leonard, D., 1995. Wellsprings of Knowledge: Building and Sustaining the Sources of Innovation. Harvard Business School Press, Boston, MA.
Liebowitz, J., 2001. Knowledge management and its link to artificial intelligence. Expert Syst. Appl. 20, 1–6.
Maponya, P., 2004. Knowledge management practices in academic libraries: a case study of the University of Natal, Pietermaritzburg Libraries. Available at: http://mapule276883.pbworks.com/f/Knowledge+management+practices+in+academic+libraries.pdf (accessed 11.05.15).
Massa, T., Testa, S., 2009. A knowledge management approach to organizational competitive advantage: evidence from the food sector. Eur. Manage. J. 27, 129–141.
Nonaka, I., 1991. The knowledge creating company. Harv. Bus. Rev. 6 (8), 96–104.
Nonaka, I., Takeuchi, H., 1995. The Knowledge-Creating Company: How Japanese Companies Create the Dynamics of Innovations. Oxford University Press, New York, NY.
Penrose, E., 1959. The Theory of the Growth of the Firm. John Wiley & Sons, New York, NY.
Polanyi, M., 1967. The Tacit Dimension. Doubleday, New York, NY.
Porumbeanu, O.-L., 2010. Implementing knowledge management in Romanian academic libraries: identifying the elements that characterize their organizational culture. J. Acad. Librariansh. 36 (6), 549–552.
Roknuzzaman, M., Kanai, H., Umemoto, K., 2009. Integration of knowledge management process into digital library system: a theoretical perspective. Libr. Rev. 58 (5), 372–386.
Sabashini, R., Rita, S., Vivek, M., 2012. The role of ICTs in knowledge management for organizational effectiveness. In: Krishna, P.V., Babu, M.R., Ariwa, E. (Eds.), Global Trends in Information Systems and Software Applications. Springer-Verlag, Berlin/Heidelberg, pp. 542–549.
Sahasrabudhe, V., 2000. Information technology in support of knowledge management. In: Srikantaiah, T.K., Koenig, M.E.D. (Eds.), Knowledge Management for the Information Professional. Information Today, Medford, NJ, pp. 269–276.
Sarrafzadeh, M., Martin, B., Hazeri, A., 2010. Knowledge management and its potential applicability for libraries. Libr. Manag. 31 (3), 198–212.
Sinotte, M., 2004. Exploration of the field of knowledge management for the library and information professional. Libri 54 (3), 190–198.

Smith, E.A., 2001. The role of tacit and explicit knowledge in the workplace. J. Knowl. Manag. 5 (4), 311–321.
Srikantaiah, T.K., Koenig, M.E.D. (Eds.), 2000. Knowledge Management for the Information Professionals. Information Today, Medford, NJ.
Sternberg, R.J., 1997. Successful Intelligence. Penguin Putnam, New York, NY.
Sullivan, P.H., 1998. Profiting from Intellectual Capital. John Wiley, New York, NY.
Van den Hoof, B., De Ridder, J.A., 2004. Knowledge sharing in context: the influence of organizational commitment, communication climate and CMC use on knowledge sharing. J. Knowl. Manag. 8 (6), 117–130.
Wijetunge, P., 2002. Adoption of knowledge management by the Sri Lankan University librarians in the light of the National Policy on University Education. Int. J. Educ. Dev. 22, 85–94.
Winter, S.G., 1987. Knowledge and competence as strategic assets. In: Teece, D. (Ed.), The Competitive Challenge: Strategies for Industrial Innovation and Renewal. Ballinger, Cambridge, MA, pp. 159–184.
Yuan, Y.C., Zhao, X., Liao, Q., Chi, C., 2013. The use of different information and communication technologies to support knowledge sharing in organizations: from e-mail to micro-blogging. J. Am. Soc. Inf. Sci. Technol. 64 (8), 1659–1670.
Zack, M.H., 1999. Managing codified knowledge. Sloan Manage. Rev. 40 (4), 45–58.
Zuboff, S., 1988. In the Age of the Smart Machine: The Future of Work and Power. Basic Books, New York, NY.

CHAPTER 6

Knowledge Management Tools for Libraries

INTRODUCTION

Knowledge management (KM) practices in any organization are based on two basic principles: (i) measurement of the intellectual capital of an organization by developing a measurement ratio or indexes and benchmarks; and (ii) knowledge mapping, ie, capturing knowledge of knowledgeable and experienced people and disseminating it throughout the organization. The first task, related to the measurement of the intellectual capital of an organization, can be accomplished by conducting a knowledge audit, ie, to identify the knowledge needs of an organization in the performance of different activities and analyse the gap between available knowledge and required knowledge. The second task, related to the capture and dissemination of knowledge throughout the organization, can be accomplished mainly through the use of information technology. Since tacit knowledge is embedded in people as regards their experiences, skills and competences, capturing and sharing this type of knowledge is one of the major challenges in every type of organization. Transfer of knowledge from experienced people to less experienced people requires face-to-face interaction and training. The best methods of transferring such knowledge and skills are communities of practice, mentoring, organization of formal or informal meetings and apprenticeships. The basic goal of KM is to harness the knowledge resources and knowledge assets of organizations to enable them to learn and adapt to a changing environment (Auster and Choo, 1995). In order to fully implement a KM system and derive the maximum benefits, organizations need to adopt a balanced approach by using two elements: (1) a technological infrastructure composed of computers, networks, databases and software applications installed in distributed environments (Uriarte, 2008) and (2) a platform for direct interactions between people by connecting them with each other (Hansen et al., 1999). However, interactions between people require investment in building networks of people, where knowledge is shared not only face to face, but also over the telephone, by e-mail, via video-conferencing, via Internet or intranet. These two elements are usually referred to as KM tools and techniques. The goal of KM tools is not to manage knowledge itself, but to facilitate the implementation of knowledge processes. KM tools are designed and built to enable easier and faster use of important processes and functionalities, such as knowledge creation, capture and codification, knowledge organization and metadata extraction, knowledge access and retrieval, knowledge transfer and sharing and so on, that are essential for the management, safeguarding and harnessing of knowledge. The effective use of these tools and techniques within an organization can improve collaboration and working environment, enhance competitive advantage and responsiveness and increase overall productivity (Uriarte, 2008). A large number of KM tools have been developed that facilitate the management of knowledge within an organization. Some tools have been designed and developed by individual organizations to suit their own requirements, and some ready-made tools are also available on the market, comprising many different features that are suitable for a number of applications in different types of organizations. In this chapter, an attempt is made to classify different KM tools and describe the important KM tools that are/may be used in libraries for managing knowledge.

KM TOOLS

KM tools are defined as "tools which support the performance of the application, activities or actions such as knowledge generation, knowledge codification or knowledge transfer" (Ruggles, 1997, cited in Tyndale, 2002, p. 183). The focus of KM tools is on assimilation, comprehension and learning by individuals who will then transform data and information into knowledge. An ideal KM tool, according to Uriarte (2008), must include such features as mobility that allows users to interact with the system from any place at any time. The first well-known human-discovered KM tool that transformed the ancient world was the alphabet, which brought with it the ability to alphabetically index information for future retrieval. Today, KM mainly deals with the creation, organization and sharing of knowledge. In order to perform these activities, various tools and techniques are used. According to Uriarte (2008), "KM tools are used to create, organize and share the knowledge that can be found, most of the time, in a document, a project report, or a memo from one employee to another" (p. 68). KM practitioners now use a wide range of information technology (IT) tools to create, codify, store and share knowledge. The trend in the development of IT for organizations is toward more communication and collaboration tools. However, all tools are not IT based, but much emphasis is placed on these tools due to their dynamic capabilities, quick evolution and organizational impact. Ruggles (1997) outlined the importance of KM technologies as tools that:

- enhance and enable knowledge generation, codification and transfer
- generate knowledge (eg, data mining that discovers new patterns in data)
- code knowledge to make knowledge available to others
- transfer knowledge to decrease problems with time and space when communicating in an organization

However, according to Rollet (2003), KM tools and technologies can potentially be used for the following purposes:

- communication
- collaboration
- content creation
- content management
- adaptation
- e-learning
- artificial intelligence and
- networking

Two major benefits of using KM tools are described by Uriarte (2008) as: (i) tactical benefits and (ii) strategic benefits. The tactical benefits include faster access to relevant information and documents at any time, resulting in accelerated organizational processes, while the strategic benefits include the competitive advantage that can result from appropriate and systematic management of the organization's knowledge.

CLASSIFICATION OF KM TOOLS

Some scholars and organizations made an attempt to classify KM tools, techniques and practices. Their classification is largely based on the different processes and practices involved in the management of knowledge. Some of the typical tools that are used in KM solutions have been described by Uriarte (2008). These tools include: (i) document management systems, (ii) enterprise portals, (iii) knowledge map and skills management, (iv) information database and lessons learned system, (v) collaboration tools and (vi) communities of practice. Jackson (1998), on the basis of a literature survey, identified 59 KM tools which were largely associated with software and technological applications in KM. These KM tools are grouped into the following six categories: (i) document management systems, (ii) information management systems, (iii) searching and indexing systems, (iv) expert systems, (v) communication and collaboration systems and (vi) intellectual asset systems. Tyndale (2002), while describing the taxonomy of KM software tools, also identified and discussed 16 technology and software-based KM tools: These included intranets, web portals, content management, document management systems, information retrieval engines, relational and object databases, electronic publishing systems, groupware and workflow systems, push technologies, agents, help-desk applications, customer relationship management, data warehousing, data mining, business process re-engineering and knowledge creation applications.

The Asian Productivity Organization (APO) (2010) proposed a five-step KM process consisting of:

1. Identifying knowledge
2. Creating knowledge
3. Storing knowledge
4. Sharing knowledge and
5. Applying knowledge

For each step, the APO suggested a list of 26 KM tools and techniques, which are summarized in Table 6.1. It may be observed from the table that there is an overlap in the grouping of KM tools and techniques in each step of KM. This means that similar tools and techniques may be applied at different stages of KM.

Similarly, Dalkir (2005) categorized different KM tools according to the particular phase of the KM life cycle. Firstly, he identified three phases of the KM life cycle: (i) knowledge capture and creation phase, (ii) knowledge sharing and dissemination phase and (iii) knowledge acquisition and application phase. He then proposed a set of tools and techniques for implementing each of these three phases of the KM life cycle. The first phase (knowledge capture and creation) does not need an extensive use of technologies. However, knowledge sharing and dissemination as well as knowledge acquisition and application phases are highly reliant on the use of a wide range of diverse KM technologies. The types of KM tools, techniques and technologies in each three phases of the KM life cycle are shown in Table 6.2.

On the basis of a review of 234 articles on KM applications published during 1995–2002, Liao (2003) outlined an interesting classification of KM tools. He classified KM tools and technologies into six categories as: (i) knowledge-based

Table 6.1 Tools and techniques in support of knowledge management processes

KM processes/steps	KM tools/techniques
Identification of knowledge	Knowledge management assessment tool Knowledge cafés Communities of practice Advanced search tools Knowledge clusters Expert locator Collaborative virtual workspaces Knowledge mapping KM maturity model Mentor/mentee
Creation of knowledge	Brainstorming Learning and idea capture Learning reviews After action reviews Collaborative physical workspaces Knowledge cafés Communities of practice Knowledge bases (wikis, etc.) Blogs Voice and voice-over-internet protocol (VOIP) Advanced search Knowledge clusters Expert locator Collaborative virtual workspaces Mentor/mentee Knowledge portal Video sharing
Storage of knowledge	Learning reviews After action reviews Knowledge cafés Communities of practice Taxonomy Document libraries Knowledge bases (wikis, etc.) Blogs Voice and VOIP Knowledge clusters Expert locator Collaborative virtual workspaces Knowledge portals Video sharing

Continued

Table 6.1 Tools and techniques in support of knowledge management processes—cont'd

KM processes/steps	KM tools/techniques
Sharing of knowledge	Peer assist Learning reviews After action reviews Storytelling Communities of practice Collaborative physical workspaces Knowledge cafés Communities of practice Taxonomy Document libraries Knowledge bases (wikis, etc.) Blogs Social networking services Voice and VOIP Knowledge clusters Expert locator Collaborative virtual workspaces Knowledge portals Video sharing Mentor/mentee
Application of knowledge	Peer assist Collaborative physical workspaces Knowledge cafés Communities of practice Taxonomy Document libraries Knowledge bases (wikis, etc.) Blogs Advanced search Knowledge clusters Expert locator Collaborative virtual workspaces Knowledge worker competency plan Mentor/mentee Knowledge portals

From Asian Productivity Organization (APO), 2010. Knowledge Management Tools and Techniques Manual, p. 3. http://www.apo-tokyo.org (accessed 12.01.16).

systems, (ii) data mining, (iii) information and communication technology, (iv) artificial intelligence or expert systems, (v) database technology and (vi) modelling. His emphasis was on the use of technology, as all the six categories are technology oriented. Different tools and systems with their application for carrying out different activities are summarized in Table 6.3.

Table 6.2 Types of knowledge management tools, techniques and technologies

Phases of KM life cycle		Techniques, tools and technologies
Knowledge creation and capture	Content creation	Authoring tools Templates Annotations Data mining Expertise profiling Blogs
	Content management	Metadata tagging Classification Archiving Personal KM
Knowledge sharing and dissemination	Communication and collaboration technologies	Telephone Fax Video-conferencing Chat rooms Instant messaging Internet telephony E-mail Discussion forums Groupware Wikis Workflow management
	Networking technologies	Intranets Extranets Web servers, browsers Knowledge repositories Portals
Knowledge acquisition and application	E-learning technologies	Computer-based training Web-based training Electronic performance support system
	Artificial intelligence technologies	Expert systems Decision support system Customization Portal personalization Push/pull technologies Recommender systems Visualization Knowledge maps Intelligent agents Automated taxonomy systems Text analysis summarization

From Dalkir, K., 2005. Knowledge Management in Theory and Practice. Butterworth-Heinemann, Burlington.

Table 6.3 Categories of knowledge management tools/systems and their application

Types of KM tools/systems	Purpose of using tools/systems
Knowledge-based systems and their application	Knowledge representation Database Knowledge engineering Quality management Risk assessment Project management
Data-mining tools and their application	Organizational learning User-guided query construction Semantic indexing Knowledge refinement Software integration Knowledge warehouse Hypermedia
Information and communication technologies and their application	Decision support Organizational memory New product development Knowledge transfer Knowledge integration Ontology Engineering design Information sharing E-learning Simulation Virtual enterprise
Expert systems and their application	Visualization Education Knowledge representation Semantic networks Human resource management Project management Knowledge engineering Information retrieval Personalization Lessons learned systems
Database technologies and their application	Hierarchical modelling Knowledge refinement Machine learning Knowledge representation Knowledge discovery Ontology Database design Knowledge reuse Knowledge repository Web applications

From Liao, S.-h., 2003. Knowledge management technologies and applications: literature review from 1995 to 2002. Expert Syst. Appl. 25, 155–164.

KM TOOLS FOR LIBRARIES

Like other organizations, libraries are also considered as a system of integrated activities and business processes that work together collaboratively in order to achieve overall organizational goals. Libraries are not only involved in collecting, storing and disseminating knowledge, but new knowledge is also created in libraries. The role of libraries and librarians in the creation of new knowledge has been formally recognized by Davenport and Prusak (1998), as well as Sinotte (2004), as they acknowledge the creation of knowledge by librarians through various activities, such as content management, organization of knowledge and evaluating the validity and reliability of information obtained from unfamiliar sources. Figueroa and González (2006) regarded libraries as learning organizations. Further, they argue that a library as a learning organization must develop the ability to create, acquire and transform knowledge. It must constantly stimulate its members to increase their capacities. According to Daneshgar and Parirokh (2007), "if librarians can conceptually value creation of knowledge and learning as useful approach for their personal and institutional development, they will change their way of thinking" (p. 23). Management of knowledge and organizational learning consists of incorporating new knowledge, recovering other knowledge that is already possessed, integrating new knowledge with existing knowledge and finally putting knowledge to its subsequent use. All of these steps are the foundation of any type of learning that implies the utilization of existing knowledge and the creation of new knowledge. Thus a library is an organization involved in the acquisition, organization, distribution and utilization of knowledge for the creation of new knowledge. The success of these activities depends on the application of effective KM tools. There are a great variety of tools and techniques described in the KM literature, and some of these have already been listed above. Broadly, KM tools can be classified into two categories: (i) IT-based KM tools and (ii) conventional or non-IT-based KM tools. These tools are commonly used as solutions for KM in most organizations. Some KM tools and techniques which are used in libraries are discussed in the next section.

IT-BASED KM TOOLS

Traditional Database Tools

A database is a collection of interrelated data stored and organized to efficiently serve many applications by centralizing the data and minimizing redundant data (McFadden et al., 2000). Chowdhury (1999) defined a database as "an organized collection of related sets of data that can be accessed by more than one user by simple means and can be searched to reveal those that touch upon a particular need" (p. 13). Modern database technologies process large volumes, multiple hierarchies and different data formats to discover in-depth knowledge from large databases (Liao, 2003). Database technology helps libraries not only to collect, organize and disseminate explicit knowledge, but also to extract tacit knowledge from different sources and make it available to end-users. Libraries maintain different types of databases to manage both explicit and tacit knowledge. Some of these databases are described in the next section.

Databases of Lessons Learned

Most libraries have created databases of their holdings to provide access to their collections for users. But the concept of databases of lessons learned is different from these traditional library databases. In a database of lessons learned, relevant experiences of employees in an organization are captured and put into a database in an organized manner to be distributed to other employees. This ensures that the appropriate persons access the right knowledge at the right time. In a library, librarians learn every day about collections, work processes and reference interaction and improve their work constantly based on the experiences they have gained. The lessons learned knowledge base (KB) forms the memory of the library. At the same time, the lessons learned system supports the process of capture and diffusion of knowledge of senior and experienced librarians. Lessons learned systems are very important in libraries, as they help to avoid redundancy and ensure the protection of the knowledge of librarians, even when an employee leaves the library or retires from the library. The protection and utilization of knowledge and expertise of people can turn a library into a learning organization.

Traditional practices to capture the collective memory of librarians, particularly reference librarians, were rather informal and generally consisted of information about frequently asked questions recorded on index cards that were filed either alphabetically or by subject (Gandhi, 2004). However, with the advancement in database technology, these practices have been replaced by the use of common knowledge databases (CKDB) (Jantz, 2001), web-based ready-reference databases (RRDs) (Stover, 2004) and the KB of Question Point (QP) (Markgren et al., 2004).

Common Knowledge Database

A CKDB has been developed by a team of reference librarians within the New Brunswick (NB) Campus Libraries of Rutgers University. This tool grew out of the need to more fully integrate the libraries on the NB campus, and to facilitate the management and use of informal knowledge that every librarian possesses. The CKDB was developed for an improved information sharing process with two major objectives: (i) to enable the acquisition and sharing of informal knowledge in order to improve reference librarianship; and (ii) to facilitate through improved communications the organizational goal of becoming one NB library system. The CKDB (consisting of the contents of specialized websites, e-mails, special guides, local databases and universal rolodex) was developed because the NB librarians felt the need to interact more fully with the librarians on the other campuses, and also to utilize their varying backgrounds and expertise by sharing the informal knowledge that every librarian possessed. They wanted to incorporate the informal knowledge so that it became part of the libraries' organizational memory and could therefore be made available and effectively reused.

Ready-Reference Database

San Diego State University developed a web-based RRD for reference services. According to Stover (the manager of the project) it is impossible for a reference librarian to be an expert in all disciplines, and therefore the ideal way to provide a quality reference service would be to have the reference desk staffed with all the subject specialists 24 h a day, 7 days a week. But no library can afford such staffing. Therefore reference librarians often answered questions outside of their areas of expertise. So, in order for reference librarians to be efficient and effective, they must document and share their KBs, which he believes to consist largely of tacit or informal knowledge. The RRD in San Diego State University Library was developed because the library was anxious to resolve the reference questions. The system was a web-accessible flat file database that was searchable by keyword and could be accessed whenever needed by any librarian. Librarians could create, acquire and share knowledge by making entries offline or capturing entries online. The system also facilitated storage and retrieval (Stover, 2004).

Question Point

QP is a virtual reference service with a KB that is used as a KM system in libraries. The QP has many features, including chat reference, issue tracking mechanism, reporting capability and a KB built from a database of completed questions and answers. The libraries of the Mount Sinai School of Medicine and the Medical Science Library at New York Medical College are using QP in reference services. These libraries were both attracted to QP, particularly the knowledge bank. However, a paramilitary study by Markgren et al. (2004) found that the KB was not heavily used. Neither library searched the KB prior to answering any reference questions, although librarians at both libraries believe that the concept of collaborating with other libraries could be of potential merit. Another study on the use of QP in the academic libraries of the United States by Ralph and Ellis (2009) reported similar findings, as the reference librarians did not generally use the KB and there was duplication of effort and no reduction in response time.

Advanced Web-Based Tools

The World Wide Web offers a very powerful platform for supporting all stages of KM. The web allows an unprecedented degree of integration of different representational and communicational media (Ghani, 2009). Web applications include both communication and collaboration technologies that consist of the Internet and intranets, as well as mobile technologies such as personal digital assistance, personal computers, telephony and videoconferencing. The main advantage of web-based technology is that it can be deployed in a networking environment within the organization. Organizations, including libraries of academic institutions, have the potential to use different platforms to deploy a KM system.

Advanced web-based tools or services include dynamic tools such as: blogs, wikis, really simple syndication (RSS) feeds and instant messaging (IM). With the enormous popularity and use of these tools, all types of libraries have explored them as a method of communication and promotion of their library collections and services for their users. According to Dickson and Holley (2010), this new method of providing library services using advanced web applications is referred to as library 2.0. The capabilities of advanced web-based applications enable users to engage the library in two-way communication and knowledge exchange. Some important web-based tools are discussed below.

Really Simple Syndication

RSS, also known as Rich Site Summary, is designed to feed users with regularly changing web content of news-like sites, news-oriented community sites and even personal weblogs without requiring users to visit multiple sites to receive updates (Stephens, 2006). RSS allows library users to subscribe to the library's content, so they can be automatically informed whenever a library adds new information to any of the sections of the website. A university library may apply this technology to provide updates to library users on new items in a collection, services provided and content in subscription databases (Maness, 2006). RSS in a university library may also be used as a form of advertisement to push library information to users who would not otherwise utilize the resources provided by libraries. This service enables users to reduce any unnecessary steps it takes to access the relevant databases. Cornell University offers MyUpdates, which is a tool to help scholars stay informed of new resources provided by the library (Kim and Abbas, 2010). The library of the University of Southampton provides a news feed on RSS to inform users about activities and events held in the university (Tripathi and Kumar, 2010).

Blogs

Blogs offer another social platform for libraries to reach university students with new services. A blog is a type of web page, usually maintained by an individual, that contains regular entries of commentary, descriptions of events or other materials such as videos (Tripathi and Kumar, 2010; Wikipedia, 2014a). Blogs have several potential uses in university libraries. Blogs encourage user interaction through their comment feature, which allows students to provide feedback regarding the information services. In one form, librarians can post news about the library as well as events occurring at the library. Blogs are also used to create subject guides as they can be easily updated to reflect the most current sources for a particular class or department. Tripathi and Kumar (2010) suggest academic libraries should use blogs to communicate with staff and users; to facilitate academic debate; to post hourly changes, events, new resources list, deadlines, etc.; to give basic search tips; and to provide links to the library websites. An interactive use of blogs may be seen at libraries of Michigan State University, where librarians regularly respond to comments by its followers, even if the goal is only marketing their services among students and not answering reference questions (Dickson and Holley, 2010).

Wikis

A wiki is defined as "a collection of web pages which allows users to add and edit content collectively" (University of Southampton, 2014). Wikis have great potential to leverage knowledge creation and sharing in the library context. According to Kim and Abbas (2010), wikis may be used in an academic library for knowledge sharing, collaborative authoring and online discussion. Although an initial survey on the use of wikis showed that academic libraries make little use of this function (Long, 2006), the overall use of this functionality in academic libraries has increased during the last few years, as seen in the findings of a recent study. Bejune (2007) observed that academic libraries mostly use wikis for collaboration across libraries. However, wikis are also used to leverage knowledge creation and sharing in the library. For example, the Ohio University Library created a Biz Wiki of business information resources for students, where both library users as well as librarians are allowed to create and edit content (Kim and Abbas, 2010). This Biz Wiki research portal includes embedded catalogue records for books, instructional videos by the liaison librarian and links to the liaison librarian's Facebook and Twitter accounts, which has enhanced collaboration between librarians and users (Chu Kai-Wah, 2009). Another example of collaboration among users is the Columbia University Library, which initiated student-developed projects on social justice movements using a wiki. This project aims to encourage students to discover knowledge on social movements and share it with the community (Kim and Abbas, 2010).

Instant Messaging

IM is defined as "a synchronous communication technology that allows users to send real-time messages to other users" (Chua et al., 2008). The most striking feature of IM is the communication that takes place between users in real time. IM may be used in academic libraries to provide chat-reference services so that users can ask questions and receive responses directly from librarians during specified contact times. Foley (2002) considers IM as an alternative for librarians seeking to reshape the delivery of reference services. Using IM, it is easily possible for libraries to reach remote users across campus and around the world as physical boundaries do not stand in the way of communication. Most academic libraries offer some form of digital reference service through e-mail or web formats. Now many libraries are moving toward an almost-immediate form of virtual reference through IM. For example, Texas Christian University's Mary Couts Burnett Library started an IM reference service, allowing faculty, staff, students and guests to send questions and get replies using six different IM protocols, including the MeeboMe widget. The MeeboMe widget is an IM box on the library's web pages that users type questions into without the need of special software or messenger accounts, and has proven to be a very popular part of the new reference service (Texas Christian University, 2014).

Knowledge Repositories

A knowledge repository is an online database that systematically captures, organizes, categorizes and provides access to knowledge-based information. Liebowitz and Beckman (1998) define a knowledge repository as an

"[...] on-line computer-based storehouse of expertise, knowledge, experience, and documentation about a particular domain of expertise." Branin (2003) termed a knowledge repository as a digital institutional repository, and defined it as "an interdisciplinary, multi-media storehouse of knowledge capital" (p. 11). Knowledge repositories were developed and used to connect people with information and expertise globally via online searchable libraries, discussion forums and other elements. They provide a central location to collect, contribute and share digital learning resources for use in instructional design and content development for both traditional and nontraditional learning environments. Using a digital institutional repository approach, Ohio State University developed a KB as a KM system. This KB is a digital institutional repository to capture all the intellectual assets of the university in a range of formats, including those that are published, unpublished, unstructured and unique (Branin, 2003).

Knowledge Portals

A knowledge portal may be defined as a gateway to codified knowledge, normally embedded in documents, databases and people, to enable the user to have one more simplified way of navigating toward the desired knowledge and expertise (APO, 2010). It serves as a single point of access to various information sources and applications. A knowledge portal helps to locate experts from a directory to help people find and connect with experts and speed up the process of learning. It facilitates more effective transfer between tacit and explicit knowledge.

Higher educational institutions and their libraries have a rich store of explicit knowledge in the form of books and journals, projects, reports, research papers, dissertations, theses and other learning material. Today, most universities have developed knowledge repositories to acquire, store, preserve and provide electronic access to locally digitized or digitally acquired library resources, including electronic books, manuscripts and other media, as well as the research output of their faculty (Alhawary et al., 2011). Availability and access to explicit knowledge in universities alone will not enable them to serve their students effectively. Universities have lacked the capacity to capture and provide access to the tacit knowledge embedded in people in the form of their expertise. Therefore it is important to have a collection of tacit knowledge from sources related to institutions in order to frame KM systems effectively. A knowledge portal can help universities to capture and transfer tacit knowledge.

The Grant MacEwan Library developed a library intranet portal for documenting and sharing information by providing a medium wherein staff can post updates that affect short-term processes and changes at the Reference desk, as well as news of interest to the Reference department staff. The library intranet portal at Grant MacEwan Library also facilitates knowledge sharing through the repository of library documents. These documents are not limited to policies or guidelines, but also include the desk schedule, meeting minutes, drafts and presentations using a file-sharing system that provides some limited search capabilities (Forcier, 2013).

Social Media Technologies

The concept of social media technologies is defined as a collection of Internet websites, services and practices that support collaboration, community building, participation and sharing (Reynol et al., 2011). Social media technologies cover a wide range of tools, all using technology to facilitate collaboration and sharing of tacit knowledge. During the last few years social media technologies have developed to encourage users to share multimedia objects from photographs to videos. Social media tools are Internet-based tools that include a range of networking platforms such as Facebook to video-sharing sites such as YouTube (Stoeckel and Sinkinson, 2013). Most social media tools allow users to create individual profiles where team-based and collaborative learning are possible through sharing of content. The findings of a study on the use of social media among faculties across the United States conducted by Pearson Learning Solutions and the Babson Survey Research Group show that two-thirds of the 2000 faculties surveyed use social media in class contexts (Mike et al., 2011). The use of social media in academic libraries is widespread in terms of marketing and broadcasting. Libraries commonly use Facebook fan pages, Twitter accounts, YouTube channels or blogs to distribute news about events, services, or resources; to alert users about new additions to collections; to provide links to articles, videos and other web content that might be relevant for users. Libraries are also actively using these mechanisms to foster relationships with users by allowing them to ask questions and providing feedback about library services (American Library Association, 2014). Librarians also post videos of library tours as well as bibliographic instruction for students, as explained by the librarian at the University of South Florida, who created a video for students demonstrating how to use a database (Ariew, 2008).

Social Bookmarking Tools

Social bookmarking is a form of link management that allows "users to collect and label information resources for both their own use and for sharing with other users" (Gilmour and Strickland, 2009). Put simply, the process of describing public documents and web page content by assigning keywords (tags) is called social bookmarking/cataloguing. Delicious is one of the most popular social bookmarking websites. By collecting, analysing and describing web content, social bookmarking websites generate valuable metadata about public documents and resources available over the Internet. Dickson and Holley (2010) suggested that librarians can use social bookmarking to create resource lists for different departments and classes that can be viewed by students. Social bookmarking is also used to create class reading lists and bibliographies by tagging the resources with the department and class number (Kroski, 2007). A link to Delicious can also be added to the library catalogue for assigning the tags from its Delicious account to the library catalogue in order to create access points for materials that are not adequately described by the existing Library of Congress Subject Headings (Dickson and Holley, 2010).

Social bookmarking is also used to enhance the features of library catalogues. LibraryThing (https://www.librarything.com/), "a social cataloguing application for book catalogue and various types of metadata" (Wikipedia, 2014b), offers libraries a solution for the enhancement of the features of their catalogues by incorporating user-generated book reviews and recommendations and providing a customizable mobile application called Library Anywhere (MacManus, 2012). LibraryThing was created by Tim Spalding in Portland in 2005. As of Oct. 2014, it has had more than 1,800,000 users and more than 95 million books catalogued (https://www.librarything.com/). The key feature of LibraryThing is the cataloguing of books by importing data from libraries through Z39.50 connections and from six Amazon.com stores. Library sources supply MARC and Dublin Core records to LibraryThing and users can import catalogue records from 700 libraries, including the Library of Congress, the National Library of Australia, the British Library, the Canadian National Catalogue and Yale University Library. For a nominal fee, LibraryThing allows member libraries to use its collective wisdom in local library catalogues. Libraries can also use LibraryThing tags to generate links between related books on their own collections by incorporating LibraryThing widgets into their online public access catalogues (Wenzler, 2007).

Knowledge Organization and Discovery Tools

Knowledge in a library is stored in the repositories and databases for preservation as well as multiple uses. A number of tools and techniques are used to facilitate the knowledge discovery, access and retrieval process. Some important techniques like indexing, taxonomies, metadata, data warehousing, data mining, knowledge mapping and knowledge discovery are used as KM tools in libraries for the organization and retrieval of knowledge (Roknuzzaman et al., 2009).

Knowledge Mapping

Knowledge in an organization is organized with the help of taxonomy or knowledge mapping. Knowledge mapping is the process of creating a knowledge map. One of the important steps in KM is the identification and mapping of intellectual assets within an organization. The knowledge-mapping process consists of five steps: data acquisition, data manipulation, data storage, data processing and data visualization (Uriarte, 2008). Librarians are acquainted with existing standard knowledge classification schemes, and also developed some special schemes of classification for specialized collections, based on the general theory of library classification developed by S.R. Ranganathan and members of the Classification Research Croup (CRG). Librarians can extend their expertise by creating and utilizing proprietary taxonomies for mapping of knowledge in KM systems. Library management systems (LMSs) and CKDB are examples of knowledge-mapping tools in libraries, as they are used to identify what information or knowledge is valuable and where it is kept, whether as a tangible entity such as a book or an intangible entity such as a named individual within the organization being acknowledged as an expert in a particular field. LMS allows end-users to search catalogues, which has enabled librarians to develop expertise in intranet and portal development. Librarians have already extended their roles towards adding value through grouping reliable websites with annotations into appropriate categories to facilitate the discovery of knowledge as well as delivery of current awareness services (Webster, 2007).

Data Warehousing

A data warehouse has been defined by Bill Inmon as "a subject-oriented, integrated, time-variant, and non-volatile collection of data in support of management's decision-making process" (Inmon, 1996, cited in Erdmann, 1997). Data warehouses are used as a medium of storage for creating a corporate memory and searching data or information from heterogeneous databases, and also serve the function of various query formulation for intensive search. They are considered as an important part of decision support systems (DSSs) or executive information systems, as they help gain new knowledge by delivering well-integrated data to analysis tools, such as online analytical processing or knowledge discovery in databases or over different network sites.

Data Mining

Data mining is defined as "the processes of extracting the hidden information and knowledge that people do not know in advance but potentially useful" (Zhou and Ouyang, 2007). Data mining technology is used to extract or discover hidden information from large databases and vast network information space in a digital library. It is also used to find previously unknown and potentially interesting patterns and relations in large databases to help information workers search for potential associations between data and find the neglected elements, which is useful for predicting trends and making decisions (Fayyad et al., 1996, cited in Awad and Ghaziri, 2004, p. 251).

Initially, data warehousing and data mining tools were used as DSSs mainly in the corporate world. Recently, some libraries (eg, Indiana University libraries and the Vanderbilt University library) have started to use data warehousing and data mining tools to strengthen administrative decision-making by facilitating the collection and analysis of data pertaining to door count statistics, circulation, interlibrary loans, collection development, acquisitions, electronic resource usage and web usage patterns (Mento and Rapple, 2003, cited in Gandhi, 2004).

Knowledge Discovery

The term 'knowledge discovery' emerged from a seminar entitled "Returning the researcher to the library, defining web-scale discovery: the promise of a unified search index for libraries", sponsored by Serials Solutions and the *Library Journal* (Infomotions Inc., 2009). As a result, several knowledge discovery systems (KDSs) were developed and are available on the market. A KDS may be defined as a preharvested central index coupled with a richly featured discovery layer that provides a single search interface across a library's local content, open access and licenced databases. In simple terms, KDS eliminates the need to search a library's local and remote (open access and subscription) content separately. KDS, with the help of its preharvested index, gathers data from multiple sources and processes it into a central index, providing a quick search for a vast range of local and remote content with relevancy ranked results. Several commercial knowledge discovery products have recently appeared on the market. Encore from Innovative Interfaces, Primo Central from Ex Libris, Summon from Serials Solutions, EBSCO Discovery Service from EBSCO and WorldCat Local from OCLC are some of the knowledge discovery products mostly used in libraries the world over.

Many studies have been published in recent years that examine the impact of KDS on the usage of online databases and journals. O'Hara (2012) examined the impact of the implementation of KDS at the University of Manitoba by studying 3 years' usage statistics of journals and found an increase in full-text journal requests. Lam and Sum (2013) also noted an increase in access to full-text content at the Open University of Hong Kong by comparing the usage of a range of databases, journals and e-books during the 12-month period before and after the implementation of KDS. However, they were uncertain whether this was due to the implementation of the KDS. Preliminary findings of a large-scale comparative study of KDS on online journal usage in the United Kingdom indicate a mixed picture of usage, with some libraries experiencing increased usage while others saw a decrease (Levine-Clark et al., 2013).

Intranets

Intranets are emerging as one of the most effective ways of sharing knowledge within an organization. An intranet is defined by Mphidi and Snyman (2004) "as a network that uses Internet concepts and technologies within an organisation in order to be accessed by employees to share knowledge" (p. 395). It is a private computer network based on the data communication standards and technologies of the public Internet. Unlike the Internet as a public network, intranets are private networks controlled by a particular organization that allow access only to authorized users. Thus an intranet is a network like the Internet, but its access is restricted to internal personnel within an organization, with the goal of fostering information and knowledge sharing.

Intranets have had a great impact on KM, particularly in the fields of information collection, collaboration and communication. Librarians can perform the role of evaluating, selecting and managing information held on an intranet and develop technical skills to publish and maintain information. Intranets provide strong platforms for libraries to organize resources in such a way which can easily be located later on and linked to other relevant resources cited (Webster, 2007). Intranets can be a valuable KM tool for libraries. Libraries develop and maintain intranets for different purposes. However, according to Weiner (1999), libraries use an intranet to provide communication support and proprietary information for use by the internal library community. An intranet is also used by libraries to improve communication and information dissemination. Mphidi and Snyman (2004) summarized some advantages of using an intranet in libraries:

- It serves as a repository of explicit knowledge in libraries, where original documents can be placed on the intranet, allowing this information to be viewed by any employee.
- It facilitates communication within the organization and reduces the use of paper.
- It encourages knowledge sharing, which leads to an improvement of employee performance.

However, the value of an intranet depends of the availability of its contents. The contents of an intranet should be relevant, accurate, informative and up to date. Mphidi and Snyman (2004) suggested a list of different types of content for a library intranet that includes training materials, management information, policies, annual budget, news, reports, bulletin boards, discussion forums and electronic magazines.

Seattle Public Library launched an intranet in Apr. 2009, and moved away from e-mail and toward the intranet as its main communications channel. Using e-mail to distribute organizational information increases productivity, consistency and accuracy, as each staff member must keep track of this information. Seattle Public Library has implemented the following communications tools on the library's intranet:

- News and Announcements: All managers throughout the library post news items that are important and system-wide.
- Message Board: A blog where any staff member can post or comment on a 'bulletin board' types of information like comings and goings, major life events or achievements, events happening around the city, etc.
- infoTALK: A moderated online discussion forum that offers the opportunity for library employees to connect and share knowledge. All employees can post topics or comment in three categories.
- Susan's Corner: A blog written by the city librarian.
- Urgent Notices: Staff alerts on closures, outages or emergencies.
- All Staff Calendar: Keeps track of major staff meetings, events and emergency contacts for the day (Seattle Public Library, 2010).

Groupware and Collaboration Tools

Groupware and collaboration tools are computer and communication network-based electronic means for eliciting, sharing and organizing quantities of information. Collaboration resembles a virtual meeting room operating in real time, in which colleagues work together, even over long distances or at different times of day. A collaborative environment enables people to share ideas and views in online workspaces, in which they use e-mail, newsgroups and mailing lists, chat systems, Internet web browsers, video-conferences and desktop applications in order to share knowledge, build closer organizational relationships and streamline work processes. Groupware represents a class of software that helps groups of colleagues attached to a communication network to organize their activities. Groupware is designed to facilitate the work of groups through communication, cooperation, coordination and problem-solving. According to Uriarte (2008), groupware is used:

- to facilitate communication and make it faster, clearer and more persuasive;
- to enable communication where it wouldn't otherwise be possible;
- to enable telecommuting;
- to cut down on travel costs;
- to bring together multiple perspectives and expertise;
- to form groups with common interests where it wouldn't be possible to gather a sufficient number of people face to face;
- to save time and cost in coordinating group work;
- to facilitate group problem-solving and
- to enable new modes of communication, such as anonymous interchanges or structured interactions.

Librarians have also taken advantage of groupware and collaboration technologies to build online communities of practice through e-mail listservs, USENET newsgroups, discussion boards and collaborative digital reference applications to manage and share their collective knowledge. An Internet-based mailing list, 'Stumpers' was created in 1992 that allows librarians to consult with hundreds of colleagues throughout the world about difficult or sticky reference questions. Therefore a question that may seem impossible to answer to one librarian may very easily be answered by another librarian who has either tackled it before or knows the answer due to a personal interest in that particular subject area. The questions and answers exchanged are stored in a searchable archive for future use and retrieval (Gandhi, 2004).

E-learning

E-learning is a modern form of distance education in which training or educational material is delivered via the Internet or an intranet to remote learners. E-learning is defined as "an instructional process that gives online learners access to a wide range of resources—teachers, other learners, and content such as readings and exercises—independently of place and time" (Xu and Wang, 2011, p. 442). An e-learning system is used to transfer knowledge, in the form of interactive teaching material. It allows the user to progress at their own pace and to receive feedback on their progress and level of understanding (Young, 2008).

There are several possibilities for libraries to apply e-learning. University libraries are committed to supporting a digitally enhanced learning environment by providing innovative solutions to integrate library content and services into existing and future course environments. Libraries currently offer a variety of services that can be customized to meet the needs of a particular class or an assignment. In addition, several pilot projects are being implemented for providing new and reformatted content that best meets the pedagogical needs of these emerging online course environments. Librarians can benefit by learning online. They can supplement their existing academic qualifications, and they can have additional training to improve their professional skills or to support their personal development and self-improvement. Additionally, online training helps library staff to acquire the latest ideas, to deal with new problems in librarianship, and to meet changing user needs. Satisfying these needs involves meeting several educational challenges, especially the possession of sufficient ICT abilities such as dealing with professional computer programs, Internet publishing, web searching and so on.

CONVENTIONAL OR NON-IT-BASED KM TOOLS

Community of Practice

The concept of community of practice was introduced by Lave and Wenger (1991) as a method to understand learning, particularly learning in the workplace. Put simply, a community of practice may be defined as a network of people who work on similar processes or in similar disciplines, and who come together to develop and share their knowledge in that field for the benefit of both themselves and their organization(s). A community of practice, according to Uriarte (2008), "consists of members exchanging knowledge and in the process they build relationships and develop a sense of belonging and mutual commitment" (p. 55). Wenger et al. (2002) described three fundamental elements of a community of practice: (i) a domain of knowledge, which defines a set of issues; (ii) a community of people who care about this domain; and (iii) the shared practice that they develop to be effective in their domain. Thus a community of practice is a platform for sharing knowledge, where a group of people come together and share each other's experience on a particular subject or a common interest.

The sharing of experience helps people to solve day-to-day problems and furnish themselves with new knowledge in areas of their work. A community of practice also helps develop a homogeneous vision and common approach to solving problems, attaining a desired objective, or designing a product (Uriarte, 2008).

Within any community, there may be subject experts who have been trained in an area of expertise and who can provide specific guidance. A group of doctors sharing each other's experiences about a complicated disease while taking coffee together in the canteen is an example of natural learning through informal community interaction. Organizations like Ericsson and ICL have successfully implemented communities of practice for sharing knowledge and unique experiences among their employees. Forming a community of practice can enable librarians to apply their expertise and to construct knowledge by collaborating with colleagues to solve problems posed by reference queries (Miller, 2001). Several groups have been formed and are available to librarians to fill the role of a community of practice within the library community. Library managers can encourage librarians to participate in both internal library groups (task forces, committees, discussion groups) and external groups from broader communities. Librarians can benefit from collective wisdom with their involvement in these groups either through face-to-face meetings or electronic discussions (Nelson, 2008).

Mentoring

The concept of 'mentoring' is derived from the term 'mentor', which means "adults who introduce students to ideas theories, tools, activities, or careers in their own fields of expertise" (Mukherjee, 2012, p. 399). Despite a wide variety of views on mentoring, there is no commonly accepted definition of mentoring. Mentoring is considered, by Hilbun and Akin (2007), as a traditional method of passing knowledge and skills from an established professional to a junior staff member. Douglas and McCauley (1999) describe mentoring as a relationship that motivates individuals to learn and grow through exposure to new opportunities and the provision of support. Ramos and Green (2007) trace the history of mentoring back to ancient Greece, where it was typically used to build a relationship between a senior and junior employee. The benefits of mentoring are explained by Mavrinac (2005) as improving "job satisfaction, career advancement, psychosocial wellbeing, induction to the organization and professionalism" in the mentee, and that the mentor often feels a sense of leaving a personal and continuing mark on the discipline through the success of their protégés (cited in Ramos and Green, 2007, p. 1). Mentoring may be distinguished as either formal or informal. The relationships in formal mentoring are arranged and supported by the library or other organization, while informal mentoring is often unplanned and unexpected, growing organically out of an existing relationship between the mentor and mentee. However, in both situations, the two staff members learn from each other's professional, personal and psychological development and goals (Ramos and Green, 2007, p. 1).

Effective relationships and learning are the mainstays of organizational success. Organizations that find meaningful ways for their employees to connect are more likely to achieve greater productivity, enhanced career growth, freely flowing innovation and overall improvement in employees' performance. A mentor with greater experience can help a novice employee to develop a mental map about what to cultivate, what to avoid and what behaviours and track records are most and least valued. All of these factors help make juniors more effective and are useful in managing their career options, as well as improving the performance of their organization.

Nelson (2008) explained the importance of mentoring from the perspective of KM by stating that "knowledge-seekers will pursue the answers they need to do their job, and the role of the apprentice is seen as that of an active learner rather than a passive recipient of knowledge" (p. 136). Douglas County Library is one institution that has adopted formal mentoring practice in the workplace (Walberg, 2004), where on the very first day at the library, new employees are matched with a mentor who will work with them each day during their first weeks in the job. Walberg (2004) describes the importance of building this type of relationship in the following way: "the mentor focuses only on the individual's training needs and, in the process, provides the moral support most of us need when starting a new job." At the end of the mentoring, the new employees are confident, skilled and well-versed in library policies and practices.

Ramos and Green (2007) described two types of mentoring that may be implemented in different library situations: peer mentoring and e-mentoring. Peer mentoring allows each participant to act as learner and teacher. Any library employee may participate in this form of mentoring. E-mentoring or virtual mentoring occurs when mentor and mentee communicate electronically rather than by meeting in person. E-mentoring may employ blogs, e-mail and real-time technology like chat and IM. One of the benefits of e-mentoring is that even people in remote locations can benefit from the knowledge and experience of a colleague regardless of time or distance (Hilbun and Akin, 2007, cited in Ramos and Green, 2007, p. 1). Mentoring provides several benefits to the library, its employees and users. Howland (1999) mentioned that "in almost all professions, and certainly librarianship, the formation of a mentoring relationship has been shown to be one of the most significant factors in contributing to retention, promotion and long-term success." Mentoring enables new employees to be more confident in their positions and often equips them for promotion and success within the library.

Storytelling

Storytelling is a powerful way to share and transfer knowledge, especially experiential and tacit knowledge. Knowledge, skills and experiences are transferred and shared among employees in an organization by narrating stories. Stories, according to Gabriel (2000), are: "[...] narratives with plots and characters, generating emotion in narrator and audience, through a poetic elaboration of symbolic material. This material may be a product of fantasy or experience, including an experience of earlier narratives. Story plots entail conflicts, predicaments, trials, coincidences and crises that call for choices, decisions, actions, and interactions, whose actual outcomes are often at odds with the characters' intentions and purposes" (p. 239, cited in Colon-Aguirre, 2012, p. 41). Storytelling may be defined as the verbal exchange of stories by a narrator or storyteller delivered to an audience. A person who has valuable knowledge tells stories of his/her experience in front of people who want to gain knowledge. According to the APO (2010), "storytelling is conveying of events in words, images, and sounds often by improvisation or embellishment" (p. 22). However, in the context of KM, storytelling is defined by Dalkir (2005) as a method to illustrate a point, convince listeners and effectively transfer knowledge by "[...] a detailed narrative of management actions, employee interactions, and other intra-organizational events that are communicated informally within the organization" (p. 86).

Storytelling can increase the potential for knowledge sharing in the workplace. It has strong and unique benefits that most other KM tools or traditional organizational communication techniques rarely have. Storytelling makes it possible for an organization to: (i) articulate emotional as well as factual content; (ii) transfer and share tacit parts of knowledge; (iii) nurture good human relationships; (iv) bring out the passion of audiences and

(v) provide learning opportunities for employees. However, to achieve the expected results from storytelling, the APO (2010) suggests five basic steps:

1. Identify the key area of knowledge you wish to transfer and share in your organization. Do not choose an unimportant knowledge area; it not only wastes your time but will send the wrong message to your organization.
2. Find the right person who has rich experience and ask him/her to tell the story. Eagerness and eloquence of the storyteller are the keys for successful storytelling.
3. Market the storytelling session to candidate participants.
4. Hold the session. It may be effective to create a more informal atmosphere than a regular meeting environment by changing layouts, serving refreshments, holding an icebreaker session, etc. You may want to hold a small social gathering after the session to help networking among the participants and the storyteller.
5. Leverage the output of the storytelling session. This step is critical to maximize the effectiveness of storytelling. This may be done by: (i) capturing the storytelling session on video and posting the video on an intranet for sharing the session among all employees and (ii) forming a community of the topic among the storyteller and participants who have a strong interest, holding a storytelling session regularly to give employees opportunities to both participate and tell a story.

Sharing of stories by librarians is important for transmitting tacit knowledge, as they most frequently deal with subjects such as how to handle problematic users or cope with difficult questions and situations. Stories are also a way for employees to empathize with their co-workers when they have to deal with frustrating situations, or after less than stellar performances. They are also a way to remember that, in the past, they or their predecessors had to endure difficult working conditions, but that most of the situations associated with these difficulties may be solved in time.

Brainstorming

When a group of people come together and generate new ideas around a specific area of interest, it is called brainstorming. Brainstorming is defined by Alex Osborn (1948) as "a conference technique by which a group attempts to find a solution for a specific problem by amassing all the ideas spontaneously by its members" (cited in Infinite Innovations Ltd, n.d.). Brainstorming sessions are conducted to capitalize on the respective insights and intuitions (tacit knowledge) of a group of individuals. By properly managing such brainstorming sessions, it is possible to produce a composite perspective on a common problem. This composite perspective can lead to innovation and new knowledge (Uriarte, 2008). Brainstorming is useful when there is a need to generate a relatively large number of options or ideas. It can also be used in almost any situation where a group (consisting of two or more people) can find a space to work together. This can be as simple as a shared desk with some blank pieces of paper (APO, 2010). Brainstorming is one of the most common techniques used to bring out the creativity and innovation in individuals. The process of brainstorming makes possible the sharing of views and ideas and mental models commonly used by individuals. It is also through this process that such ideas, views and mental models can be challenged and defended, and further elaborated or modified.

After Action Review

The concept of after action review (AAR) was originally developed and extensively used by the US Army. Now AARs are extensively used for learning processes to help support a learning organization. AAR is a technique to evaluate and capture the lessons learned upon completion of a project. Dalkir (2005) defined AAR as a professional discussion of an event that enables participants to understand what worked well, what did not and what they learned from the experience. An AAR is conducted upon completion of the project or upon achievement of any key milestones of a long-duration project. It is the basis for learning from a project's successes and failures. Members of the project team can identify strengths and weaknesses and determine how to improve performance in the future by focusing on the desired outcome and describing specific observations. On the basis of a review of the project, the project team can document the lessons learned and make it available to the rest of the organization to improve decision-making.

Knowledge Audit

A knowledge audit is carried out by an organization to identify the needs of core knowledge, the availability of existing knowledge and uses of knowledge for different activities. On the basis of a knowledge audit, an organization identifies knowledge gaps, duplications and flows, and how it contributes to achieve business goals. Mukherjee (2012) defines a knowledge audit as "[a] systematic process to identify an organization's knowledge needs, resources and flows as a basis for understanding where and how better knowledge management can add value" (Mukherjee, 2012, p. 400). Uriarte (2008) identified three key components of a knowledge audit:

(i) knowledge map (internal supply) and knowledge gap analysis (supply-demand gap), (ii) stakeholder analysis (external supply and demand) and (iii) learning organization diagnostics (culture and practices). A knowledge audit is one of the most important components of KM, as it identifies owners, users, uses, and key attributes of core knowledge assets in an organization. The knowledge audit equates with a KM assessment, which provides a baseline on which one can develop a KM strategy. Organizations often conduct a knowledge audit for one of the following purposes:

- to identify the core knowledge assets and flows (who creates, who uses)
- to identify the gaps in information and knowledge needed to manage the core business activities effectively
- to identify the areas of information policy and ownership that needs refinement
- to identify the possibilities of reducing information-handling costs
- to identify methods for improving coordination and access to commonly needed information
- to develop a clearer understanding of the contribution of knowledge to business results

Conference, Formal or Informal Meetings, Training Programmes, Seminars and Workshops

Acquisition and sharing of knowledge by employees in an organization is an important factor in the KM implementation process. Knowledge can be acquired and enhanced by providing training or learning opportunities to the staff. Continuous learning and acquiring knowledge through professional training courses, workshops and seminars are important methods of acquiring knowledge and developing competencies among employees for their involvement in KM practice. These events help employees to share their experience and views of their day-to-day work. In this way, tacit knowledge of their employees is shared amongst themselves, which improves their performance, in turn benefitting the organization.

SUMMARY

One of the most important objectives of KM is to transform an organization into a learning and knowledge-sharing organization by linking people together and creating a flow of knowledge generated by people in different units. The most valuable knowledge of an organization resides in its employees and workers, and transfer and utilization of this knowledge is one of the major challenges for most organizations. However, organizations can make best use of this knowledge either by converting it into explicit knowledge or by providing a platform for sharing knowledge directly with others. For this, they use different tools and techniques to capture and transfer knowledge. Knowledge may be shared either face to face or remotely with the help of information and communication technologies. Communities of practice, apprenticeships, mentoring, informal and informal meetings, conferences, seminars, workshops, etc. are some methods of sharing knowledge face to face. Telephony, video-conferencing, e-mail, intranets and social networking are some important ICT-based tools for sharing knowledge virtually. KM tools are designed and built to enable easier and faster use of important processes and functionalities, such as knowledge creation, capture and codification, knowledge organization and metadata extraction, knowledge access and retrieval, knowledge transfer and sharing and the like. These tools are essential for the management, safeguarding and harnessing of knowledge. The KM tools and techniques have an important enabling role in ensuring the success of KM applications. A number of tools and techniques presented in this chapter address the phenomenon of emergence that can help discover existing valuable knowledge, experts, communities of practice and other valuable intellectual assets that exist within an organization. Once these tools are effectively implemented, the intellectual assets can be better accessed, leveraged and utilized.

REFERENCES

Alhawary, F.A., Irtaimeh, H.J., Hamdan, K.B., 2011. Building a knowledge repository: linking Jordanian Universities e-library in an integrated database system. Int. J. Bus. Manag. 6 (4), 129–135. http://www.ccsenet.org/ijbm (accessed 19.01.16).

American Library Association, 2014. The 2012 state of America's libraries: a report from American Library Association. Am. Libr. 2012 (special issue). http://www.ala.org/news/sites/ala.org.news/files/content/StateofAmericasLibrariesReport2012Finalwithcover.pdf (accessed 02.01.16).

Ariew, S., 2008. Joining the YouTube conversation to teach information literacy. In: Godwin, P., Parker, J. (Eds.), Information Literacy Meets Library 2.0. Facet Publications, London, pp. 125–132.

Asian Productivity Organization (APO), 2010. Knowledge Management Tools and Techniques Manual. http://www.apo-tokyo.org (accessed 12.01.16).

Auster, E., Choo, C.W., 1995. Managing Information for Competitive Age. Neal Schuman, New York.

Awad, E.M., Ghaziri, H.M., 2004. Knowledge Management. Pearson, Upper Saddle River, NJ.

Bejune, M., 2007. Wikis in libraries. Inf. Technol. Libr. 26, 26–38.

Branin, J.J., 2003. Knowledge management in academic libraries: building the knowledge bank at the Ohio State University. J. Libr. Adm. 39 (4), 41–56.

Chowdhury, G.G., 1999. Introduction to Modern Information Retrieval. Library Association, London.
Chu Kai-Wah, S., 2009. Using Wikis in academic libraries. J. Acad. Librariansh. 35 (2), 170–176.
Chua, A.Y.-K., Hoe-Lian Goh, D., Lee, C.S., 2008. The prevalence and use of Web 2.0 in libraries. In: Proceedings of ICADL, Vol. 5362 of Lecture Notes in Computer Science. Springer, New York, pp. 22–30.
Colon-Aguirre, M., 2012. Organizational Storytelling in Academic Libraries: Roles, Addressees and Perceptions. PhD Dissertation, University of Tennessee, Knoxville, TN. http://trace.tennessee.edu/utk_graddiss/1470 (accessed 25.12.15).
Dalkir, K., 2005. Knowledge Management in Theory and Practice. Butterworth-Heinemann, Burlington.
Daneshgar, F., Parirokh, M., 2007. A knowledge schema for organizational learning in academic libraries. Knowl. Manag. Res. Pract. 5, 22–33.
Davenport, T.H., Prusak, L., 1998. Working Knowledge: How Organizations Manage What They Know. Harvard Business School Press, Boston, MA.
Dickson, A., Holley, R.P., 2010. Social networking in academic libraries: the possibilities and concerns. New Libr. World 111 (11/12), 468–479.
Douglas, C.A., McCauley, C.D., 1999. Formal developmental relationship: a survey of organizational practices. Hum. Resour. Dev. Q. 10 (1), 203–220.
Erdmann, M., 1997. The Data Warehouse as a Means to Support Knowledge Management. http://www.dfki.uni-kl.de/~aabecker/Final/Erdmann/dwh_km.doc.html#692651 (accessed 23.01.16).
Fayyad, U.M., 1996. Advances in Knowledge Discovery and Data Mining. AAAI Press, Menlo Park, CA.
Figueroa, L.A., González, A.B., 2006. Management of knowledge, information and organizational learning in university libraries: a case study. Libri 56, 180–190.
Foley, M., 2002. Instant messaging reference in an academic library: a case study. Coll. Res. Libr. 63 (1), 36–45.
Forcier, E., 2013. The Shoemaker's Son: A Substantive Theory of Social Media Use for Knowledge Sharing in Academic Libraries. Master Thesis, Department of Humanities Computing, School of Library and Information Studies, Edmonton, AB.
Gabriel, Y., 2000. Storytelling in Organizations: Facts, Fictions, and Fantasies. Oxford University Press, Oxford.
Gandhi, S., 2004. Knowledge management and reference services. J. Acad. Librariansh. 30 (5), 368–381.
Ghani, S.R., 2009. Knowledge management: tools and techniques. DESIDOC J. Libr. Inf. Technol. 29 (6), 33–38.
Gilmour, R., Strickland, J., 2009. Social bookmarking for library services: bibliographic access through Delicious. Coll. Res. Libr. News 70 (4), 234–237.
Hansen, M.T., Nohria, N., Tierney, T., 1999. What is your strategy for managing knowledge? Harv. Bus. Rev. 106–116.
Hilbun, J., Akin, L., 2007. E-Mentoring for librarians and libraries. Tex. Libr. J. 83 (1), 28–32.
Howland, J.S., 1999. Beyond recruitment: retention and promotion strategies to ensure diversity and success. Libr. Adm. Manag. 13 (1), 414.
Infinite Innovations Ltd, n.d. What is Brainstorming? Available at: http://www.brainstorming.co.uk/tutorials/whatisbrainstorming.html (accessed 01.01.06).
Infomotions Inc., 2009. Web-scale Discovery Indexes and Next Generation's Library Catalogs. http://infomotions.com/musings/web-scale/ (accessed 15.05.15).
Inmon, W.H., 1996. Building the Data Warehouse, second ed. Wiley, New York.
Jackson, C., 1998. Process to product: creating tools for knowledge management. 2nd International Conference on Technology Policy and Innovation, Assessment,

Commercialization and Application of Science and Technology and the Management of Knowledge, 3–5 August, Lisbon, Portugal.
Jantz, R., 2001. Knowledge management in academic libraries: special tools and processes to support information professionals. Ref. Serv. Rev. 29 (1), 33–39.
Kim, Y.-M., Abbas, J., 2010. Adoption of Library 2.0 functionalities by academic libraries and users: a knowledge management perspective. J. Acad. Librariansh. 36 (3), 211–218.
Kroski, E., 2007. The social tools of Web 2.0: opportunities for academic libraries. Choice 44 (12), 2011–2021.
Lam, M.S., Sum, M., 2013. Enhancing access and usage: the OUHK's experience in resource discovery service. In: Paper Presented at IFLA World Library Information Congress, 17–23 August 2013, Singapore. http://library.ifla.org/76/1/106-lam-en.pdf (accessed 11.01.16).
Lave, J., Wenger, E., 1991. Situated Learning: Legitimate Peripheral Participation. Cambridge University Press, Cambridge.
Levine-Clark, M., McDonald, J., Price, J., 2013. Discovery or displacement? A large scale longitudinal study of the effect of discovery systems on online journal usage. In: Paper Presented at Charleston Conference, November 7, 2013. http://wwwslideshare.net/MichaelLevineClark/mlc-jdm-jsp-charleston-2013-slideshare-28161600 (accessed 11.01.16).
Liao, S.-h., 2003. Knowledge management technologies and applications: literature review from 1995 to 2002. Expert Syst. Appl. 25, 155–164.
Liebowitz, J., Beckman, T.J., 1998. Knowledge Organizations: What Every Manager Should Know. CRC Press, Boca Raton, FL.
Long, S.A., 2006. Exploring the wiki world: the new face of collaboration. New Libr. World 157, 157–159.
Macmanus, R., 2012. The Social Library: How Public Libraries Are Using Social Media, September 18, 2012. http://readwrite.com/author/richard-macmanus (accessed 05.01.16).
Maness, J.M., 2006. Library 2.0: the next generation of web-based library services. LOGOS: J. World Book Community 17 (3), 139–145.
Markgren, S., Ascher, M.T., Crow, S.J., Lougee-Heimer, H., 2004. Asked and answered online: how two medical libraries are using OCLC's question point to answer reference questions. Med. Ref. Serv. 23 (1), 13–28.
Mavrinac, M.A., 2005. Transformational leadership: peer mentoring as a values based learning process. Portal 5 (3), 391–404.
Mcfadden, F.R., Hoffer, J.A., Prescott, M.B., 2000. Modern Database Management, fifth ed. Prentice-Hall, New York.
Mento, B., Rapple, B., 2003. SPEC Kit 274: Data Mining and Data Warehousing. Association of Research Libraries, Washington, DC.
Mike, M., Seaman, J., Tinti-Kane, H., 2011. Teaching, Learning, and Sharing: How Today's Higher Education Faculty Use Social Media. Pearson, Boston.
Miller, R.E., 2001. Reference communities: applying the community of practice concept to development of reference knowledge. Public Serv. Q. 7 (1). http://dx.doi.org/10.1080/15228959.2011.572772.
Mphidi, H., Snyman, R., 2004. The utilization of an intranet as a knowledge management tool in academic libraries. Electron. Libr. 22 (5), 393–400.
Mukherjee, B., 2012. Information Communication and Society. Ess Ess Publications, New Delhi.
Nelson, E., 2008. Knowledge management for libraries. Libr. Adm. Manag. 22 (3), 135–137.
O'Hara, L., 2012. Collection usage pre- and post-Summon implementation at the University of Manitoba libraries. Evid. Based Libr. Inf. Pract. 7 (4), 25–34.

Osborn, A.F., 1948. Your Creative Power: How to Use Imagination. C. Scribner's Sons, New York.
Ralph, L.L., Ellis, T.J., 2009. An investigation of a knowledge management solution for the improvement of reference services. J. Inf. Inf. Technol. Org. 4, 17–38.
Ramos, M., Green, R., 2007. Mentoring in libraries: library worklife. HR E-News Today's Lead. December, 1–2. http://alaapa.org/newsletter/2007/12/16/mentoringinlibraries/ (accessed 12.01.16).
Reynol, J., Heiberger, G., Loken, E., 2011. The effect of Twitter on college student engagement and grades. J. Comput. Assist. Learn. 27 (2), 119–132. http://dx.doi.org/10.1111/j.1365-2729.2010.00387.x.
Roknuzzaman, M., Kanai, H., Umemoto, K., 2009. Integration of knowledge management process into digital library system: a theoretical perspective. Libr. Rev. 58 (5), 372–386.
Rollet, H., 2003. Knowledge Management Processes and Technologies. Kluwer, Norwell, MA.
Ruggles, R., 1997. Knowledge Management Tools. Butterworth-Heinemann, Oxford.
Seattle Public Library, 2010. Improving Communication through the Library's Intranet. http://www.urbanlibraries.org/improving-communication-through-the-library-s-intranet-innovation-587.php?page_id=76 (accessed 05.01.16).
Sinotte, M., 2004. Exploration of the field of knowledge management for the library and information professional. Libri 54 (3), 190–198.
Stephens, M., 2006. Web 2.0 & Libraries: Best Practices for Social Software. American Library Association, Chicago, IL.
Stoeckel, K.S., Sinkinson, C., 2013. Social media. Tips Trends. Summer, http://www.ala.org/acrl/sites/ala.org.acrl/files/content/aboutacrl/directoryofleadership/sections/is/iswebsite/projpubs/tipsandtrends/2013summer.pdf (accessed 02.01.16).
Stover, M., 2004. Making tacit knowledge explicit: the ready reference database as codified knowledge. Ref. Serv. Rev. 32 (2), 164–173.
Texas Christian University, 2014. Using Instant Messaging at an Academic Library Reference Desk: Successes, Challenges, and Future Directions. http://www.lib.lsu.edu/sci/chem/vbulletin_real/bond.pdf (accessed 22.10.15).
Tripathi, M., Kumar, S., 2010. Use of Web 2.0 tools in academic libraries: a reconnaissance of the international landscape. Int. Inf. Libr. Rev. 42, 195–207.
Tyndale, P., 2002. A taxonomy of knowledge management software tools: origin and applications. Eval. Program Plan. 25, 183–190.
University of Southampton, 2014. Using Wikis Within Blackboard. http://www.southampton.ac.uk/isolutions/computing/elearn/wikis/ (accessed 22.10.15).
Uriarte, F.A., 2008. Introduction to Knowledge Management. ASEAN Foundation, Jakarta.
Walberg, N., 2004. A commitment to 'best practices'. Colo. Libr. 30 (2), 1517.
Webster, M., 2007. The role of library in knowledge management. In: Rikowski, R. (Ed.), Knowledge Management: Social, Cultural and Theoretical Perspectives. Chandos Publishing, p. 77–91.
Weiner, S.T., 1999. The university intranet. Econtent 22 (2), 66–69.
Wenger, E., McDermott, R.A., Snyder, W., 2002. Cultivating Communities of Practice: A Guide to Managing Knowledge. Harvard Business School Press, Boston, MA.
Wenzler, J., 2007. LibraryThing and the library catalogue: adding collective intelligence to the OPAC, CARL, NITIG, September 7, 2007. http://wff1.ff.unilj.si/oddelki/biblio/oddelek/osebje/dokumenti/MercunZumer08_New_generation_of_catalogues_for_the_new_generation_of_users.pdf (accessed 25.08.15).
Wikipedia, 2014a. Definition of Blog. http://en.wikipedia.org/wiki/Blog (accessed 22.10.15).

Wikipedia, 2014b. LibraryThing. http://en.wikipedia.org/wiki/LibraryThing (accessed 05.01.16).

Xu, D., Wang, H., 2011. Integration of knowledge management and e-learning. In: Schwartz, D.D., Te'eni, D. (Eds.), Encyclopedia of Knowledge Management, second ed. Information Science Reference, Hershey, NY, pp. 442–451.

Young, T., 2008. Knowledge Management for Services, Operations and Manufacturing. Chandos, Oxford.

Zhou, S., Ouyang, F., 2007. Analysis of the feasibility of data mining application in academic digital library. Lib. Work Coll. Univ. 27, 36–38.

CHAPTER 7

Knowledge Management Competencies

INTRODUCTION

Knowledge management (KM) has emerged as an interdisciplinary concept, which includes human resource management (HRM), information and communication technology (ICT), information science, and information management (IM). Librarianship is often described as the organization of recorded knowledge (Corrall, 1998), while KM:

> *[…] involves the management of explicit knowledge (i.e. knowledge that has been codified in documents, databases, web pages, etc.) and the provision of an enabling environment for the development, nurturing, utilization and sharing of employees' tacit knowledge (i.e. know-how, skills, or expertise).*
>
> ***(Ajiferuke, 2003, p. 1)***

In the present knowledge environment, library and information science (LIS) professionals are experiencing the consequences of the following three major paradigm shifts, as explained by Raina (2000):

- The transition from paper to electronic media as the dominant form of information dissemination, storage, and retrieval is the first shift. Convergence of different media, such as text, graphics, and sound, into multimedia resources has a direct impact on this transition.
- Increasing demand for accountability, with focus on quality customer services, performance measurement, benchmarking, and continuous improvement, is the other shift. Shrinking financial resources for providing quality library and information support services have a direct bearing on this shift.
- New forms of work organization such as end-user computing, work-teams, downsizing, reengineering, outsourcing, etc. is the result of the third shift.

LIS professionals will benefit if they pay serious attention towards developing and enhancing their core competencies. Hence:

LIS professionals can enhance the productivity of those engaged in knowledge creation and its dissemination by playing a more "proactive" role rather than "passive" one. In this changed dimension, LIPs will have to assume the role of analyzers, synthesizers and interpreters of knowledge/information, rather than be content with acquiring, organising and providing information when asked for. Further, the role of traditional librarianship is changing into cybrarianship to include the tasks of scanning, filtering, selecting, organizing and packaging the flood of information. In keeping with their changing role from "gatekeepers" to gateways to "information," LIPs should be performing such tasks as information audits, training in information, literacy, information of best practices/competencies and helping their users to navigate through the world of information, more meaningfully.

(Gulati and Raina, 2000)

Although LIS professionals play the role of information managers in handling organizations' documents and explicit knowledge, to establish a strong position in a KM environment they need to extend their roles by managing employees' tacit knowledge on the basis of their distinctive information and knowledge-handling skills (Al-Hawamdeh, 2005). However, to help LIS professionals be involved more successfully in KM activities and to maximize their prospects for success in what is a very competitive field, the acquisition of a number of additional competencies in the field of management, business operations, and ICT are required. This chapter describes the concept of KM skills and competencies, and the requirements of different types of KM competencies among LIS professionals to facilitate their involvement in KM practice.

CONCEPT OF KNOWLEDGE MANAGEMENT SKILLS AND COMPETENCIES

Competencies encompass knowledge, skills, and personal traits. Competencies are defined as descriptions of skills, know-how, abilities, and personal qualities acquired through deliberate, systematic, and sustained efforts to smoothly and adaptively perform a particular role and carry out complex activities or job functions successfully (Todd and Southon, 2001).

Gulati and Raina (2000) defined competencies as "the interplay of knowledge, understanding skills and attitudes required to do a job effectively from the point of view of both the performer and the observer." The skills, knowledge, and personal attributes that contribute to an individual's success in a particular position are described as core competencies by Giesecke and McNeil (1999). However, they suggest that the competencies must relate to the organizational goals, objectives, and strategies.

REQUIREMENTS OF GENERAL COMPETENCIES IN THE LIS PROFESSION

There is a growing need to understand the requirements of competencies in the LIS profession. Flynn and Shirey (1983) identified the following competencies in the LIS profession:

(a) understanding of principles, fact, concepts, and procedures, and problem-solving using the principles of information transfer;
(b) appreciation of the general role of the profession, and knowledge of clients' capacity to establish systematic relationships;
(c) self-understanding and self-reliance;
(d) critical attributes towards the profession's rationale and tools/technologies;
(e) continued growth; and
(f) identification and use of ethical principles.

Griffiths and King (1984) in their study pointed out several types of knowledge and understanding considered critical to information work:

- basic knowledge in such areas as language, communication, and arithmetic operation;
- subject knowledge of the primary subject field of the user served, such as medicine, chemistry, law, etc.;
- LIS knowledge, such as definition, structure, and format of information;
- knowledge about information work environments, such as the information community, its participants, and their social, economic, and technical interrelationships;
- knowledge of what work is done, such as that required to provide and produce products and services;
- knowledge of how to do work, such as how to perform various activities, apply techniques, use materials and technology; and
- knowledge of organization or the user community served, such as mission, goals, and objectives, users' information needs and requirements.

TYPES OF COMPETENCIES

Mukherjee (2012) classified the necessary skills and competencies in the LIS profession into three categories: professional competencies, personal competencies, and core competencies.

Professional competencies: These competencies relate to the practitioner's knowledge of information resources, access, technology, and management, and the ability to use this knowledge as a basis for providing the highest quality information services. There are four major types of professional competencies, each augmented with specific skills:

(a) managing information organizations;
(b) managing information resources;
(c) managing information services; and
(d) applying information tools and technologies.

Personal competencies: These competencies represent a set of attitudes, skills, and values that enable practitioners to work effectively and contribute positively to their organizations, users, and profession. These competencies range from being strong communicators, to demonstrating the added value of their contributions, to remaining flexible and positive in an ever-changing environment.

Core competencies: Core competencies are those things that an organization knows how to do well, that provide a competitive advantage. These are situated at a tactical level. Some examples would be a process, a specialized type of knowledge, or a particular kind of expertise that is rare or unique to the organization (Liebowitz, 2011). LIS professionals are expected to develop core competencies in the following two areas:

1. They should contribute to the knowledge base of the profession by sharing best practices and experiences, and continue to learn about information products, services, and management practices throughout the life of their career.
2. They should commit to excellence and ethics, and to the values and principles of the profession.

NEED FOR KNOWLEDGE MANAGEMENT SKILLS AND COMPETENCIES FOR LIS PROFESSIONALS

Competencies that emanate from the deliberate use and management of the organization's knowledge resources with the aim of gaining competitive advantage are referred to as KM competencies (Zheng, 2005; Luthra, 2008). KM as a mainstream discipline operates in a largely different context and differs significantly from the theory and practice of librarianship, IM, and information resource management. Though traditional skills of LIS professionals are considered important in KM practice, some other types of skills are needed in the knowledge environment. Loughridge (1999) stated that:

KM differs clearly from the theory and practice of librarianship, information management, and information resource management. It requires a new set of skills among LIS professionals if they wished to have any effective role in this domain (p. 245).

LIS professionals have the expertise to create the file management, databases, and archives (repositories) to enable knowledge capture and sharing for digital and online information sources, and to make these available to a wider audience. The experience or skills of LIS professionals in organization of knowledge via metadata, understanding of user needs, knowledge of integrated and federated searching, and professional skills must be extended beyond recorded information (Blair, 2002). In the present knowledge age, LIS professionals are expected to effectively identify, capture, and utilize an organization's knowledge assets that may be embedded in people, processes, procedures, and routines.

Koenig (1999) highlights the importance of both traditional skills of librarianship in the information environment and additional skills in the business environment. LIS professionals' skills in the fields of indexing, cataloging, authority control, and database management are still relevant for the organization and structuring of information, but they need to acquire some additional skills and competencies in management, leadership, interpersonal skills for leveraging intellectual assets, fostering innovation and change, and creating a culture in the organization for the sharing of knowledge.

To maximize the application of their traditional skills of librarianship in the business world and to take advantage of new opportunities, LIS professionals need to be more creative and imaginative in the application of their traditional skills, and be able to make critical decisions, but also must be capable of shifting to what is frequently a strategic mindset. However, according to Sarrafzadeh (2008), this requires:

the ability to appreciate the wider environment in which organizations operate, including the role of the organization and its clients and the role of information and knowledge in achieving corporate success.

(Sarrafzadeh, 2008, p. 59)

The application of traditional skills of librarianship in a new knowledge environment is further explained by Abell and Wingar (2005) as:

the professional and technical skills of LIS graduates need to be applied with much more understanding of the context, about the way they contribute to the business of the organization ... An organization expects candidates to have an acceptable level of professional and technical skills ... interpersonal skills and transferable "organizational skills"-skills and behaviours that enable professional skills to be applied effectively – are key (p. 175).

One research project by Hill (1998) has compared KM market needs with the traditional skills that have been considered necessary in the LIS profession. The project findings conclude that:

> *an information professional will possess not just the tangible skills required (i.e., research, quick reference skills, source knowledge, collection development, Netscape, online, IT) but also the intangible ones (communication, customer services orientation, organizational understanding, business knowledge, interpersonal skills).*
>
> ***(Hill, 1998, p. 151)***

This statement is supported by a survey of newspaper advertisements in Australia for the first 6 months of 2005 (Jan. to Jun.), which revealed 21 positions with the word "knowledge" in the position title (a relatively small number, given that most of the major Australian newspapers were surveyed).

Thus, in the present knowledge environment, the LIS sector needs to develop a range of interpersonal and business skills in its staff to work in knowledge-based organizations. Rooi and Snyman (2006) pointed out that LIS professionals have an opportunity to play an important role in KM on the basis of the training and experience they have developed and used for many years. However, they need to extend and renew their skills and link those with the processes and core operations of the business in order to be successful in the field of KM. Morris (2001) also noted that LIS professionals already possess the essential theoretical and practical skills to work in KM. They have opportunities to use these skills in creative and imaginative ways to influence information strategies at boardroom level and in corporate decision-making, but they have to gain other skills related to management, business operations, and ICTs to take advantage of their emerging roles in the knowledge economy.

However, if LIS professionals remain reluctant to gain new skills, they will become irrelevant to their organization and will probably lose out in competition for employment to people of other fields, like scientists, engineers, and IT professionals, as pointed out by Sarrafzadeh (2005). Thus LIS professionals will encounter rapidly changing environments that require diverse skills, new thinking and broader perspectives, and must be prepared to develop innovative ideas for the capture, processing and sharing of knowledge, and demonstrate good management practices if they want to remain relevant in the emerging knowledge age (Smythe, 1999). LIS professionals need a substantial expansion of their thinking, knowledge, and a broadening of their skills to benefit from the opportunities that have emerged from KM, and make themselves more relevant to their organizations.

TYPES OF KM SKILLS AND COMPETENCIES

It is clear from the above discussion that the traditional skills of LIS professionals are still in demand, but these skills have to be expanded to handle new digital formats and the online (especially internet) environment to use new metadata schemes and cataloging of digital and Internet resources. Bishop (2001) points out that managing knowledge in libraries requires a mix of technical, organizational, and interpersonal skills. In making knowledge more accessible, it is useful to have knowledge of the organization, user service orientation, and training skills (Koina, 2003). Based on a literature survey, different types of understandings, skills, and competencies are identified, which are discussed below.

Teng and Hawamdeh (2002) summarize different types of understanding and skills that are needed by a LIS professional in a knowledge-based environment. These may be grouped into four categories:

1. IT literacy—that is, knowing how to use the appropriate technology to capture, catalog, and disseminate information and knowledge to the target audience, and knowing how to translate that knowledge into a central database for employees of the organization to access.
2. A sharp and analytical mind.
3. Innovation and an inquiring mind.
4. Enabling knowledge creation, flow and communication within the organization, and between staff and the public (p. 195).

Todd and Southon (2001) investigated the understanding and key skills required for KM in LIS professionals. Based on the findings of their study, they identified five specific categories of understanding related to knowledge, information, people, cognitive issues, organization and business, and management and technology for effective KM. These categories of understanding clearly emphasize the significance of people and organizational factors over technology:

- understanding of human knowing (knowledge about knowledge),
- understanding the knowledge dynamics of people,
- understanding the organization as a knowledge generating and using entity,
- understanding the fundamental principles of IM, and
- understanding technology.

They have also identified six specific categories of skills for KM:

1. people-centered skills, such as those of negotiation, sharing, teamworking, and communication;
2. skills associated with aspects of management of the organization as a whole (management skills);

3. information processing skills;
4. cognitive skills;
5. organization and business skills; and
6. information technology skills.

Reporting on the proceedings of the 1999 ALA Congress on Professional Education, Prentice (1999), from a long list, highlighted the following as values that need to be acknowledged in LIS courses:

- ability to deal with IT
- communication skills
- management skills
- the ability to deal with change

The Department of Information Science at Loughborough University (UK) produced the following ranked list of required experience and skills for KM:

- relevant industrial experience
- interpersonal skills
- highly developed oral/written communication skills
- project management skills
- team player
- change management
- analytical skills
- ability to work to strict deadlines/prioritization skills
- people management
- training skills
- negotiating skills (Morris, 2004, p. 120)

However, Abell (2000) compiled a list of KM enabling skills and competencies as listed below:

- business process identification and analysis,
- understanding the knowledge process within the business process,
- understanding the value, context, and dynamics of knowledge and information,
- knowledge mapping and flows,
- change management,
- leveraging ICT to create KM enablers,
- an understanding of support and facilitation of communities and teams,
- project management,
- information structuring and architecture,
- document and IM and workflows,
- an understanding of IM principles, and
- an understanding of information technology opportunities (p. 36).

Another study conducted in Canada by Ajiferuke (2003) investigated the required skills for KM from the viewpoint of information professionals. Ajiferuke identified teamworking, communication, and networking skills as the key organizational skills required for information professionals in order to participate in KM programs.

Jain (2009), after reviewing the relevant literature, suggests the following skills for LIS professionals in the 21st century:

- good communication and interpersonal skills;
- understanding flexible needs of customers and employers and developing creative solutions;
- ability to market the concept of KM and its benefits;
- negotiation skills, for dealing with suppliers and licensers;
- creativity and long-term vision;
- general management skills: IM, HRM, project management, change management, strategic planning, financial management;
- liaison and negotiation skills (Jain, 2009);
- analytical and lateral thinking ability; and
- cultural adaptability skills.

In developing countries, we can also find several works dealing with the competencies necessary for KM. A study conducted by Mahmood (2003) has identified a set of KM competencies for entry-level professionals in academic libraries in Pakistan. Based on the respondents' opinion, he found that seven out of the ten most essential KM competencies for academic librarians were in the information technology category. Most of the respondents, whether they possess these competencies themselves or not, expect information technology, interpersonal communication and leadership skills from academic librarians of Pakistan to involve in KM practice.

Findings of a study on "competencies for successful KM applications in Nigerian academic libraries" conducted by Ugwu and Ezema (2010) show that cultural skills, leadership skills, strategic skills, and restructuring skills are the most essential requirements for LIS professionals involved in KM. Further, they suggest that LIS professionals should acquire these skills for involvement in KM in Nigerian university libraries. Siddike and Islam (2011) carried out a survey to identify the core competencies needed for information professionals involved in KM in libraries/information institutions in Bangladesh. Most respondents believe that competencies, including those in communication, facilitation, coaching, mentoring, networking, negotiating, consensus building and teamworking, are essential for KM in libraries in Bangladesh. The authors, on the basis of the findings of this study, suggested that the Department of

Information Science and Library Management of Dhaka University and Rajshahi University should introduce KM course(s) either at graduate or post-graduate level. According to Yaacob et al. (2010), middle and top managers of the large libraries of Malaysia perceive that librarians in Malaysian libraries lack leadership and IT skills which influence the success of knowledge-sharing efforts in organization.

INVESTIGATION OF THE REQUIRED KM COMPETENCIES FOR LIS PROFESSIONALS[1]

An analytical study by Gulati and Raina (2000) establishes the set of professional competencies that need to be developed among LIS professionals in India in various areas of operations and services such as knowledge capture, knowledge processing (and dissemination), and knowledge application. Further, they have also recommended the development of need-based and tailor-made short-term training programs for existing professionals, to hone their skills and develop their expertise. A few studies in India (Gulati and Raina, 2000; Subramanian, 2007; Thanuskodi, 2010) acknowledge the importance of developing skills and competencies among LIS professionals in order to perform their job more effectively in the knowledge age; however, no empirical study has been conducted in India to examine the requirements of skills and competencies for LIS professionals involved in KM practice.

It has emerged from the literature reviewed and the discussion above that traditional skills of librarianship are still relevant in the management of information, but LIS professionals need to acquire other types of competencies to work with knowledge-intensive organizations. The findings of some studies suggest a need to introduce formal education and training programs for LIS professionals to develop a strong and shared understanding of the nature of KM, its underpinning assumptions and values, and its multifaceted relationship to existing information work (Todd and Southon, 2001; Jain, 2007; Rehman, 2006; Hazeri et al., 2007; Martin, 1999). Some studies in India (Gulati and Raina, 2000; Subramanian, 2007; Thanuskodi, 2010) acknowledge the importance of developing skills and competencies that enable LIS professionals to perform their jobs more effectively in the knowledge age; however, no empirical study has been conducted to examine the requirements of skills and competencies for the involvement of LIS professionals in KM practices.

[1]This section of the chapter is based on an article by Nazim and Mukherjee (2013).

According to Rehman et al. (1997), competence identification and validation processes provide an objective framework for the design of education and training programs. They also provide guidelines to determine appropriate educational and training levels for intake and graduation. Education and training programs can be evaluated against validated sets of competencies. The LIS curriculum has always been criticized in India, as it has been implemented without any feedback from the LIS community (Singh, 2009). According to Chakraborty and Sarkhel (2009), the courses offered by LIS schools in India are not sufficient to develop a proper understanding of the concept of KM, as well as to hone the requisite skills for LIS students to become practically involved in KM practices. Identification and validation of KM competencies may help the academic community to reconsider LIS curricula and teaching methods, and modify existing curricula to impart a wide range of competencies among students. Therefore an attempt is made to prepare a list of KM competencies and to validate this list based on the perceptions of the academic community.

A web-based questionnaire survey method was used to achieve the objectives of the study. A questionnaire was designed and distributed through FreeOnlineSurveys.com. For this purpose a list of 78 universities offering up to master degree level courses in LIS was prepared using the latest available directory (ie, university handbooks, published by the Association of Indian Universities, 2010). The sample size was identified by searching the Internet and consulting the websites of LIS schools to identify those teachers who had some specialization in KM and its related areas. The details of 65 LIS schools and their faculty are available on the Internet. After consulting the websites of the LIS schools of 65 universities, the details (including name, designation, e-mail, specialization, etc.) of the LIS teachers were noted. As of Jun. 30, 2011, this number represented 177 teachers from 65 universities. Of 177 teachers, the present study chose all of the 95 teachers who mentioned their specialization in KM and its related areas as the sample for this study. A list of 25 competencies was prepared based on an extensive review of the literature. Special attention was given to those competencies that had already been validated in Asian or other developing countries, including Pakistan (Mahmood, 2003), Malaysia (Yaacob et al., 2010), Bangladesh (Siddike and Islam, 2011), Nigeria (Ugwu and Ezema, 2010), and Thailand (Tanloet and Tuamsuk, 2011). The list was divided into five categories:

(1) KM culture competencies
(2) Management competencies
(3) Interpersonal competencies

(4) Leadership and strategic competencies
(5) IT competencies

Respondents were asked to nominate the level of importance of each proposed KM competency a holder of a Master of Library and Information Science (MLIS) degree should possess, bearing in mind the needs of KM applications in academic libraries in India. The level of importance of each competency was measured using a five-point Likert scale, where 1 represented "not needed" and 5 denoted "most needed." For validation purposes, the mean value 3.45 (based on a method designed and used by Sarrafzadeh et al., 2010) was fixed as the cut-off point, meaning that a competency would be considered "needed" if it had an average mean score greater than 3.45.

A link for the survey (list of KM competency statements) to the validation of competencies was sent via electronic mail to the teachers (95 in numbers) of 65 LIS schools. A total of 43 or ~45% of responses were received. Of the 43 respondents, 24 (55.8%) were assistant professors (including two lecturers), 13 (30.2%) were associate professors (including three readers), and 6 (14.0%) were professors. Of a total of 43 respondents who completed the questionnaire, 27 (62.8%) were male and 16 (37.2%) were female. Their duration of teaching experience was between 4 months and 35 years, with the majority (71.1%) having between 6 and 30 years of experience in teaching. The majority of respondents (81.4%) had a Ph.D. as the highest degree, followed by a Master's degree (16.3%), and M.Phil. degree (2.3%) in LIS. Table 7.1 illustrates the demographic profile of the respondents.

Although the perceptions of the respondents on each competency statement were different, they validated all competencies because the smallest mean score a competency statement obtained was 3.56, above the cut-off point of 3.45. Thirteen competencies had mean scores of 4 or more (the list is presented in Table 7.2). This trend of validation shows that respondents anticipated the need for interpersonal and management competencies in LIS professionals, as communication skills in the interpersonal competency category was rated number one in the list of 25 competencies, with a mean score of 4.67.

Three competencies from the management competency category, which were in second, third, and fourth positions in the list of the top 13, were HRM skills, change management skills, and project management skills, with mean scores of 4.58, 4.53, and 4.51 respectively.

Table 7.1 Demographic profile of the respondents

	Frequency	%
By designation		
Assistant professors (including lecturers)	24	55.8
Associate professors (including readers)	13	30.2
Professors	6	14.0
By gender		
Male	27	62.8
Female	16	37.2
By years of experience		
0–5	8	18.6
6–10	10	23.2
11–19	15	34.9
20–29	6	14.0
30 and over	4	9.3
By highest degree		
Master's degree in library and information science	7	16.3
M.Phil. degree in library and information science	1	2.3
Ph.D. degree in library and information science	35	81.4

Table 7.2 Ranked list of the top 13 knowledge management competencies

Rank	Category	Competencies	Mean
1	Interpersonal	Communication skills	4.67
2	Management	Human resource management skills	4.58
3	Management	Change management skills	4.53
4	Management	Project management skills	4.51
5	KM culture	Teamwork skills	4.42
6	Interpersonal	Mentoring skills	4.40
7	Management	Leadership skills	4.33
8	KM culture	Ability to foster a knowledge-sharing and learning environment	4.30
9	KM culture	Ability to motivate employees	4.26
10	Leadership and structural	Ability to develop social networks or communities of practice	4.19
11	IT	Ability to design and develop web-based content for online use	4.19
12	Leadership and structural	Ability to develop performance-based reward systems	4.16
13	IT	Ability to develop web-based portals or gateways	4.12

KM Culture Competencies

The validation data of 25 KM competencies for the five categories are presented in Tables 7.3–7.7. As Table 7.3 shows, the highest scoring KM competency of the five in the KM culture competency category was teamwork skills. With a mean score of 4.30, the ability to foster a knowledge-sharing and learning environment was the second most important competency in this category, closely followed by the ability to motivate employees, with a mean score of 4.26. The ability to build trust and relationship and to resolve conflict were given comparatively low rankings.

Management Competencies

In the management competency category, HRM skills topped the list of the five competencies, with a mean score of 4.58 (Table 7.4). The other important competencies in this category were change management skills, project management skills, and leadership skills, with mean scores of 4.53, 4.51, and 4.33 respectively. Knowledge about marketing and publicity of information products and services was given low importance, receiving a mean score of 3.98.

Interpersonal Competencies

Good interpersonal skills such as communication and mentoring were given high ratings among the competencies belonging to the interpersonal category, with mean scores of 4.67 and 4.40 respectively (Table 7.5). Other competencies, which were given a lower rating, in the interpersonal competency category include interviewing skills (mean 3.93), judgment and evaluation skills (mean 3.91), and presentation skills.

Leadership and Strategic Competencies

Table 7.6 shows the competencies needed for the strategic planning and restructuring of academic libraries. As shown in Table 7.6, the ability to develop social networks or communities of practice and the ability to develop performance-based reward systems were rated as the important competencies of LIS professionals, with mean scores of 4.19 and 4.16 respectively. These were closely followed by the ability to link knowledge with strategic results, the ability to develop KM policy, and the ability to create value from an organization's knowledge-based assets, with mean scores of 3.88, 3.77, and 3.72 respectively.

Table 7.3 Results for competencies related to organizational culture

Competencies	Mean
Teamwork skills	4.42
Ability to foster a knowledge-sharing and learning environment	4.30
Ability to motivate employees	4.26
Ability to build trust and relationships	3.98
Ability to resolve conflicts	3.56

Table 7.4 Results for management competencies

Competencies	Mean
Human resource management skills	4.58
Change management skills	4.53
Project management skills	4.51
Leadership skills	4.33
Knowledge about marketing and publicity of information products and services	3.98

Table 7.5 Results for interpersonal competencies

Competencies	Mean
Communication skills	4.67
Mentoring skills	4.40
Interviewing skills	3.93
Judgment and evaluation skills	3.91
Presentation skills	3.61

Table 7.6 Results for leadership and strategic competencies

Competencies	Mean
Ability to develop social networks or communities of practice	4.19
Ability to develop performance-based reward systems	4.16
Ability to link knowledge with strategic results	3.88
Ability to develop KM policy	3.77
Ability to create value from an organization's knowledge-based assets	3.72

IT Competencies

Table 7.7 shows the competencies needed for the use and application of IT in the implementation of KM systems in academic libraries in India. Competencies which received high mean scores were design and development of web-based content for online use, development of web-based portals or subject gateways, and use of digital library software to create

Table 7.7 Results for information technology competencies

Competencies	Mean
Ability to design and develop web-based content for online use	4.19
Ability to develop web-based portals or gateways	4.12
Ability to use digital library software to create institutional or knowledge repositories	3.98
Ability to design and maintain in-house databases	3.95
Expertise to evaluate performance of information systems	3.58

institutional or knowledge repositories, with mean scores of 4.19, 4.12, and 3.98 respectively. Competencies that were given comparatively less importance were the design and maintenance of in-house databases and expertise to evaluate the performance of information systems, with mean scores of 3.95 and 3.58 respectively.

Comparison of the Mean Scores of KM Competencies (Five Categories)

An average mean of each competency category was calculated. The results, presented in Table 7.8, show that there is a minor difference in the average mean scores of the five types of competencies, but the respondents validated the requirements of competencies in the five areas. However, respondents were of the opinion that the need for management competencies in LIS professionals is the most essential requirement (mean 4.38). This is closely followed by interpersonal competencies (mean 4.25); KM culture competencies (4.18), and leadership and strategic competencies (mean 4.08). It is important to note that the use of information technology has been recognized in the literature as the foundation of KM, but the necessity of competencies relating to the use and application of IT had a low mean (3.98) among the five categories of competencies identified and validated.

Discussion

KM competencies are needed in five areas of competency building (management, KM culture, interpersonal, leadership and strategic, and information technology) for the practice of KM in academic libraries. The findings on the requirements of KM competencies in these areas indicate that, although there are minor differences in the mean scores in the five categories of competencies, all of these categories were validated as being necessary. This means the academic community believes that LIS professionals in India

Table 7.8 Results for different types of competencies

Competencies	**Mean**
Management competencies	4.38
Interpersonal competencies	4.25
KM cultural competencies	4.10
Leadership and strategic competencies	4.08
Information technology competencies	3.98

need to develop competencies in all these five areas. However, respondents were of the opinion that development of management competencies is the most essential requirement for LIS professionals.

It is important to mention here that IT has been recognized as one of the most important enablers of KM by the respondents of a study conducted in India by Nazim and Mukherjee (2011), but the necessity of competencies relating to the use and application of IT was rated the lowest among the five types of competencies identified and validated in the present study. Martens and Hawamdeh (2010) rightly remark that IT skills are necessary but not sufficient for KM as a profession. The five categories of KM competencies investigated and validated clearly emphasize managerial, interpersonal, and organizational/cultural factors over IT. Although the use and application of IT is essential, that alone does not ensure successful KM in the absence of skills relating to the organizational culture, and business and leadership to develop a strategy for the implementation of KM in academic libraries. Roknuzzaman and Umemoto (2013), based on the findings of a study on incorporating KM education into the LIS curriculum, remark that since KM is being developed through inputs from many other disciplines, it would be a tough challenge for LIS professionals to succeed in incorporating KM unless they have knowledge of business and management.

The findings of the study show that the list of necessary KM competencies, based on the work already done in developed as well as some developing countries, is acceptable to the academic community of India. When comparing the findings with previous studies, it may be observed that competencies in the areas of communication, HRM, change management and project management, which are validated with the high mean ratings in the present study, are closely associated with the findings of earlier studies on the requirements of KM competencies in LIS professionals as investigated by Abell (2000) and Ajiferuke (2003). They found that these competencies are required for collaboration within an organization to facilitate the processes of sharing, exchange, and use of knowledge. The findings of the present study are also closely related to the findings of other studies conducted to investigate KM competencies in LIS professionals in Africa by Maponya (2004), in Malaysia by Yaacob et al. (2010), in Nigeria by Ugwu and Ezema (2010), in Bangladesh by Siddike and Islam (2011), and in Thailand by Tanloet and Tuamsuk (2011).

The competencies that are identified and validated in the present study are essential for the proper repositioning of LIS professionals to face the challenges of present-day realities. A focus on the transfer of traditional LIS skills, for example in knowledge organization, to the management of tacit knowledge could greatly enhance the influence of LIS professionals in the KM field and contribute to their overall understanding of the need for knowledge both at organizational and personal levels. These competencies may also be objectively applied for the evaluation of current LIS educational programs and starting new courses to impart such competencies among LIS students.

SUMMARY

Traditional skills of librarianship and IM may be considered useful for initiating KM practice in libraries, but there is a need to impart additional skills and competencies for LIS professionals regarding their involvement in KM, including those relating to communication, HRM, change management, project management, teamwork, mentoring, presentation, and leadership. The necessity for a wide range of competencies may be considered as an indication of the multidisciplinary nature of KM, and along with this there is a need for integrated and comprehensive KM educational programs. A partial or improper understanding of KM among LIS professionals and a lack of realization of the value of KM education in LIS students and the academic community are key issues facing KM education in the LIS sector. To solve these problems, LIS schools need either to restructure the existing LIS curricula or to provide courses in KM to impart competencies in LIS students. The sets of competencies validated by the respondents in a case study presented in this chapter may be used as groundwork for redefining the curricula of LIS educational programs. These can also be objectively applied to the evaluation of current LIS educational programs. Course curricula imparted at all levels in the discipline of LIS need to undergo a sea change to incorporate newer approaches/concepts. Existing professionals need to be provided with state-of-the-art exposure to the art and science of the profession through various in-service (continuing education) programs. All existing as well as future professionals will need to be groomed to take on the role of "knowledge managers." Importance of KM education for LIS professionals is discussed in the next chapter.

REFERENCES

Abell, A., 2000. Skills for knowledge environments. Inf. Manag. J. 34 (3), 10–12.

Abell, A., Wingar, L., 2005. The commercial connection: realizing the potential of information skills. Bus. Inf. Rev. 22, 172–181.

Ajiferuke, I., 2003. Role of information professionals in knowledge management programs: empirical evidence from Canada. Inform. Sci. J. 6, 247–257.

Al-Hawamdeh, S., 2005. Designing an interdisciplinary graduate program in knowledge management. J. Am. Soc. Inf. Sci. Technol. 56 (11), 1200–1206.

Association of Indian Universities, 2010. Universities Handbooks, 32nd ed. Association of Indian Universities, New Delhi.

Bishop, K., 2001. Information Service Professionals in Knowledge-Based Organizations in Australia: What Will We Manage? University of Technology, Sydney.

Blair, D.C., 2002. Knowledge management: hype, hope, or help. J. Am. Soc. Inf. Sci. Technol. 50 (12), 1019–1028.

Chakraborty, S., Sarkhel, J.K., 2009. LIS education in India: an appraisal of the parity between the syllabus and the market demands. In: Paper Presented at 75th IFLA General Conference and Council, Milan, Italy, August 23–27.

Corrall, S., 1998. Knowledge management: are we in the knowledge management business? Ariadne 18. www.ariadne.ac.uk/issue18/knowledge-mgt/ (accessed 16.09.15).

Flynn, R., Shirey, D.L., 1983. Towards a paradigm for education in information science. In: Debons, A., Larson, A. (Eds.), Information Science in Action: System Design. Martinus Nijhoff, Boston, pp. 703–706.

Giesecke, J., Mcneil, B., 1999. Core competencies and the learning organization. In: Faculty Publications, Paper 60. UNL Libraries, University of Nebraska, Lincoln. http://digitalcommons.unl.edu/libraryscience/60 (accessed 15.12.15).

Griffiths, J.-M., King, D.W., 1984. Educating the information professionals of the future: challenges to the information society. In: Proceedings of the 47th ASIS Annual Meeting, vol. 22. Knowledge Industry Publication, White Plains, NY, pp. 68–74.

Gulati, A., Raina, R.L., 2000. Professional competencies among librarians and information professionals in the knowledge era. World Libr. 10 (1), 11–18.

Hazeri, A., Sarrafzadeh, M., Martin, B., 2007. Reflections of information professionals on knowledge management competencies in the LIS curriculum. J. Edu. J. Edu. Libr. Inf. Sci. 48 (3), 168–186.

Hill, S., 1998. Knowledge management: a new career path for the information profession. In: Graham, C., (Ed.), Proceedings of 22nd International Online Information Meeting. London, pp. 149–156.

Jain, P., 2007. An empirical study of knowledge management in academic libraries in East and Southern Africa. Libr. Rev. 56 (5), 377–392.

Jain, P., 2009. Knowledge management for 21st century information professionals. J. Knowl. Manag. Pract. 10 (2). http://www.tlainc.com/artic1193.htm.

Koenig, M.E.D., 1999. Education for knowledge management. Inf. Serv. Use 19 (1), 17–32.

Koina, C., 2003. Librarians are the ultimate knowledge managers. Aust. Libr. J. 52 (3). Available at: http://alianet.alia.org.au/publishing/alj/52.3/full.text/koina.html.

Liebowitz, J., 2011. Introduction to knowledge management. In: Dalkir, K., Liebowitz, J. (Eds.), Knowledge Management in Theory and Practice. MIT Press, Boston, MA, pp. 1–30. http://www.jstor.org/stable/j.ctt5hhhx9.4 (accessed 12.01.2016).

Loughridge, B., 1999. Knowledge management, librarians and information managers: fad or future? New Libr. World 100 (6), 245–253.

Luthra, P., 2008. Understanding the process of building KM competencies—drawing on the resource-based view of the firm. http://ssrn.com/abstract=1126118 (accessed 15.12.15).

Mahmood, K., 2003. A comparison between needed competencies of academic librarians and LIS curricula in Pakistan. Electron. Libr. 21 (2), 99–109.

Maponya, P., 2004. Knowledge management practices in academic libraries: a case study of the University of Natal. In: Pietermaritzburg Libraries. University of KwaZulu Nata, Durban. http://citeseerx.ist.psu.edu/viewdoc/download?doi=10.1.1.137.8283&rep=rep1&type=pdf (accessed 11.06.15).

Martens, B.V., Hawamdeh, S., 2010. The professionalization of knowledge management. In: Pankl, E., Theiss-White, D., Bushing, M.C. (Eds.), Recruitment, Development, and Retention of Information Professionals: Trends in Human Resources and Knowledge Management. Business Science Reference, Hershey, PA, pp. 139–156.

Martin, W., 1999. New directions in education for LIS: knowledge management programs at RMIT. J. Educ. Libr. Inf. Sci. 40 (3), 142–150.

Morris, A., 2001. Knowledge management: opportunities for LIS graduates. In: Paper Presented at 67th IFLA Council and General Conference, Boston, MA, August 16–25.

Morris, A., 2004. Knowledge management: employment opportunities for IS graduates. In: Hobohm, H.C. (Ed.), Knowledge Management: Libraries and Librarians Taking Up the Challenge. Saur, Munich, pp. 115–125.

Mukherjee, B., 2012. Information Communication and Society. Ess Ess Publications, New Delhi.

Nazim, M., Mukherjee, B., 2011. Implementing knowledge management in Indian academic libraries: perceptions of applications and challenges. J. Knowl. Manag. Pract. 12 (3). Available at: http://www.tlainc.com/articl269.htm.

Nazim, M., Mukherjee, B., 2013. Knowledge management competencies required among library and information science professionals: an Indian perspective. Libr. Rev. 62 (6/7), 375–387.

Raina, R.L., 2000. Competency development among librarians and information professionals. In: Paper of XIX IASLIC Seminar, Bhopal, 2000, pp. 211–216.

Rehman, S.U., 2006. New age competencies for information professionals. In: Paper Presented at the Asia-Pacific Conference on Library and Information Education and Practice, Singapore, April 3–6.

Rehman, S.U., Majid, S., Baker, A.B.A., 1997. Competences for future library professionals of academic libraries in Malaysia. Libr. Rev. 46 (6), 381–393.

Roknuzzaman, M., Umemoto, K., 2013. Incorporating KM education into LIS curriculum: perspectives from LIS academics. VINE: J. Inf. Knowl. Manag. Syst. 43 (1), 111–124.

Rooi, H.V., Snyman, R., 2006. A content analysis of literature regarding knowledge management opportunities for librarians. Aslib Proc. 58 (3), 261–271.

Sarrafzadeh, M., 2005. The implications of knowledge management for the library and information professions. ActKM Online J. Knowl. Manag. 2 (1), 92–102. www.actkm.org/actkmjournal_vol2iss1.php (accessed 15.12.15).

Sarrafzadeh, M., 2008. The Implications of Knowledge Management for the Library and Information Professions. Ph.D. Dissertation, RMIT University. Available at: https://researchbank.rmit.edu.au/eserv/rmit:13384/Sarrafzadeh.pdf (accessed 15.02.15).

Sarrafzadeh, M., Martin, B., Hazeri, A., 2010. Knowledge management and its potential applicability for libraries. Libr. Manag. 31 (3), 198–212.

Siddike, M.A.K., Islam, M.S., 2011. Exploring the competencies of information professionals for knowledge management in the information institutions of Bangladesh. Int. Inf. Libr. Rev. 43, 130–136.
Singh, J., 2009. Leadership competencies for change management in libraries: challenges and opportunities. http://crl.du.ac.in/ical09/papers/index_files/ical-51_250_732_3_RV.pdf (accessed 10.12.15).
Smythe, D., 1999. Facing the future: preparing new information professionals. Inf. Manag. J. 33 (2), 44–48.
Subramanian, N., 2007. Knowledge and Information Management in Libraries: A New Challenge for the Library and Information Professionals in the Digital Environment. www.igcar.ernet.in/igc2004/sird/redit2007.pdf (accessed 19.12.15).
Tanloet, P., Tuamsuk, K., 2011. Core competencies for information professionals of Thai academic libraries in the next decade (AD 2010–2019). Int. Inf. Libr. Rev. 43 (3), 122–129.
Teng, S., Hawamdeh, S., 2002. Knowledge management in public libraries. Aslib Proc. 54 (3), 188–197.
Thanuskodi, S., 2010. Knowledge management in academic libraries: an overview. In: Paper Presented at 6th International Conference on Webometrics, Informetrics and Scientometrics and Eleventh COLLNET Meeting, University of Mysore, India, October 19–22.
Todd, R.J., Southon, G., 2001. Educating for a knowledge management future: perceptions of library and information professionals. Aust. Libr. J. 50 (4), 313–326.
Ugwu, C.I., Ezema, I.J., 2010. Competencies for successful knowledge management applications in Nigerian academic libraries. Int. J. Libr. Inf. Sci. 2 (9), 184–189.
Yaacob, R.A., Jamaluddin, A., Jusoff, K., 2010. Knowledge management and challenging roles of academic librarians. Manag. Sci. Eng. 4 (4), 14–23.
Zheng, W., 2005. A conceptualization of the relationship between organizational culture and knowledge management. J. Inf. Know. Manag. 4 (2), 113–124.

FURTHER READING

Al-Hawamdeh, S., Foo, S., 2001. Information professionals in the information age: vital skills and competencies. In: Paper Presented at International Conference for Library and Information Science Educators in the Asia Pacific Region (ICLISE 2001), Kuala Lumpur, Malaysia, June 11–12.

CHAPTER 8

Knowledge Management Education

INTRODUCTION

The library and information science (LIS) community is still debating whether knowledge management (KM) is a new discipline or simply a re-branding of librarianship or information management (IM). The perceptions and attitudes in the LIS community towards KM are varied. However, they view KM from a more positive angle, calling for full involvement of LIS people in KM programs, arguing for the enhancement of LIS skills and competencies beyond IM, and taking advantage of the new opportunities emerging from the origins of KM. As the relevance of KM to the LIS community has already been well established, a number of scholars have called for the full involvement of LIS professionals in KM both for individual career development and overall advancement of the LIS profession (Abell and Oxbrow, 2001; Butler, 2000; Sarrafzadeh et al., 2006a; Southon and Todd, 2001; White, 2004). It may, however, be noted that a gap exists between the skills required for LIS professionals' involvement in KM and what is currently being taught in LIS master's degree programs (Wormell, 2004), a fact that was also emphasized by Roknuzzaman and Umemoto (2008). In fact, the multidisciplinary nature of KM requires a mix of skills and competencies in LIS, as have been applied to KM in other disciplines (Kebede, 2010). Responding to the exciting and emerging phenomenon of KM, some LIS schools have adopted KM as an academic program at different levels of education. In this context, this chapter aims to explore the current state of KM education offered by LIS schools globally and investigate the perceptions of the LIS community in India toward the provision of KM education within LIS courses.

THE LIS PROFESSION AND THE EMERGENCE OF KM

LIS is a discipline that combines the common principles of both library and information sciences. Library science concentrates on the theory and fundamental principles of librarianship, while librarianship is concerned with library practice (Langridge, 1978). Information science, as a discipline, is concerned with the study of information in any information system. It investigates the properties and behavior of information, the forces governing the flow of information, and the means of processing information for optimum accessibility and usability. Library science as a discipline includes: selection, organization, planning, and management of library resources; guidance in their use; and historical, philosophical, and legal aspects (Carnovsky, 1964). Information science deals with the collection, organization, storage, retrieval, interpretation, transmission, transformation, and utilization of information (Borko, 1968). Roknuzzaman and Umemoto (2008) define LIS as "an interdisciplinary field of study which promotes information processing activities to provide people with access to library and information resources in any form, either in printed or in electronic form" (p. 281).

The major challenge for the LIS profession is the distinct possibility of isolation triggered by the emergence of a parallel and more sophisticated KM profession. There has been a paradigm shift in the ways in which knowledge is created, acquired, accessed, communicated, disseminated, and utilized. New information technologies are playing a central and key role in the emergence of a range of mechanisms (with a wider range of labels that include libraries and other such institutions, digital libraries, institutional repositories, digital archives, open archives, KM systems, learning resource centers, knowledge resource centers, to mention just a few); a range of careers and a new industry centered on the knowledge of people (tacit knowledge). Information systems of all kinds, including libraries and KM systems, are fields of institutional investment: they are major commitments of resources to developing and using certain facilities. This can only be justified in terms of the extent to which these facilities augment and enhance human and organizational capabilities, or in terms of the disadvantages, losses, and negative impact resulting from not having these facilities. The same argument may be used for investment in institutional mechanisms aiming to train manpower to work in libraries and information systems. Their utility and value has to be measured in terms of their ability to train suitable and relevant manpower for the emerging job market. Judging by the significant amount being invested by major organizations to augment their KM/information facilities, it indeed appears that organizations have begun to see investment in KM as important for their growth. Since this knowledge sector is not limited to libraries or information centers, it is a potential job market for the information manpower being trained. The important question is whether this sector will look to LIS schools and their educational programs for their knowledge manpower needs. According to Raghavan (2007), there are three factors that are likely to have a bearing on manpower development programs in the information field:

- the requirements of emerging information systems and emerging job markets
- the changing manpower needs and requirements in traditional libraries
- the nature of job positions being occupied by students of LIS schools

KM EDUCATION

KM, as an interdisciplinary subject, integrates a range of concepts, theories, and practices from different disciplines, including management, LIS, information technology (IT), communication, and business (Al-Hawamdeh, 2005). KM is also associated with system engineering, organizational learning, and decision support systems (Ponzi and Koenig, 2002). According to Roknuzzaman and Umemoto (2008), the nature of KM is interdisciplinary because several disciplines are involved in the promotion of KM education and research. Theories and practices of different disciplines, such as business theory and economics, cognitive sciences, cybrary sciences (library science and cyberspace), ergonomics, information sciences, knowledge engineering, artificial intelligence, management sciences, and social sciences are also supporting KM (Wiig, 1999). Some authors have tried to identify the contribution and involvement of different disciplines in the advancement of KM. Wilson (2002) examined the current nature of KM by analyzing 242 papers from the Web of Science published in 2001 on the subject of "knowledge management." These 242 papers were distributed over 106 journals covering 26 subject fields. Of these 26 subjects, more than five journal titles appeared in five fields, including computing and information systems (26); information science, information management, and librarianship (18); management (13); artificial intelligence (10); and engineering (8). The participation of such a wide range of different subjects clearly indicates the strength of the interdisciplinary nature of KM. On the other hand, it also offers a challenge as to what types of courses might need to be introduced in KM education programs.

Despite the challenges involved in the provision of KM education, a growing number of schools around the world are now offering master's or other degrees in KM, keeping in mind the demands of the KM market (Sarrafzadeh, 2008; Sarrafzadeh et al., 2006b). However, the nature of KM programs is varied, with a range of diversified course contents emphasizing different disciplinary perspectives. Chaudhry and Higgins (2001) examined the disciplinary association of 37 KM courses, and found that the highest number of KM courses (40%) were in the discipline of information systems or studies, followed by business management (35%), computer science/engineering (14%), and others (11%). They show differences in perspectives and emphases in the course contents and curriculum areas varying from more technology-oriented courses in computing schools to a management orientation in LIS and business schools. They categorized frequently listed KM topics into five main curriculum areas: KM foundations, technology, process (codification), applications, and strategies. In their study, Roknuzzaman and Umemoto (2008) found that KM graduate programs vary from school to school with various course titles, curricula, and contents. They categorized KM programs into five major areas (Table 8.1): KM core elements, library and information studies, information system/computing, business and management, and organizational behavior.

Olszak and Ziemba (2010) proposed the teaching courses for bachelor's and master's degree studies in KM in Poland. The aim of these courses is to meet the assumptions underlying knowledge-based organizations. Although these courses are designed specifically to suit the requirements of KM education in the universities of Poland, they may be applicable to other universities in the world. These courses are listed in Table 8.2.

Chaudhry and Higgins (2001), in their study on KM courses in the curriculum of academic disciplines of business, computing, and information science in the universities of Australia, Canada, Singapore, UK, and the United States, found that courses in KM are mainly offered at graduate level. Of the total of 37 KM courses, only 7 are at undergraduate level, while 30 courses are at graduate level, which are designed as part of a master's program. These KM courses are in the areas of business, computing, and information. These courses are part of the curriculum in the departments of information systems (either in computing or business schools) and the divisions of information studies (generally in schools of LIS, with a couple of exceptions). The highest number of KM courses, as identified, is found to be a master's degree in information systems or studies (40%), followed by a master in business administration (35%), and computer science/engineering (14%). The remaining 11% of KM courses are offered by other schools.

Table 8.1 Nature of KM educational programs at graduate level

Serial no.	Curriculum areas	Examples of courses
1	KM core elements	Foundation of KM, KM principles, KM processes, KM tools and technologies, KM practices, etc.
2	Library and information science/information management	Content management, classification and cataloging, taxonomies and codification, indexing and abstracting, record management, information retrieval, etc.
3	Information systems/ computing/IT	IT management, database management systems (DBMS), system analysis, data mining, knowledge engineering, Internet technology, etc.
4	Business and management	Business administration, business/ competitive, intelligent e-commerce, business process management, management information systems (MIS), etc.
5	Human and organizational behavior	Communication and organizational behavior, organizational learning, intellectual capital, human resource management (HRM), leadership, culture and change management, etc.

From Roknuzzaman, M., Umemoto, K., 2008. Knowledge management's relevance to library and information science: an interdisciplinary approach. J. Inf. Knowl. Manag. 7 (4), 279–290.

Based on a review of the contents of KM courses offered by business, computing, and information science schools, Chaudhry and Higgins (2001) classified frequently listed topics into five main curriculum areas:

1. concepts relating to knowledge;
2. tools to exploit the potential of knowledge;
3. processes that facilitate the acquisition, creation, mapping, and sharing of knowledge;
4. strategies employed by organizations to manage knowledge; and
5. support systems needed to sustain KM initiatives.

Topics that are frequently listed in these categories are shown in Table 8.3.

Table 8.2 KM courses for bachelor's and master's degree programs

Level of courses	Serial no.	Courses
Bachelor's degree courses/ obligatory courses	1	Management of information resources in a knowledge-based organization
	2	Information collection methods and techniques
	3	Information technology support for business processes
	4	Use of the Internet in a knowledge-based economy
	5	Information-processing methods
	6	Business intelligence
	7	Information technologies in knowledge management
Bachelor's degree courses/ optional courses	1	Communication on the Internet
	2	Online information search systems
	3	Online information search systems
	4	Business intelligence using computer tools
	5	Online business portals
Master's degree courses/ obligatory courses	1	Customer relationship management
	2	Audit of information resources
	3	Corporate portals for a knowledge-based organization
	4	Security and protection of information resources
Master's degree courses/ optional courses	1	E-business strategies and models
	2	Simulations and computer decision-making games
	3	Information project management

From Olszak, C.M., Ziemba, E., 2010. Knowledge management curriculum development: linking with real business needs. Issues Inform. Sci. Inf. Technol. 7, 235–248.

THE NEED FOR KM EDUCATION: CHALLENGES FOR LIS PROFESSIONALS

The participation of LIS professionals in KM requires multidisciplinary knowledge and skills, because many positions arising from KM seem to fit other professional settings like LIS. The findings of a study by TFPL (1999) revealed that the involvement of LIS professionals in KM at a strategic level was extremely rare, as these professionals lacked business understanding, the breadth of required experience, and the necessary mindset. They were more concerned with external information and to some extent the management

Table 8.3 Fundamental areas and topics covered in KM curricula

Main curriculum areas	Course descriptions/topics
Foundations	Definitions and complexity of knowledge
	Forms of knowledge (tacit, explicit)
	Sources of knowledge (best practices, communities of practice)
	Knowledge workers
	Intellectual capital
	Knowledge-based organizations
	KM processes
	KM enablers
	Knowledge-sharing models
Technology	General overview of commonly used technologies
	Selection and design considerations for KM-enabling technologies
	KM architecture
	KM tools and applications
	Collaboration (groupware tools)
	Business intelligence (data analysis tools)
	Document management systems
	Intranets/portals/websites
Process (codification)	Knowledge audit
	Capture and acquisition of knowledge
	Knowledge mapping
	Organization and categorization of knowledge resources
	Developing and maintaining knowledge repositories
	Search and retrieval, use, and reuse of knowledge
Applications	Case studies and success stories of KM applications in consulting firms and IT companies
	Considerations for KM applications in different sectors and industries
	Implementing a KM project in an organization
Strategies	Integrating knowledge into organizational work to gain leverage from organizational knowledge resources
	Steps for sustaining KM work
	Institutionalization of KM activities
	Human resources and support (role and responsibilities of knowledge professionals)
	Measurement of knowledge assets

From Chaudhry, A.S., Higgins, S.E., 2001. Perspectives on education for knowledge management. Paper Presented at the 67th IFLA Council and General Conference, 16–25 August, Boston, MA.

of records and documents. In order for them to thrive in a KM environment, they had to develop the confidence to apply their skills in unfamiliar situations; develop understanding of organizational strategies and challenges; comprehend the complex array of knowledge and information available within an organization; develop new skills for working with knowledge teams; and acquire the attributes needed to succeed in knowledge culture. Raghavan (2007), on the basis of some recent job notifications on the Web, identified different skill sets for different positions that are expected of LIS professionals working in a knowledge environment (Table 8.4). It may be observed from Table 8.4 that the nature of this requirement is significantly

Table 8.4 Skills and knowledge expected of LIS professionals

Job title	Skill and knowledge required
Electronic Service Librarian	Web architecture principles, database design, web authoring and graphic design, scripting language, developing complex websites, macromedia MX, hardware and software for text and image digitization
Preservation Field Services Officer	Preservation education, word processing, spreadsheets, software programs, web design and maintenance
Associate Director of Public Services	Knowledge of electronic and print reference sources, technology for reference services, library user education, digital technology, web authoring tools and standards, foreign language expertise
Automation Librarian	Horizon databases, OPACs, Sybase SQL, Unix, Novell Netware and Windows, W/MCSE certification
Library Director	Management of Voyager integrated library system, scientific databases and e-journals, MARC tag field, OCLC cataloging, LC subject heading, MS Access, Excel, PowerPoint, Word
Bibliographic and Technical Services Coordinator	OCLC cataloging, metadata, ILL, MARC format, batch loading, retrospective conversion, computer applications in libraries
Programmer/Analyst, Digital Library Development	Apache, Tomcat, Java/JSP, database design, MySql/Postgres, XML, XSLT, CSS, Perl, metadata standards such as METS, MARC and MIX, and digital library protocols such as OAI, web design, digital repositories (DSpace preferred), working in a Unix/Linux environment, working with digital images, in particular JPEG 2000

Table 8.4 Skills and knowledge expected of LIS professionals—cont'd

Job title	Skill and knowledge required
Web Developer	HTML, DHTML, XML, CGI, and Java, web development tools such as Acrobat, Dreamweaver, and Fireworks, relational database systems such as Oracle and MySQL, CSS, RSS
Digital Librarian/ Cyber Infrastructure for Biodiversity and Ecosystems	Digital formats, conversion alternatives, metadata standards, access and navigation tools, digital preservation issues, digitization and multimedia/ nontext formats, building electronic libraries in cyberspace, biodiversity/biology/ecology/ conservation biology
Digital Library Programmes Head	Digital library services/digital image conversion projects, management and delivery of electronic full text, web delivery of multimedia formats, and metadata file management, image capture and delivery technologies, full-text mark-up and searching methods, database management systems, HTML, SGML, XML, CGI, programming languages: SQL, C, C++, Java, and Perl, hardware and software applications in DOS, Windows and Unix environments, library and information standards (eg, MARC, Z39.50), library integrated systems, and issues and developments in digital library development
Web Development Librarian	Database design and development, eg, Microsoft Access and SQL, web database middleware development (eg, cold fusion), Internet technologies, subject indexing and classification including metadata schema, web user-interface design and evaluation
Librarian for Digital Repository	Digital libraries, electronic archives, institutional repositories, or equivalent open-access vehicle, basic metadata schemas, especially Dublin core, HTML

From Raghavan, K.S., 2007. Education for the information management profession: challenges and opportunities. DESIDOC Bull. Inf. Technol. 27 (2), 21–26.

different from what normally constitutes the course contents in LIS education programs at master's level.

KM skill sets, as identified by Abell and Oxbrow (2001), include:

- strategic and business skills
- IM skills
- thinking and learning skills

- management skills
- communication and interpersonal skills
- IT literacy
- KM awareness

On the basis of the analysis of graduate programs in KM, Saito (2007) proposed four sets of corresponding KM activities and capabilities that may be reflected in curricula:

1. information-oriented perspective (information manager profile)
2. human-oriented perspective (learning facilitator profile)
3. computing-oriented perspective (knowledge systems developer profile)
4. strategy-oriented perspective (profile of the KM manager)

When analyzing the relevance of KM education for LIS professionals, Roknuzzaman and Umemoto (2008) broadly categorized KM skills and competencies into five areas:

1. core skills of KM
2. ICT literacy and skills
3. core skills of LIS/IM
4. business and management skills
5. communication and behavioral skills

This clearly suggests that there are certain common denominators that will drive the demand for LIS professionals in the future. These are:

- New methods and forms of work organization requiring effective communication skills.
- The need for and desire to put to effective use the tools and technologies for harnessing and utilizing both tacit and explicit knowledge in organization-building activities.
- The emergence of the corporate sector as a major destination for LIS professionals. This naturally comes with a higher demand for accountability, performance measurement, etc.
- The transition from paper to digital and multimedia resources.
- Disintermediation of the process of searching for and accessing information.
- The increasing demand for specialization within the LIS profession and the shift from "ownership" to "access" via networks in traditional libraries.

Familiarity with the use of IT appears to be an essential requirement at all levels and for all positions. There is also a need to examine manpower development programs for LIS professionals. It does indeed appear that there is a profound gap between the course contents, the knowledge, and the skills most students learn in schools and the knowledge and skills they need to work effectively and efficiently in typical 21st century communities and workplaces (Raghavan, 2007). One of the major challenges for the LIS profession and LIS schools in the near future, as Raghavan (2007) predicted, is the distinct possibility of isolation triggered by the emergence of a parallel KM profession. There is a need to redefine the boundaries of our profession in order to continue to be relevant in terms of developing and providing human resources for 21st century workplaces, which require knowledge and skills of a different kind and of a different order. To be an active player in the competitive KM market and remain relevant in changing marketplaces, LIS schools and LIS professionals urgently need to:

- focus on value-addition processes;
- find new applications for established and proven techniques/processes that librarianship has developed over a century and more;
- innovate with the structure of specializations that are being offered in our educational programs;
- incorporate KM education in all LIS schools, and practice KM in libraries;
- develop education and training that will meet the new professional demands of KM and demonstrate the relevance of courses and understanding of competences which must be developed in KM students; and
- attain both theoretical and practical knowledge, skills and competencies that are needed for collaboration, sharing, innovation, problem-solving, and decision-making in a KM environment.

KM EDUCATION IN LIS EDUCATIONAL PROGRAMS

Several universities from different parts of the world have started offering KM educational programs in the form of degrees, specializations, or courses. These programs are offered by different schools of studies, including business, information systems, computer science, and LIS (Rehman and Chaudhry, 2005). A number of LIS schools all over the world have also started offering KM education at certificate, diploma, undergraduate, and postgraduate levels. The major objectives of LIS-based KM programs, as outlined by Roknuzzaman and Umemoto (2008), are to:

- promote understanding of KM theories, techniques, technologies, and their applications;

- provide leadership roles in managing intellectual capital, establishing a knowledge-sharing culture, and promoting KM practices within the organization;
- prepare graduates with multidimensional skills and competencies so that they can compete in the job market with other KM players; and
- to prepare innovative, service-oriented knowledge professionals for diverse environments, etc.

Rehman and Chaudhry (2005) examined the initiatives offering KM educational programs by different LIS schools in North America, the UK, and selected countries of the Pacific region. Websites of LIS schools were analyzed to find the different types of KM educational programs. They identified 12 academic programs in KM, as listed in Table 8.5. As indicated in Table 8.5, 7 of the 12 LIS programs had graduate-level degrees or coursework in KM. Two of them also had a graduate diploma in KM. Three of these schools had KM components in their undergraduate courses.

Roknuzzaman and Umemoto (2008) also identified in their study 12 LIS-based graduate KM programs. Of these 12 KM programs, four were in the United States, three from the UK, two from Australia, and one each from Canada, Israel, and Singapore. Of the 12 programs, 8 have an M.Sc./MA in KM, while 4 have masters in LIS/information studies with a KM concentration or specialization. They have also observed that KM programs at the University of Oklahoma, Dominican University, Kent State University, Nanyang Technological University, Loughborough University, University of Denver, McGill University, University of Canberra, and Bar-Ilan University are offered by LIS schools/units. The rest of the programs are offered by information-related units like IM, and their objectives and contents are related to LIS. Of the total of 115 core or compulsory and elective course titles selected from five major LIS-based graduate KM programs of the University of Oklahoma, Dominican University, Kent State University of the USA, Loughborough University of the UK, and Nanyang Technological University of Singapore, the top 30 course titles (26%) are related to information systems/computing/IT followed by LIS/IM (26 courses with 23%), and business and management (17 courses with 15%). Fifteen courses (13%) included each of human and organizational behavior, and other categories including research methods, special topics, seminars, practicum/internship, etc. The remaining 12 (10%) titles are concerned with KM foundation courses. The details of these courses are given in Table 8.5.

Table 8.5 Graduate-level KM programs in LIS-based schools

Name of university	College/school/ faculty/dept.	Name of the course/ program
University of Oklahoma	School of Library and Information Studies	M.Sc. in KM
Dominican University Graduate	School of Library and Information Science	M.Sc. in KM
Kent State University	College of Communication and Information, School of Library and Information Science	M.Sc. in information architecture and KM
Nanyang Technological University, Singapore	Division of Information Studies, School of Communication and Information	M.Sc. in KM
Loughborough University	Department of Information Science	M.Sc. in information and KM
University of Denver	College of Education, Library and Information Science Program	Master of LIS-KM Specialization
McGill University	Graduate School of Library and Information Studies	Master of LIS-KM Specialization
University of Canberra, Israel	Faculty of Communication and International Studies	Information studies program, master of information studies in KM
Bar-Ilan University	Department of Information Science	Master in information science—specialization in KM and organizational information
Robert Gordon University	Aberdeen Business School, Department of Information Management	M.Sc. in KM
University of Technology Sydney	Faculty of Humanities and Social Sciences, Information and KM	MA in information and KM
London Metropolitan University	Department of Applied Social Sciences, Information Management School	M.Sc. in information and KM

From Roknuzzaman, M., Umemoto, K., 2008. Knowledge management's relevance to library and information science: an interdisciplinary approach. J. Inf. Knowl. Manag. 7 (4), 279–290.

KNOWLEDGE MANAGEMENT EDUCATION FROM AN INDIAN PERSPECTIVE[1]

This section aims to explore the relevance of KM education in LIS educational courses in India. Despite the opportunities and challenges involved in the provision of KM education, a growing number of schools around the world now offer master's degrees in KM, keeping in mind the demands of the KM market (Sarrafzadeh, 2008; Sarrafzadeh et al., 2006b). No such provision, however, exists in Indian LIS schools, despite the assertion of academicians (Chakraborty and Sarkhel, 2009). Therefore the perceptions of the LIS community in India regarding the provision of KM education in LIS courses were examined.

The introduction of LIS education in India was reported as early as 1911, when the first Library School was started in Baroda (Gujarat) under the patronage of Sayajirao Gaekwad III. In 1915, a 3-month apprentice training program for working librarians was started by Punjab University, Lahore (now in Pakistan) (Satija, 1993). This was the first university course in LIS in India. Madras Library Association started a 3-month certificate course in librarianship at Madras in 1929. Madras University, under Dr S.R. Ranganathan, took over the certificate course from Madras Library Association in 1931. The course was subsequently converted into a postgraduate course of 1-year duration in 1937. It served as a model for the development of Library Science courses in pre-independent India, like those at Andhra University in 1935, Banaras Hindu University in 1941, Bombay University in 1946, the University of Delhi in 1947, and Aligarh Muslim University in 1952 (Mollah, 2013; Shrivastava 2002). At the time of independence, there were five universities in India providing 1-year postgraduate diploma course in library science.

Post-independence, India has seen a spurt in the development of LIS courses, starting with certificate and diploma courses offering bachelor's and master's degrees. The university of Delhi in 1948, under the guidance of Dr Ranganathan, started a master's course in library science in India, and Aligarh Muslim University was the first to provide a bachelor course in LIS in the country. The University of Delhi is again credited as the

[1]This section of the chapter is based on an article by Shabahat Husain and Mohammad Nazim, 'Exploring the need of knowledge management education within library and information science educational courses', published in *New Library World* (2015), Vol. 116, No. 11/12, pp. 711–727.

first to start a research program and to award M.Phil. and Ph.D. degrees (Naushad Ali and Bakshi, 2006). The first master's degree in library science was started at the University of Delhi by Dr S.R. Ranganathan in 1948, followed by M.Phil. and Ph.D. courses. The first Ph.D. in LIS was awarded in 1958 by the University of Delhi. Six new departments of library science came into existence between 1956 and 1959; the figure successively rose to 19 in 1960, 20 in 1970, and 24 in 1974 (Shrivastava, 2002).

At present, bachelor degree courses are offered by more than 120 universities, with 78 master's degrees, 21 integrated master's degrees, 16 M.Phil. and 63 Ph.D. degrees in LIS (Sarkhel, 2006; Singh and Shahid, 2010; Association of Indian Universities, 2010). Parallel to this, certain reputed institutions like the National Institute for Science Communications and Information Resources (NISCAIR, New Delhi), the Documentation Research and Training Centre (DRTC, Bangalore), the National Centre for Science Information (Bangalore) and the International School of Information Management (ISIM, Mysore) have been imparting specialized training in LIS education for creation of information and communication technology (ICT)-equipped librarians and information scientists of the 21st century (Chakraborty and Sarkhel, 2009). LIS education in India has now reached a pinnacle with many universities and institutions offering bachelor's, master's, M.Phil., and Ph.D. courses. In addition, other ICT-oriented courses like bachelor of library and information science (Hons), certificate in ICT applications in libraries, and a PG diploma in library automation and networking are also being offered.

KM Education Within LIS Educational Programs

Since the 1990s, India has witnessed an economic as well as cultural awakening through its liberalization, globalization, and market-centered progression. Today, India is becoming the knowledge capital of the world, as more than 300 multinational corporations have already set up R&D facilities, while many more are expected to do likewise. This is mainly because of the availability of world-class skilled workers at comparatively low salaries (Malhan, 2006). Such developments have made a tremendous impact on LIS job opportunities in India and abroad. Consequently, academics in LIS are moving to the corporate sector as knowledge managers, while library professionals from the private sector are taking up government jobs.

Some libraries of corporate sector organizations and research laboratories operated by the Council of Scientific and Industrial Research, the Indian Council of Medical Research, and the Indian Council of Agricultural Research have adopted KM systems. But the libraries of public sector organizations and academic institutions have lagged far behind in the use of KM systems, as reflected in the LIS literature. Some studies (Nazim and Mukherjee, 2013a; Raja et al., 2009) identified the following major barriers to incorporating KM into Indian academic library practice:

- lack of understanding of KM concepts;
- lack of a knowledge-sharing attitude due to insecurity and fear of losing their importance by passing their tacit knowledge to colleagues;
- library professionals' reluctance to set their minds to cooperate or share resources;
- lack of technical skills in ICT;
- lack of appropriate tools and technologies;
- lack of sufficient funds;
- lack of collaboration and team spirit;
- lack of a centralized policy for KM; and
- lack of top management interest in KM activities.

The current LIS education model in India mainly focuses on the functionality of procurement, organization and supply of documents, database development, and Internet search assistance. LIS schools in India are not responding adequately to the emerging information scenario created by electronic publishing and the dynamics of the knowledge society. Olszak and Ziemba (2010) explained that, in the age of knowledge, LIS graduates are expected to know and use different types of skills to:

- manage an organization's information resources;
- supervise an information policy and manage information in an organization;
- design and carry out reengineering of an organization's information infrastructure;
- design and carry out reengineering of business processes;
- control and carry out audits of various areas of an organization's activities;
- supervise information projects within an organization; and
- plan, implement, and use e-business solutions.

LIS educational courses in India are designed to prepare human resources, mainly for libraries and information centers, whereas demand for the management of knowledge is surfacing from different sectors. To fulfill the demands of different sectors for managing knowledge, LIS schools should carry out a periodic assessment of their courses and modify them accordingly (Chakraborty and Sarkhel, 2009). This would certainly help LIS graduates to get jobs, not only with libraries and information institutions but also enterprises, consulting firms, research agencies, business intelligence agencies, banks and financial institutions, and public administration offices (Malhan, 2011).

Specific Issues of KM Education in India

A need for the inclusion of KM in professional education for LIS has been identified by many researchers (Hazeri et al., 2007, 2009b; Jain, 2007; Martin, 1999; Raghavan, 2007; Rehman, 2006; Roknuzzaman and Umemoto, 2013; Sarrafzadeh et al., 2006a,b; Todd and Southon, 2001). However, there remains a degree of uncertainty as to the extent to which this needs to be incorporated in LIS education. Some scholars in India have also acknowledged the importance of imparting knowledge and skills in management, business operations, and information and communication technologies to LIS professionals to perform their job more effectively in knowledge-intensive organizations (Gulati and Raina, 2000; Malhan, 2011; Nazim and Mukherjee, 2013b; Subramanian, 2007; Thanuskodi, 2010). During recent decades, LIS schools in India have responded in a variety of ways by educating LIS professionals to develop appropriate KM-related skills and capabilities. However, there seems to be a gap between the knowledge and skills that LIS students acquire through existing LIS educational courses and those that are required in the present knowledge era. Recognizing these potential issues, we examined the requirements of KM education in LIS educational courses with specific reference to India. The specific objectives are as follows:

- to identify the need for KM education within LIS educational courses;
- to investigate the perceptions of the academic community towards incorporating KM education within the curricula of LIS courses;
- to understand the need for modifications of the curricula of LIS courses with respect to the emergence of KM as a multidisciplinary subject;
- to identify the most meaningful approach with respect to the revision of course content for incorporating KM education within the curricula of LIS courses.

The methodology includes a quantitative approach. To explore the viewpoints of the academic community regarding the requirements of KM education in LIS courses, a web-based questionnaire survey method was used. A short and structured, both open- and close-ended, questionnaire was designed and distributed through FreeOnlineSurveys.com. For this purpose, a list of 78 universities, offering up to master's degree-level courses in LIS, was prepared using the latest available directory (ie, Universities Handbooks, 32nd ed., 2010) published by the Association of Indian Universities. The sample size was identified by searching the Internet and consulting the websites of LIS schools to identify those teachers who had some specialization in KM-related areas. The details of 65 LIS schools and their faculties were available on the Internet. After consulting the websites, the details (including name, designation, e-mail, specialization, etc.) of LIS teachers were noted. In Jun. 30, 2011, a list of 177 teachers was prepared. Of the 177 teachers, all of the 95 teachers having a specialization in KM-related areas were selected as the sample for study.

A link for completing the survey was sent via electronic mail to the 95 teachers all over India, and 43 responses were received. This resulted in a 45% response rate, which is typical for an online survey as stated by Gravetter and Forzano (2008), who found that the typical response rate for an online survey is only about 18%. The responses were analyzed using descriptive statistics and are presented as tables. However, comments received from the respondents were also thematically analyzed and classified into four categories.

Of the total of 43 respondents, 24 (55.8%) were assistant professors (including two lecturers), 13 (30.2%) were associate professors (including three readers), and six (14.0%) were professors. Of all the respondents, 27 (62.8%) were men and 16 (37.2%) were women. Their teaching experience was between 4 months and 35 years. A majority of respondents (71.1%) had 6–30 years of experience in teaching. In terms of level of education, the majority of the respondents (81.4%) had a Ph.D. as the highest degree, followed by a master's degree (16.3%) and M.Phil. degree (2.3%) in LIS. Details of the respondents participating in the study are shown in Table 7.1 in Chapter 7.

This research has certain limitations as regards the generalization of the findings. Although the intention of researchers was to collect responses from the different stakeholders (eg, LIS schools, libraries, library associations, societies, and industries) involved in offering LIS education, training and KM practice, but the investigation succeeded mainly in obtaining responses from LIS schools, due to time and financial constraints. Thus the results of this study are not representative of all stakeholders associated with LIS education and KM practice, and therefore cannot be generalized as such. Moreover, despite the questionnaire being distributed to 95 teachers, the sample size is still relatively small. Thus both the quantity and variety of responses may be too small in some instances to draw meaningful conclusions.

Findings

Need for incorporating KM education in LIS educational courses. Respondents were asked for their opinions on whether LIS curricula should be revised to incorporate KM education in LIS educational courses. As shown in Table 8.6, 97.7% (a high majority) of respondents replied "Yes" to this question, which means that there is a strong preference in the academic community for the inclusion of KM education in LIS educational courses.

Justifications for incorporating KM education in LIS educational courses. Further, respondents were asked to indicate their level of agreement with statements regarding the justifications for incorporating KM education in LIS educational courses using a five-point Likert scale, where 1 represents "strongly disagree" and 5 "strongly agree." The results are shown in Table 8.7. As indicated in the table, more than 66% of respondents agreed (including strongly agreed) that "Current LIS curricula are

Table 8.6 Results for KM education in LIS educational courses

Respondents' opinion	Frequency	%
Yes	42	97.7
No	1	2.3
Not sure	0	0
Total	43	100

Table 8.7 Justifications for changes in LIS educational programs

Statement	Mean	Overall mean[a]
Current LIS curricula are outdated and do not include content related to KM in the curricula of LIS courses	3.95	Agree
Without making changes in the curricula of LIS courses, LIS graduates would lose the opportunity to become knowledge managers, and they may be supplemented by those having a management and information systems and technology background	3.93	Agree
More business and information system and technology-oriented curricula are needed	3.67	Agree

[a] For the purpose of marking the overall perceptions of respondents, the following scoring system designed by Sarrafzadeh et al. (2010) was used: mean 1–1.44 = strongly disagree; mean 1.45–2.44 = disagree; mean 2.45–3.44 = don't know; mean 3.45–4.44 = agree; mean 4.55–5 = strongly agree.

outdated and do not include content related to KM in the curricula of LIS courses." A total of 77% (either agreed or strongly agreed) respondents believe that a more business-oriented curriculum is needed. Combining both "agree" and "strongly agree" responses, a slightly lower percentage (68.8%) of respondents believe that, without making changes in the curricula of LIS courses, LIS graduates will lose the opportunity to play a role as knowledge managers and they may be supplemented by those having a management and information systems and technology background.

Approaches to KM education with respect to LIS educational courses. To identify the most meaningful approach to KM education in LIS educational courses, respondents were asked to choose from a list of the approaches to KM curricula which would best meet the needs of LIS students and maximize their prospects to succeed in this career. As shown in Table 8.8, a majority of respondents (53.5%) expected to have "A curriculum that embodies core elements of LIS, management, and information systems and technology." This may be interpreted as the necessity for a multidisciplinary system of education that may include education in LIS as well as allied subjects, including management and information systems and technology.

However, 30.2% of respondents believe that "A curriculum based largely on LIS (acquisition, organization, storage, retrieval, etc.) and supplemented with modules on organizational behavior, knowledge, and the knowledge-based economy" would meet the requirement of LIS

Table 8.8 Approaches to KM education in LIS curricula

Statement	%
A curriculum based largely on LIS (information dissemination, retrieval, etc.) and supplemented with modules on organizational behavior, knowledge, and the knowledge-based economy	30.2
A curriculum based largely on the management domain (human resources, strategy, marketing, etc.) supplemented with modules on information and knowledge and the knowledge-based economy	4.7
A curriculum largely based on the information systems domain (databases, advanced and web-based systems) supplemented with elements of natural language processing, artificial intelligence, and the design and use of web technologies	11.6
A curriculum that embodies the core elements of all three examples	53.5
Total	100

students to get jobs in knowledge-based organizations. Some respondents (11.6%) also indicated a preference for:

> *A curriculum largely based in the information management systems domain (databases, advanced and Web-based systems) supplemented with elements of natural language processing, artificial intelligence and the design and use of Web technologies.*

It may be useful for students of LIS to find job opportunities outside the library sector. A few respondents (4.7%) believe that "A curriculum based largely on the management domain (human resources, business strategy, marketing, etc.) supplemented with modules on information and knowledge and the knowledge-based economy" could be the basis for LIS students to perform their role as knowledge managers in different types of organizations.

Analysis of Respondents' Additional Comments

In addition to the data presented above, we received a considerable number of additional comments from the respondents, which are classified into four categories on the basis of the analysis of the content of each comment:

LIS educational courses do not require any change. Some respondents indicated that LIS educational courses have already included the necessary concepts of management techniques and KM which best suited the requirements of LIS professionals. One respondent specifically mentions that LIS curricula already include KM-related concepts such as human resource management, total quality management and ICT, and believes that no more changes to LIS curricula are needed. Specific comments in this category are as follows:

- LIS curricula do not require any change. They are best suited to the requirements of library professionals. Libraries require librarians not business managers or IT experts.
- LIS curricula already include modules on many management and ICT techniques such as financial management, HRM, TQM, KM, and use of ICTs in library operations and services. I think there is no need to accommodate anything more.
- I think LIS curricula sufficiently include the necessary concepts of management techniques and KM. LIS should focus on knowledge acquisition, organization, and dissemination. No more emphasis is required on business management.

Practical training should be provided in LIS educational courses. Some respondents believe that LIS courses should focus on practical aspects of ICT applications, particularly in designing web portals, subject gateways, intranets, library websites, database creation and management, which would facilitate their entry into the job market outside of libraries. There was also support in the literature for such assertions, with the results of Ajiferuke's study on the role of information professionals in KM programs indicating that the ability to use ICT is necessary for information professionals to perform some of the roles mentioned above (ie, web design, development of subject gateways, management of content of an intranet, database creation, and searching). Specific comments in this category are as follows:

- Instead of accommodating more business or IT aspects to LIS curricula, there should be provision of practical training to LIS students in IT-based and corporate libraries. This may help library students to acquire practical knowledge as well as to get jobs in areas other than libraries.
- LIS graduates lack practical applications of ICTs in a library environment. Practical training is a necessity for LIS professionals to apply the latest technologies in library services. LIS curricula must focus on the practical aspects of ICT applications, particularly in designing web portals, subject gateways, intranets, library websites, database creation and management, etc.
- It requires teamwork and LIS professional skills alone cannot complete the task. A combination of skills is necessary.

The LIS faculty should be motivated to acquire knowledge and understanding of KM from a business perspective. Some respondents believe that LIS faculties should update their knowledge and skills by attending specialized courses and training programs on KM. Sanchez (2001) stated that continuous learning through professional training courses or attending methodical workshops is an important method of acquiring knowledge and developing skills in the field of KM. But acquiring knowledge through professional training is a time-consuming process. Therefore hiring a visiting faculty from management schools may be an option to teach business-oriented concepts like KM to LIS graduates, as mentioned by one respondent. Specific comments in this category are as follows:

- I think teachers should be motivated to acquire knowledge and understanding of KM from a business perspective. They should be encouraged to attend specialized courses and training programs on KM to enhance their expertise.
- I think a visiting faculty from management schools should be hired to teach LIS graduates because LIS faculties are not equipped to teach more business-oriented concepts such as KM.

LIS education courses should include business-oriented concepts and management of e-resources. According to some respondents' comments, LIS education courses should include the concepts of knowledge taxonomies, human resources management, project management, database management, institutional repositories, and digital libraries in LIS educational courses. Specific comments in this category are:

- The modules of KM should be expanded to some extent to include knowledge taxonomies, human resources management, project management and IT, etc.
- LIS curricula should include modules of business information systems, rediscover taxonomies and include more concepts and core elements of digital librarianship in their wider perspective. But efforts should be practical not theoretical.
- Some elements of the use of modern ICT tools, particularly database management, IR, and digital libraries, may be included.

Discussion

KM education has been recognized as one of the factors of potential survival for the LIS profession. In the present knowledge-based environment, LIS education providers are thinking of redesigning LIS courses to incorporate the concepts of KM in LIS educational programs. The LIS literature reveals some notable benefits of KM education for LIS professionals, such as the potential broadening of professional perspectives to wider areas, entry of LIS professionals into knowledge-based organizations, and enhancement of the image of LIS professionals both within and outside the profession (Hazeri et al., 2009a; Roknuzzaman and Umemoto, 2013). Realizing the potential of KM in the LIS profession, many LIS schools, particularly in North America, Europe and the Pacific region, have adopted KM education in 140 different degree programs, with KM components (Roknuzzaman and Umemoto, 2010). A recent study by Siddike and Islam (2011) on the requirements of KM competencies for information professionals in the libraries/information institutions of Bangladesh has also suggested introducing KM course(s) at graduate and postgraduate levels by different departments of information science and library management in Bangladesh.

As KM, as a multidisciplinary subject, is still at the early stages of development in India, debate continues on its academic status, including its relevance to the LIS profession. Some educational institutions in India, particularly Indian Institutes of Technology, Indian Institutes of Management and Indira Gandhi National Open University, have recently started offering

KM courses, but the role of LIS schools in imparting KM education is almost negligible. The academic community in India believes that current LIS educational courses do not include content related to KM in the curricula of LIS courses, and there is a need to incorporate KM education in LIS courses to develop an understanding of KM concepts among LIS students.

The findings indicate that LIS courses in India are outdated and do not provide sufficient KM education in LIS educational programs to develop KM competencies among LIS students (Table 8.3). Issues of the inaccuracy of LIS courses regarding the provision of KM education for LIS students have also been mentioned in the literature by many researchers. Singh (2009), along with Chakraborty and Sarkhel (2009), mentioned that LIS professionals are facing an identity crisis due to dual challenges both from technology experts and market information suppliers. Further, they observed that the courses offered by LIS schools in India do not provide sufficient knowledge and skills required for KM.

The findings also indicate that there is a need to restructure LIS courses to provide an opportunity to LIS graduates so that they are able to perform their role as knowledge managers in knowledge-based organizations. If LIS schools remain reluctant to restructure their courses, they may be supplemented by technology-oriented courses in computing schools and management-oriented courses in business schools, as reflected in the LIS literature, as well as in the responses of the respondents of this study (Table 8.3). Although Bangalore University (India) has recently introduced two elective papers of "web technology" and "digital resources management" to cater for the needs of information technology skills for LIS students, information technology skills alone are not sufficient for KM as a profession, as mentioned by Van der Veer Martens and Hawamdeh (2010). In fact, LIS professionals require a mix of technical, organizational and interpersonal skills, which provide opportunities for LIS professionals to take up new positions in knowledge-based organizations and other related fields. LIS schools, along with other academic units, can play a significant role in realizing the potential of KM for LIS professionals.

Findings related to the most appropriate approaches to KM education, as have emerged in this study, revealed that some changes in LIS courses are essential to equip LIS students to become involved in KM practice. The reasons for this, as mentioned by Koenig (1999), are:

- to prepare students with a proper understanding and expectation of the corporate culture and its environment;
- to develop an understanding of the knowledge process within the business process and to develop the ability to identify these processes; and
- to analyze business processes as a core competency in the practice of KM.

However, some respondents in the present study argued that LIS education should not be entirely diverted from its mainstream objectives, such as acquisition, organization, and retrieval of knowledge. As well as the arguments for or against the incorporation of KM education in LIS educational programs, some respondents in the present study also emphasized practical training relating to the use of ICT in libraries, encouraging LIS faculties to acquire knowledge and understanding of KM concepts from business and management perspectives, and hiring visiting faculties from business schools to teach LIS students. Thus the findings of this study indicate a need to incorporate business elements into LIS education, a fact that has been emphasized by other authors as well (Ajiferuke, 2003; Koenig, 1999; Roknuzzaman and Umemoto, 2013; Sarrafzadeh et al., 2006a). Koenig (1999) stated that, to be significant players in KM, LIS professionals need knowledge of information technology and applications, corporate culture and change agents, as well as a business and economic background. Since KM is emerging as a multidisciplinary subject, it is a tough challenge for LIS schools to succeed in incorporating all elements of KM into LIS courses, unless LIS teachers have knowledge of all those subjects. Collaboration by LIS schools with business schools and industry may be a useful step in providing KM education to LIS students, as suggested by Hazeri and Martin (2009).

Thus the findings of the present study acknowledge a need to incorporate KM in LIS educational courses to develop an understanding of the concept of KM among LIS students for the practical application of KM in libraries and other organizations. The findings of the present study are akin to those of previous studies. A study by Southon and Todd (2001) concludes that LIS educational courses should provide theoretical frameworks and also the professional skills required for the effective management of information in the context of KM initiatives. Another study by Hazeri et al. (2009a,b) also acknowledges the multidisciplinary character of LIS education and the need to incorporate KM courses in LIS educational programs to focus on tacit knowledge and the human dimensions of KM, as well as on business, management, and organizational issues.

SUMMARY

The emerging knowledge environment offers enormous opportunities for LIS professionals to create economic value through KM. But LIS education and training programs in India are not sufficiently oriented to these objectives. LIS schools in India have been slow to restructure their curricula and to face up to the challenges of preparing knowledge workers to serve the needs of knowledge-based organizations. The results of this study indicate a need for the inclusion of elements of KM education within professional education of LIS for the greater understanding of the concept of KM and its related aspects. However, there remains a degree of uncertainty as to the extent to which this will happen in existing LIS educational courses.

As KM has been recognized as a fully fledged discipline, and some institutions/universities in India have started to offer courses in KM at graduate and postgraduate levels, it would be unwise for LIS schools in India to incorporate it comprehensively into their existing LIS courses. Although the responses of respondents regarding the potential inclusion of KM education in LIS courses vary according to the extent to which they interpret the concept of KM, they felt the need to extend opportunities for their students by incorporating nontraditional subjects. However, there is a degree of consensus on the inclusion of KM education in LIS educational courses to provide better job prospects for their students. As the nature of KM is multidisciplinary, there remain serious difficulties concerning the proposed nature and content of these programs. However, the research findings reported in this study affirm the need for a multidisciplinary approach to KM education in LIS educational courses by incorporating the core elements of LIS, business and information systems, and technology to help make students more employable. But it seems unlikely that all three of these areas can be treated comprehensively within a single LIS program. Hence, first of all, there is a need to clarify the roles that LIS professionals can play within the spectrum of KM activities, and then amend or expand educational courses to meet these requirements.

Finally, on the basis of the different issues discussed in this chapter, it is suggested that library schools and the profession at large should identify the requirements of KM competencies for LIS professionals and work out the ways of embodying coverage of these elements in future courses. Library schools must develop a strong interdisciplinary collaboration with other academic units having KM interests to overcome the challenge of the multidisciplinary nature of KM. Library schools must adapt an integrated approach to KM education by engaging other partners, including practitioners and industries. Involvement of other stakeholders would be useful for integrating practice and research into teaching. While the needs of KM education for LIS students may be catered by LIS schools, there are limited opportunities for working LIS professionals in India to learn about KM and acquire the necessary levels of KM competencies to engage in KM activities. Besides the involvement of library schools in KM education, professional associations and organizations, such as the Indian Library Association, Academic Staff Colleges, Information and Library Network, and National Institute of Science Communication and Information Resources, could introduce short-term skill enhancement programs and workshops for working professionals to equip them with the required skills in KM. Equal opportunities should be provided to all professionals of their grades and designations to participate in such programs.

REFERENCES

Abell, A., Oxbrow, N., 2001. Competing With Knowledge: The Information Professionals in the Knowledge Management Age. Library Association Publishing, London.

Ajiferuke, I., 2003. Role of information professionals in knowledge management programs: empirical evidence from Canada. Inform. Sci. J. 6, 247–257.

Al-Hawamdeh, S., 2005. Designing an interdisciplinary graduate program in knowledge management. J. Am. Soc. Inf. Sci. Technol. 56 (11), 1200–1206.

Association of Indian Universities, 2010. Universities Handbooks, 32nd ed. Association of Indian Universities, New Delhi.

Borko, H., 1968. Information science: what is it? Am. Doc. 19 (1), 3–5.

Butler, Y., 2000. Knowledge management: if only you knew what you knew. Aust. Libr. J. 49 (1), 31–43.

Carnovsky, L., 1964. Role of public library: implications for library education. Libr. Q. 34, 315–325.

Chakraborty, S., Sarkhel, J.K., 2009. LIS education in India: an appraisal of the parity between the syllabus and the market demands. In: Paper Presented at 75th IFLA General Conference and Council, 23–27 August, Milan.

Chaudhry, A.S., Higgins, S.E., 2001. Perspectives on education for knowledge management. In: Paper Presented at the 67th IFLA Council and General Conference, 16–25 August, Boston, MA.

Gravetter, F.J., Forzano, L.A.B., 2008. Research Methods for the Behavioral Sciences. Wadsworth, Cenage Learning, Belmont, CA.

Gulati, A., Raina, R.L., 2000. Professional competencies among librarians and information professionals in the knowledge era. World Libr. 10 (1), 11–18.

Hazeri, A., Martin, B., 2009. On the need for collaboration in KM education in the LIS sector: some professional perspectives. Int. J. Inf. Manag. 29 (5), 380–388.

Hazeri, A., Sarrafzadeh, M., Martin, B., 2007. Reflections of information professionals on knowledge management competencies in the LIS curriculum. J. Educ. Libr. Inf. Sci. 48 (3), 168–186.

Hazeri, A., Martin, B., Sarrafzadeh, M., 2009a. Integration of knowledge management with the library and information science curriculum: some professional perspectives. J. Educ. Libr. Inf. Sci. 50 (3), 150–163.

Hazeri, A., Martin, B., Sarrafzadeh, M., 2009b. Exploring the benefits of KM education for LIS professionals. Educ. Inf. 27, 1–20.

Jain, P., 2007. An empirical study of knowledge management in academic libraries in East and Southern Africa. Libr. Rev. 56 (5), 377–392.

Kebede, G., 2010. Knowledge management: an information science perspective. Int. J. Inf. Manag. 30, 416–424.

Koenig, M.E.D., 1999. Education for knowledge management. Inf. Serv. Use 19 (1), 17–32.

Langridge, D.W., 1978. Teaching and organization of knowledge. In: Peter, G. (Ed.), Education for Librarianship: Decisions in Organizing a System of Professional Education. The Shoe String Press, Hamden, CT, pp. 104–114.

Malhan, I.V., 2006. Strategic planning for developing Indian university libraries into knowledge resource and service centres. In: Paper Presented at 72nd IFLA General Conference and Council, 20–24 August, Seoul. Available at: www.ifla.org/IV/ifla72/index.htm (accessed 15.12.13).

Malhan, I.V., 2011. Challenges and problems of library and information science education in India: an emerging knowledge society and developing nation if Asia. Libr. Philos. Pract. Available at: http://digitalcommons.unl.edu/cgi/viewcontent.cgi?article=1744&context=libphilprac (accessed 15.06.14).

Martin, B., 1999. New directions in education for LIS: knowledge management programs at RMIT. J. Educ. Libr. Inf. Sci. 40 (3), 142–150.

Mollah, N., 2013. LIS education in India: a chorological and chronological study. e-Library Sci. Res. J. 10, 10–14.

Naushad Ali, P.M., Bakshi, S.I., 2006. Problems and prospects of LIS education in India with special reference to distance mode. Available at: www.bibliotheksportal.de/fileadmin/user_upload/content/bibliotheken/international/dateien/_ind4_indien_1.pdf (accessed 07.07.15).

Nazim, M., Mukherjee, B., 2013a. Librarians' perceptions of knowledge management in developing countries: a case with Indian academic libraries. Int. Inf. Libr. Rev. 45, 63–76.

Nazim, M., Mukherjee, B., 2013b. Knowledge management competencies required among library and information science professionals: an Indian perspective. Libr. Rev. 62 (6/7), 375–387.

Olszak, C.M., Ziemba, E., 2010. Knowledge management curriculum development: linking with real business needs. Issues Inform. Sci. Inf. Technol. 7, 235–248.

Ponzi, L.J., Koenig, M., 2002. Knowledge management: another management fad? Inf. Res. 8 (1). Available at: http://informationr.net/ir/8-1/paper145.html (accessed 05.05.07).

Raghavan, K.S., 2007. Education for the information management profession: challenges and opportunities. DESIDOC Bull. Inf. Technol. 27 (2), 21–26.

Raja, W., Ahmad, Z., Sinha, A.K., 2009. Knowledge management and academic libraries in IT era: problems and positions. In: Poster Paper at International Conference on Academic Libraries, 5–8 October, University of Delhi. Available at: http://crl.du.ac.in/ical09/papers/index_files/ical-124_198_418_2_RV.pdf (accessed 22.04.15).

Rehman, S.U., 2006. New age competencies for information professionals. In: Paper Present at the Asia-Pacific Conference on Library & Information Education & Practice, 3–6 April, Singapore. pp. 27–34.

Rehman, S.U., Chaudhry, A.S., 2005. KM education in LIS programs. In: Paper Presented at the 71st IFLA General Conference and Council, 14–18 August, Oslo, Norway.

Roknuzzaman, M., Umemoto, K., 2008. Knowledge management's relevance to library and information science: an interdisciplinary approach. J. Inf. Knowl. Manag. 7 (4), 279–290.

Roknuzzaman, M., Umemoto, K., 2010. Knowledge management education at library and information science schools: an analysis of knowledge management master's programs. J. Educ. Libr. Inf. Sci. 51 (4), 267–280.

Roknuzzaman, M., Umemoto, K., 2013. Incorporating KM education into LIS curriculum: perspectives from LIS academics. VINE 43 (1), 111–124.
Saito, A., 2007. Educating knowledge managers: a competence-based approach. Unpublished doctoral dissertation, Graduate School of Knowledge Science, Japan Advanced Institute of Science and Technology, Japan.
Sanchez, R., 2001. Knowledge Management and Organizational Competence. Oxford University Press, New York.
Sarkhel, J.K., 2006. Quality assurance and accreditation of LIS education in Indian universities: issues and perspectives. In: Khoo, C., Singh, D., Chaudhry, A.S. (Eds.), Proceedings of the Asia Pacific Conference on Library and Information Education and Practice. School of Communication & Information, Nanyang Technological University, Singapore, pp. 427–431.
Sarrafzadeh, M., 2008. The Implications of Knowledge Management for the Library and Information Professions. PhD Dissertation, RMIT University. Available at: https://researchbank.rmit.edu.au/eserv/rmit:13384/Sarrafzadeh.pdf (accessed 15.02.15).
Sarrafzadeh, M., Hazeri, A., Martin, B., 2006a. Knowledge management education for LIS professionals: some recent perspectives. J. Educ. Libr. Inf. Sci. 47 (3), 218–237.
Sarrafzadeh, M., Hazeri, A., Martin, B., 2006b. LIS professionals and knowledge management: some recent perspectives. Libr. Manag. 27 (9), 621–635.
Sarrafzadeh, M., Martin, B., Hazeri, A., 2010. Knowledge management and its potential applicability for libraries. Libr. Manag. 31 (3), 198–212.
Satija, M.P., 1993. Research in librarianship before and after Ranganathan. In: Navalani, K., Satija, M.P. (Eds.), Pettits Petals: A Tribute to S R Ranganathan. ABC Publishing House, New Delhi.
Shrivastava, B.P., 2002. Library & Information Science Education in Indian Universities. Commonwealth Publication, New Delhi.
Siddike, M.A.K., Islam, M.S., 2011. Exploring the competencies of information professionals for knowledge management in the information institutions of Bangladesh. Int. Inf. Libr. Rev. 43, 130–136.
Singh, J., 2009. Leadership competencies for change management in libraries: challenges and opportunities. Available at: http://crl.du.ac.in/ical09/papers/index_files/ical-51_250_732_3_RV.pdf (accessed 28.12.14).
Singh, J., Shahid, S.M., 2010. Changing needs of library science curricula in India. Libr. Philos. Pract.(accessed 15.02.15).
Southon, G., Todd, R., 2001. Library and information professionals and knowledge management: conceptions, challenges and conflicts. Aust. Libr. J. 50 (3), 259–282.
Subramanian, N., 2007. Knowledge and information management in libraries: a new challenge for the library and information professionals in the digital environment. Available at: http://library.igcar.gov.in/readit2007/conpro/s1/S1_5.pdf (accessed 19.12.13).
TFPL, 1999. Skills for knowledge management; a report by TFPL Ltd. TFPL, London.
Thanuskodi, S., 2010. Knowledge management in academic libraries: an overview. In: Paper Presented at 6th International Conference on Webometrics, Informetrics and Scientometrics & Eleventh COLLNET Meeting, 19–22 October, University of Mysore, Mysore.
Todd, R.J., Southon, G., 2001. Educating for a knowledge management future: perceptions of library and information professionals. Aust. Libr. J. 50 (4), 313–326.
Van der Veer Martens, B., Hawamdeh, S., 2010. The professionalization of knowledge management. In: Pankl, E., Theiss-White, D., Bushing, M.C. (Eds.), Recruitment, Development, and Retention of Information Professionals: Trends in Human Resources and Knowledge Management. IDEA Group Publishing, Hershey, PA, pp. 139–156.
White, T., 2004. Knowledge management in an academic library: based on the case study KM within OULS. In: Paper Presented at 70th IFLA General Conference and Council, 22–27 August, Buenos Aires.

Wiig, K.M., 1999. What future knowledge management users may expect? J. Knowl. Manag. 3 (2), 155–165.

Wilson, T.D., 2002. The nonsense of knowledge management. Inf. Res. 8 (1). Available at: http://informationr.net/ir/8-1/paper144.html (accessed 12.02.08).

Wormell, I., 2004. Skills and competencies required to work with knowledge management. In: Hobohm, H. (Ed.), Knowledge Management: Libraries and Librarians Taking up the Challenge. K.G. Saur, München, pp. 107–114. IFLA Publication 108.

CHAPTER 9

Knowledge Management in Libraries

INTRODUCTION

Academic libraries have long been described as the heart of their universities because of the strategic position they occupy. They were established to support the mission of their universities by providing resources to aid teaching, learning, and research. However, the environment in which academic libraries operate today and the way people search and access information have changed due to the rapid developments in information and communication technologies (ICT). Development of the Internet, the World Wide Web, user-friendly databases, and search engines have not only made a profound impact on the structure and functioning of academic libraries, but also have challenged the status of academic libraries as the only provider of information. This is because of the alternatives, such as Google Scholar, that are available for people to locate and access scholarly literature from commercial publishers. Technological changes, along with the external pressure of market forces, have forced academic libraries to transform their structures and implement new managerial processes. These changes have helped them to become more flexible and thereby stimulate innovation and performance to survive in the face of competition from emerging groups of information suppliers and ever increasing levels of user expectations (Sarrafzadeh et al., 2010). Knowledge management (KM) is one of the processes which is recognized worldwide as a very useful solution for the survival and success of academic libraries (Porumbeanu, 2010).

KM is defined as the process through which organizations generate value from their intellectual knowledge-based assets (Santosus and Surmacz, 2001). The concept of KM emerged in the mid-1980s and was mainly used in the corporate sector (Rus and Lindvall, 2002). Due to the appearance of new knowledge producers in the education sector, universities have also started to apply KM practice to support every part of their mission (Kidwell et al., 2000). Libraries are not lagging behind in this race. Increasingly, library and information professionals are being referred to as knowledge managers, and libraries and information centers as knowledge centers (Jain, 2007). Academic libraries contain vast amounts of organizational knowledge about their users, processes, products and services, as well as knowledge of their employees as key knowledge assets. However, librarians are reluctant to consider organizational knowledge as a resource in the same way as their library collections and facilities. Traditionally, their functions were mainly confined to the identification and acquisition of information to satisfy the information needs of the academic community (Townley, 2001). Library and information professionals in India are still involved in the traditional practices of knowledge organization and information management (Nazim and Mukherjee, 2011). There is also a lack of understanding of various dimensions of KM, and a lack of competencies among library and information professionals to develop and apply KM tools and techniques (Malhan, 2006).

This chapter is divided into three parts. The first part highlights a number of important issues facing academic libraries. The second part looks at what KM is about and how its practices can be applied in academic libraries. Finally, the attitudes of librarians towards KM in developing countries are examined.

THE CHANGING ENVIRONMENT AND ISSUES FACING ACADEMIC LIBRARIES

The environment in which academic libraries work is continuously changing, and there are several issues to be faced by academic libraries. Some of these issues are discussed in the next section.

Information Is Created in Many Formats

Media of scholarly communication and information communication technology are changing at regular intervals and replacing existing media with cheap and advanced versions very quickly. It appears that the world of electronic information seems to be built on shifting sands. New resources are developing each year, existing resources evolve in new forms, and more information is being contained in different electronic formats, which are even accessible through mobile centric applications and interfaces. As we know, in many cases electronic resources require software and hardware support to access them. So often changes in the form of electronic resources require specific software and hardware to access or view. The situation becomes more critical for librarians, particularly in developing and underdeveloped countries, where the authorities do not provide additional budgets to support hardware and software associated with these new resources.

Over the past few years, the Internet and the World Wide Web have had a tremendous effect on the growth of information and the speed of transmission. The problem with the Internet is that there is no real organization of information as in the case of libraries. New means to deliver information over the Internet poses a challenge to librarians in terms of helping students make sense of the information found on websites.

As the nature of information sources becomes more varied, this provides a challenge to academic libraries. The changes in the nature of information, in research strategies, and in the structure of higher education are affecting academic libraries. These changes define much of the shifting context. The changes brought about by electronic media necessitate a transformation in the way librarians think about their jobs, the users of information, and the communication process of which they are a part (Budd, 1998, cited in Maponya, 2004). Academic librarians must strive to remain competent navigators of each medium in order to assist library users.

Other challenges facing academic libraries in the networked online environment are to exploit all forms of digital and telecommunication technologies, and find new ways and means to provide feasible forms of collections, services, and access to library materials (Foo et al., 2002). These technologies, however, represent a greater responsibility for librarians. The challenge for librarians is to manage services, which offer users a carefully selected mix of multiple formats and media. Academic libraries should rethink their role in the overall university community. There is a need to support the needs of users since the teaching and learning patterns in universities have changed.

New Scholarly Communication and Publishing Models

Worldwide commercial publishers are coming up with new scholarly communication and publishing models at an ever-faster pace. This requires libraries to be actively involved or to be left behind. New publishing models are being explored for journals, scholarly monographs, textbooks, and digital materials, so that the demands of new-generation users may be fulfilled without affecting the library budget. As we know, education paradigms are shifting towards online learning, hybrid learning, and collaborative models to meet the need of an increasing number of students. Students and faculties want to use their own technology for learning, and expect to be able to work, learn, and study whenever and wherever they want on their choice of devices. Massive open online courses are being widely explored as alternatives and supplements to traditional university courses, particularly in the disciplines of science, technology, engineering, and medicine. So libraries are facing a challenge to manage the new scholarly communication and publishing models and have the opportunity to be involved.

Opportunities for academic libraries burgeoned with the development of the Internet, and some research and academic libraries are now becoming publishers, and have started to develop programs offering a set of core publishing services to editors and partners. Libraries are supporting these services by reallocating resources, partnering, seeking synergies with related services, and developing modest revenue streams. Now some academic libraries are taking an active role in changing the scholarly communication environment by creating or expanding their publishing services. In 2011 a survey of member institutions of the ARL, the Oberlin Group, and the University Libraries Group found that approximately half of the respondents had or were developing library publishing services. Three-quarters published journals, while half published monographs, and/or conference proceedings. The libraries commonly provided digital repository services, author copyright advice, digitization services, and management of research datasets, as well as metadata creation, cataloging, and digital preservation (Judith, 2013).

Ever Changing Information Needs of Users

Due to societal and technological developments, traditional teaching increasingly has to change in terms of creating learning environments. Students participate in flexible learning processes via more "indirect" contacts with teachers and facilities, including scientific information (Maponya, 2004). Additionally, teaching and learning patterns have developed towards greater modularization and place an emphasis on self-directed, independent study, and student-centered learning. This places greater demands on the library, which is increasingly being used for group work, and librarians face increased pressure on their enquiry services and a greater need for user support and education. Academic libraries have to provide information services for users acting in a changing academic environment.

Traditional library services are not sufficient to meet the information service requirements of library users who prefer to use library services online either at the university campus or outside the campus. Therefore academic libraries have to initiate the next generation of library services as desired by their users by extending their services beyond the traditional library walls to reach out to users through the use of ICT. Academic librarians need to liaise with library users, faculties, and schools to support effective teaching, learning, and research in universities. Liaison is important in a world of resource-based learning where students are encouraged to carry out more independent work and make wider use of a range of learning resources (including electronic information resources). Academic libraries are expected to offer user-friendly ICT-oriented facilities (like remote access to information and services), analyze changing user needs, and provide support to users in new academic environments.

New Models of Information Organization and Delivery

Recent developments in ICTs have brought significant changes in the ways libraries organize and disseminate information, as well as the ways that users access and make use of information (Chowdhury and Chowdhury, 2003; Nazim, 2008). The traditional methods for providing library and information services have also changed significantly in recent years because of the development and application of new technologies, especially the Internet and web applications (Dickson and Holley, 2010). The demands and expectations of users have also changed accordingly. Keeping pace with the changing scenario, librarians all over the world are using Web 2.0 applications (blogs, wikis, Really Simple Syndication (RSS), Instant Messaging (IM), etc.), social networking websites (Facebook, MySpace, etc.), social media websites (YouTube, Flickr, etc.), social bookmarking and cataloging (LibraryThing, Delicious, etc.), and resource discovery services (RDS) for offering new-generation library services. Due to the availability and delivery of information sources and services via the Internet, students hardly feel the need to step inside the physical library or to use a librarian in their research. Meredith Farkas is a strong supporter of using these tools and services in libraries for reaching users where they are. According to Farkas (2007a):

> *If libraries are not the first place our prospective users go to do research, they will likely miss any marketing we do on our own Web sites. This is why we must start looking beyond these sites and toward putting our content where our users actually are.*

Web-based applications or services refer to dynamic tools that include: blogs, wikis, RSS feeds, and IM. With the enormous popularity and use of these tools, all types of libraries have explored them as a method of communication and promotion of their library collections and services for their users. This new method of providing library services, according to Dickson and Holley (2010), is referred to as library 2.0.

Changing Role of Academic Librarians From Information Managers to Knowledge Managers

Academic libraries are changing in a changing environment of scholarly publishing, information delivery models, and technologies. The use of the Internet for academic and research purposes has increased this change, and it is now happening at regular intervals. This change has forced decision-makers at academic libraries, particularly the librarians involved in collection development decisions and implementing information technology (IT) infrastructures, to be aware of the changes taking place at global level as regards ICT, publishing, cloud computing, data curation, preservation, and management of big data so that they may develop their resources, collection, and services to satisfy the needs of a new generation of users.

In the midst of these changes, important new roles are emerging for librarians. One of the major roles of librarians in the knowledge economy is that of knowledge managers. It is evident that librarians can no longer meet the information needs of the university community through the traditional avenue of simply adding to their library collections. Librarians need to go the extra mile. They need to understand the information and knowledge needs of users. They should be in a position to map internal and external knowledge that would assist them in increasing their efficiency. In other words, librarians should extend their information management roles and enhance their KM competencies. Foo et al. (2002) argue that librarians as knowledge workers need to play active roles in searching for innovative solutions to the issues involved in adapting to new environments.

Khoo (2005) posited that librarians still need traditional skills, but also noted that these skills should be expanded to handle new digital functions and the online environment because the development of ICT networks is accompanied by a corresponding increase in knowledge. Consequently the role of librarians and information professionals as both user-educators and mediators is vital in this environment (Hashim and Mokohtar, 2012). On the other hand, Cao (1999) emphasized that, in the knowledge economy era, libraries will carry out research on the development and application of information resources, the construction of virtual libraries, and the protection of intellectual property rights in the electronic era, thus creating a basis for knowledge innovation. All these tasks will have to be carried out by librarians because, according to Lawal (2004), library staff as human capital embody the knowledge, skills and abilities of the library, and it is the knowledge, skills, and abilities of individuals that create value. Corroborating this, Seonghee (1999) claimed that the most valuable knowledge sources in the organization are the people themselves, and they should participate actively in organization-wide knowledge collection and a knowledge-sharing network.

Librarians therefore will have to add more value to their work by evaluating, filtering, extracting, analyzing, summarizing, synthesizing, and packaging information into a form that is ready for immediate use (Khoo, 2005). Moreover, to cope with the present information environment, Hashim and Mokohtar (2012) stated that new-era librarians must be knowledge-based practitioners who use research as a foundation for their own professional practice. Hence information professionals (including university librarians) will move from information work to knowledge work and this will have a direct impact on their users and on the effectiveness and competitiveness of their parent organization—the library (Khoo, 2005). The changing roles of university librarians also demand that they have to be broad minded and know something about everything. Consequently they need to collaborate effectively with other colleagues and utilize each other's knowledge to provide services for their users.

KM PRACTICES IN ACADEMIC LIBRARIES[1]

Academic libraries have vast amounts of organizational knowledge about their users, processes, products and services, as well as knowledge of their employees as key knowledge assets. However, librarians are reluctant to consider organizational knowledge as a resource in the same way as their library collections and facilities. Traditionally, their functions were mainly confined to the identification and acquisition of information to satisfy the information needs of the academic community (Townley, 2001). The aim of KM in academic libraries is to effectively utilize the available knowledge resources to help librarians to manage their tasks efficiently and effectively. It aims to extend the role of librarians to manage all types of information and knowledge for the benefit of the library. KM may transform the library into a more efficient knowledge-sharing organization. Academic libraries manage their knowledge assets to avoid duplication of efforts. The processes of KM revolve around the creation, capture, sharing, and utilization of knowledge.

There is a group of scholars who strongly argue that librarians, on the basis of their skills in information handling, can apply and incorporate KM

[1]This section of the chapter is based on an article by Mohammad Nazim and Bhaskar Mukherjee "Librarians' perceptions of knowledge management in developing countries: A case with Indian academic libraries" published in *The International Information & Library Review* (2013) Vol. 45, pp. 63–76.

practice in several areas of an academic library, including administrative and support services (Townley, 2001; Yi, 2006), technical services (Ralph and Ellis, 2009; White, 2004), reference and information services (Gandhi, 2004; Jantz, 2001; Markgren, et al., 2004; Ralph and Ellis, 2009; Stover, 2004), knowledge resource management (Lee, 2005), resource sharing and networking (Jain, 2007), and use of information technology for the development of knowledge repositories (Lee, 2005). The logic behind the application of KM practice in libraries is that it can help librarians to utilize their expertise for finding information for people through reference interview skills and adding value to information through such services as evaluation, prioritization, and summarization, which is more relevant for those seeking to create new knowledge (Schwarzwalder, 1999; Sinotte, 2004).

Relevance of KM to Academic Libraries

Although KM initiatives may vary from one organization to another, all types of organizations including business organizations, academic and research institutions, government bodies, and public service organizations have adopted the practice of KM (Aurum, et al., 2008; Chua, 2009; Rowley, 2007). Some researchers in the library profession have also identified potential benefits of KM for academic libraries and librarians. According to Townley (2001), KM offers many opportunities for academic libraries to manage knowledge for improving organizational effectiveness, both for themselves and their parent institutions. KM in academic libraries has also been recognized as: (1) a survival factor to overcome the challenges librarians are facing in a changing and competitive environment (Porumbeanu, 2010; Sarrafzadeh et al., 2010); (2) a solution for improving future prospects (Roknuzzaman and Umemoto, 2009; Wen, 2005); (3) a method of improving knowledge-based services for internal and external users by creating an organizational culture of sharing knowledge and expertise within the library (Roknuzzaman et al., 2009; Teng and Hawamdeh, 2002); (4) a solution for developing and applying organizational knowledge to improve library operations and services, and promote knowledge innovation by leveraging knowledge (Shanhong, 2000; Townley, 2001); and (5) a means for transforming an academic library into a more efficient and knowledge-sharing organization (Jantz, 2001).

Use of KM Systems in Academic Libraries

Formal initiatives to apply KM practices are relatively scarce in libraries. Librarians are experts in IM, yet libraries lack the infrastructure to foster effective KM within their own walls (Levinge, 2005). Approaches to KM applications in libraries are general in nature and are unlikely to show how KM really works in libraries. Gandhi (2004) describes the value of capturing the tacit knowledge of reference librarians and describes the early efforts of reference librarians in capturing tacit knowledge through old information tools like card files of frequently asked questions. However, with the recent developments in ICT, these practices have been replaced by the use of common knowledge databases (Jantz, 2001), web-based ready-reference databases (Stover, 2004), and knowledge base of Question Point (Markgren et al., 2004). Recently, intranets and advanced web applications have provided an excellent platform to share knowledge both within and outside libraries. Increasingly, libraries are using blogs, wikis, RSS, social media, and other web applications for knowledge-sharing purposes (Bejune, 2007; Chu Kai-Wah, 2009; Kim and Abbas, 2010; Tripathi and Kumar, 2010). The findings of a study on the existing state of practices in tacit knowledge sharing in university libraries conducted by Parirokh et al. (2008) indicate that intranets, telephone lines, and traditional face-to-face communication methods have been used by most librarians, but knowledge-sharing initiatives had not been institutionalized in a majority of the libraries that participated in the study. In a recent study, Kim and Abbas (2010), on the basis of 230 randomly selected academic library websites, found that RSS and blogs have been widely adopted by academic libraries.

The Problems of Adopting KM Practice in Academic Libraries

Despite the similarities between KM and IM, not all librarians have the ambition necessary to gain access to more senior KM roles (Ferguson, 2004). The challenges for librarians lie in applying the competencies used in managing information to the broader context of managing knowledge (Bishop, 2001). According to Sarrafzadeh (2005), if LIS professionals remain reluctant to acquire new skills, they will become irrelevant to their organization and will probably lose out in a competition for employment to people from other fields. Traditionally, librarians' roles have been limited to the identification, acquisition, and organization of explicit or recorded knowledge. Although library and information professionals have been performing the role of information managers in handling organizations' documents and explicit knowledge, to establish a strong position in a KM environment they have to extend their role by managing employees' tacit knowledge on the basis of acquiring professional competencies in the fields of knowledge capture, knowledge processing, and knowledge application (Gulati and Raina, 2000). Management of the "tacit" intuitions and "know-how" of people or knowledge workers in an organization is a great challenge for librarians (Bishop, 2001; Maponya, 2004). The most frequently mentioned challenges to the successful applications of KM practice in libraries are: inadequately trained staff and lack of expertise; reluctance of library professionals to accept changes; lack of understanding of the KM concept and its benefits; lack of a knowledge-sharing culture; lack of incentives or rewards for innovation and sharing of knowledge; lack of guidelines on KM implementation; lack of top management commitment; lack of collaboration; and lack of resources (financial, human, and technological) (Jain, 2007, 2012; Maponya, 2004; Roknuzzaman et al., 2009; Sarrafzadeh et al., 2010; Sinotte, 2004; Ugwu and Ezema, 2010).

KM INITIATIVES IN INDIA

India is moving quickly towards becoming a knowledge society as the government of India is paying due attention to transform India into a global knowledge superpower. The government of India took a landmark step by creating a National Knowledge Commission (NKC) in 2005 with the objective to transform India into a vibrant knowledge-based society (Isaac, 2008). The NKC seeks to develop appropriate institutional frameworks to strengthen the education system, promote domestic research and innovation, and facilitate knowledge application in sectors like health, education, agriculture, water and energy, and industry. It also aims to leverage ICT to enhance governance and connectivity. Its prime focus is on five key areas of the knowledge paradigm: access to knowledge, knowledge concepts, knowledge creation, knowledge application, and development of better knowledge services (Malhan, 2006; National Knowledge Commission, 2007).

KM is not an unknown phenomenon to organizations in India. With an increase in information technology usage, many organizations have started KM initiatives in India. Results of a survey on the use of KM practice of Fortune 100 companies in India show that more than 75% of these companies had or were considering a KM program (Knowledge Management Research Report, 2002). This early survey shows that Indian organizations are not too far behind in the race for KM application. Wipro Technologies Limited developed a KM engagement and effectiveness index that gives top management a clear view both at the organizational level as well as at each of the business unit levels (Chatzkel, 2004). Similarly, Tata Steel Limited developed the Knowledge Manthan Index to measure the effectiveness of its initiative by capturing aspects like involvement of people, sharing of ideas, quality of implementation, etc. (Khanna et al., 2005).

Another Indian IT giant, Infosys Technologies Limited, has conceived, developed, and internally deployed an elaborate architecture for KM that aims to take the company to a "learn once, use anywhere" paradigm (Goswami, 2004). Infosys Technologies Limited has created an internal metric known as the knowledge maturity model (KMM) to track its progress on KM initiatives. The KMM is a series of steps and aspirations that Infosys would like to accomplish. KMM includes various levels to determine the state of KM implementation (Mehta et al., 2007). According to Chawla and Joshi (2010), the starting point is where the organization does not have a KM system in place, followed by firms' ability to be reactive, aware (data-driven decision-making), be convinced (ability to sense and respond proactively to changes in the technology and business environment), and ready to share (shape technology and business environment). This KM framework encompasses business strategy, people, processes and technology, and follows a principle of incremental change and not forcing employees to use the system (Suresh and Mahesh, 2008). Tata Consultancy Services Limited has also developed a KM maturity model known as 5iKM3 to access and harness the organization's ability to manage knowledge. According to Mohanty and Chand (2005), the states of knowledge maturity can be achieved by systematically addressing the three pillars of KM, that is, people (people's mindset and culture); process (process, policy, and strategy); and technology (technology and infrastructure).

A large number of organizations, particularly private sector organizations, in India have successfully adopted and implemented KM. On the contrary, there is not much literature available on KM initiatives in Indian public sector organizations, particularly in academic institutions and libraries. Though there are some success stories involving KM in libraries of the corporate sector and research laboratories, under the auspices of the Council of Scientific and Industrial Research (CSIR), Indian Council of Medical Research (ICMR), and Indian Council of Agricultural Research (ICAR), KM is still in its infancy in academic libraries. Little effort has been devoted to the study of how to improve library operations through KM. Some scholars in India (Aswath and Gupta, 2009; Malhan, 2006; Malhan and Gulati, 2003; Rah et al., 2010; Raja et al., 2009; Singh, 2009; Subramanian, 2007; Thanuskodi, 2010; Tripathy et al., 2007; Vijayakumar and Vijayakumar, 2003) have discussed and identified the problems and prospects of KM in an Indian academic library context. The KM literature reveals the following major barriers to incorporating KM into Indian academic library practice:

- lack of understanding of the KM concept;
- lack of a knowledge-sharing attitude due to insecurity and fear of passing their tacit knowledge to colleagues and losing their status;
- library professionals' reluctance to set their minds to cooperate or share resources;
- lack of technical skills in ICT;
- lack of appropriate tools and technologies;
- lack of sufficient funds;
- lack of collaboration and team spirit;
- lack of a centralized policy for KM;
- lack of top management interest in KM activities.

LIBRARIANS' PERCEPTIONS TOWARDS KM

The perceptions of KM, emerging from the review of the literature presented above, are varied and there is no consensus on the concept of KM. This has resulted in, among other things, a lack of universal consensus on some of the key issues of KM, including the concept of KM and its applications to libraries. There are a host of working definitions of KM which create confusion not just for corporations, but also for libraries and non-profit information centers. Though several studies have been conducted on KM and its applications to academic libraries (see, eg, Branin, 2003; Clarke, 2004; Daneshgar and Parirokh, 2007; Jantz, 2001; Mphidi and Snyman, 2004; Porumbeanu, 2010; Stover, 2004; Wen, 2005; White, 2004; Yi, 2006), but most of these studies were conducted in developed countries. Therefore it is necessary to discover its relevance and importance from a developing country's perspective, such as in India. It is also important to know what concepts of KM prevail among librarians in India and how this understanding might be developed effectively to respond to the KM challenge.

When something is not defined clearly, it is also difficult to apply. Academic institutions, particularly universities, have significant opportunities to apply KM practice to support every part of their mission. According to Kidwell et al. (2000), there are five key areas of KM applications in universities, which include research, curriculum development, administrative services, alumni services, and strategic planning. Although the concept of KM is relatively new to academic libraries in India, it is important to identify its applications in academic libraries. Although there are several benefits of KM applications for academic libraries as have emerged from a review of the literature (see, eg, Porumbeanu, 2010; Sarrafzadeh et al., 2010; Townley, 2001; Roknuzzaman and Umemoto, 2009; Wen, 2005; Jantz, 2001), but it is important to know how librarians in India perceive the benefits of KM.

Over the years, several IT-based tools and social practices have evolved and are being used to support the processes of knowledge capture, codification, and sharing. Intranets, web portals, blogs, wikis, social media, groupware, knowledge directories, and communities of practice are increasingly used in libraries as knowledge-sharing tools, reported in the findings of previous studies (Ajiferuke, 2003; Anderson, 2007; Farkas, 2007b; Foo and Ng, 2008; Kim and Abbas, 2010; Mphidi and Snyman, 2004; Singh, 2007; Tripathi and Kumar, 2010). Use of these tools and practices helps academic libraries to improve their performance and fulfill their mandate. However, there is uncertainty about the extent to which they are being used in Indian academic libraries.

Library and information professionals in India are still involved in the traditional practices of knowledge organization and information management (Nazim and Mukherjee, 2011). There is also a lack of understanding of various dimensions of KM and lack of competencies among library and information professionals to develop and apply KM tools and techniques (Malhan, 2006). There are several challenges of KM applications in Indian academic libraries as identified from the review of the literature. But it is also important to analyze whether these challenges are common to all types of libraries or whether librarians in academic libraries in India perceive different challenges.

Research Questions

The study focused on the following research questions (RQ):

RQ1. What is the concept of KM as understood by librarians?

RQ2. In the view of university librarians, what are the potential applications and methods of incorporating KM practice in academic libraries?

RQ3. What are the potential benefits of incorporating KM into academic library practice as perceived by librarians?

RQ4. What are the barriers to incorporating KM practice as perceived by librarians?

RQ5. How are academic librarians involved in KM at their institutions?

This study answers these questions using data collected from university librarians. The findings of the study will be useful to library practitioners and also help to identify important variables to examine in future empirical studies. Since the words university and academic libraries are used interchangeably, the present study is limited to central university libraries in India.

Methods of Research

The study employed a combination of quantitative and qualitative research methods using a structured questionnaire which includes both open- and close-ended questions. Academic institutions and their libraries in India are numerous when considering a sample for any research. Therefore only central university libraries were included in this study, keeping in mind that these are funded by the central government and might have advanced library infrastructure and facilities. Of the total of 42 central university libraries in India, we chose 30 libraries on the basis of collections, infrastructure, and services at various locations within India using purposive sampling methods in order to investigate the perceptions of librarians on KM and its applications in academic libraries. The university librarians of these universities were selected as respondents. However, in the absence of a university librarian an official up to the rank of assistant librarian was allowed to participate in the survey. A total of 30 questionnaires were delivered by post, of which only 15 were returned (50% response rate). The libraries which participated in the study were from nine different states of the country, four from Uttar Pradesh, four from Delhi, one each from Andhra Pradesh, West Bengal, Kerala, Chhattisgarh, Manipur, Mizoram, and Meghalaya, spread over a distance of 4000 km, and serve an extended community of users but are still very different libraries in terms of staff, users etc. The data for the present study was collected during Jun. to Dec. 2011. As it was not a large amount of data, data analysis was done by simple frequency counting and presented in tables.

The details of the libraries participating in the study are shown in Table 9.1. Column A gives the name of the University. Column B lists the years when each university and its library were established. Column C provides an indication of the relative size of each library based on total collections. Column D indicates the total number of sanctioned posts and the number of staff currently working in the participating libraries.

Study Findings

The next section presents the major findings of the study.

Librarians' Understanding of the Concept of KM

In order to learn the respondents' understanding of the concept of KM, they were asked to choose one of three definitions provided in the questionnaire. These definitions were derived from the KM literature and describe the relationship of KM with learning organizations. Space was also provided to

Table 9.1 List of participating libraries ($N=15$)

A	B		C	D	
	Year established			Library staff	
Name of the University library	University	Library	Total collection	NPS[a]	NSW[b]
Aligarh Muslim University (AMU), Aligarh	1920	1960	1,186,139	121	100
Allahabad University (ALU), Allahabad	1837	1913	653,164	88	44
Babasaheb Bhimrao Ambedkar University (BBAU), Lucknow	1996	1996	13,000	9	7
Banaras Hindu University (BHU), Varanasi	1916	1917	1,061,378	159	122
Guru Ghasidas University (GGS)	1983	1984	110,000	22	19
Indira Gandhi National Open University (IGNOU), New Delhi	1985	1986	130,000	17	17
Jamia Millia Islamia University (JMIU), New Delhi	1920	1920	340,000	59	50
Jawaharlal Nehru University (JNU), New Delhi	1968	1969	560,000	99	78
Manipur University (MPU), Imphal	1980	1980	160,000	25	18
Maulana Azad National Urdu University (MANUU), Hyderabad	1998	1998	32,498	22	22
Mizoram University (MU), Mizoram	2001	2001	87,431	26	20
North Eastern Hill University (NEHU), Shillong	1973	1973	250,000	73	63
Pondicherry University (PU), Pondicherry	1985	1986	251,000	53	36
University of Delhi (UOD), Delhi	1922	1922	1,475,729	416	126
Visva Bharati (VB), Shanti Niketan, West Bengal	1921	1925	376,511	42	28
Total				1122	700

[a] Number of posts sanctioned.
[b] Number of staff working.

the respondents so that they could write their own definitions, if desired. It was believed that gaining an understanding of the concepts of KM among librarians would help to understand the concepts of KM that prevail among librarians.

As shown in Table 9.2, more than half of the respondents chose option B, which described KM as: *A process of creating, storing, sharing, and reusing organizational knowledge (know-how) to enable an organization to achieve its goals and objectives*. However, 26.6% of respondents feel that KM deals with: *The creation and subsequent management of an environment which encourages knowledge to be created, shared, learnt, enhanced, and organized for the benefit of the organization and its customers*. Option C, *KM is an activity concerned with strategy and tactics to manage human-centered assets*, was chosen by 13.3% of the respondents. Some respondents also suggested their own definitions of KM, a list of which is given in Table 9.3.

Applications and Methods of KM Practice in Academic Libraries

A group of studies (see, eg, Townley, 2001; Yi, 2006; Ralph, 2008) reported that the use of KM in libraries may be extended to areas such as administration or support services, where libraries have had little impact in the past. In order to identify the potential areas of KM practice in Indian academic libraries, respondents were asked to indicate any combination of the five tentative areas listed by being allowed to check more than one option. Additionally, they were also provided with the space to write their own comments. The results are shown in Table 9.4.

Some respondents also expressed their own views regarding potential areas of KM applications in academic libraries, as summarized in Table 9.5.

In the next step we tried to find how KM is applied in academic libraries. As shown in Table 9.6, 86.6% of respondents agreed that "providing training

Table 9.2 Definitions of KM

	Which definition of KM do you find most suitable?	**%**
A	The creation and subsequent management of an environment which encourages knowledge to be created, shared, learnt, enhanced, and organized for the benefit of the organization and its customers	33.6
B	KM is a process of creating, storing, sharing, and reusing organizational knowledge (know-how) to enable an organization to achieve its goals and objectives	60.0
C	KM is an activity concerned with strategy and tactics to manage human-centered assets	13.3

Table 9.3 Definitions of KM as provided by respondents

Creation of a digital repository to preserve organizational knowledge for easy retrieval, use, and retention for activities such as problem-solving, strategic planning, and decision-making
Management and organization of information sources with the use of information and communication technologies
Management and organization of all types of knowledge resources, such as books, journals, theses, manuscripts, etc. KM is not a new concept for information professionals, since they have been managing knowledge for a long time, but today the focus is on content management, digitization, etc. So the application of ICT to the storage and access of information is called KM
The term KM is confusing and very close to information management and knowledge organization, which are the primary activities of libraries. I think the term IM is more appropriate for libraries; however, the business community coined this term and library professionals are blindly using it
Knowledge is difficult to manage; only information can be managed. Knowledge which individuals hold can only be shared and transferred to others through communication, discussions, meetings, etc. In organizations people usually do not share knowledge for several political and cultural reasons. For the effectiveness of knowledge sharing and transfer, organizations must create a conducive environment for their workers

Table 9.4 Potential areas of KM applications

In what aspect is KM applied to academic libraries?	**%[a]**
Reference and information services	53.3
Policy and decision making	46.6
Technical services	33.3
Administrative services	33.3
Planning of information services	26.6

[a] The overall percentage is greater than 100% because multiple answers were allowed.

and learning opportunities to the employees for acquiring new knowledge and developing competencies" is the most suitable method to implement KM practice in academic libraries. A great majority of respondents (73.3%) also agreed that the provision of rewards and incentives would encourage employees to share knowledge with their colleagues. About 50% of respondents believe that KM can be applied in academic libraries using ICT to support the creation and access to internal knowledge. Forty percent of respondents think that KM can be applied in academic libraries by extending access to external information/knowledge resources through library

Table 9.5 KM applications in academic libraries: relevant comments

Digital and online library services, particularly web-based information and reference services such as e-mail alerts, CAS, SDI, answers to frequently asked questions
E-learning
Human resource management
Project management
Cataloging by downloading catalogs from other libraries to avoid duplication of work
Initiating new information services such as creating subject-based portals, institutional repositories, interactive online reference services, etc.
Value-added services such as evaluation and summarization of information for specialized users
Information literacy programs

Table 9.6 Methods of KM application in academic libraries

How is KM applied in academic libraries?	%[a]
Providing training and learning opportunities to employees to acquire new knowledge and develop competencies (ie, through training programs, participation in communities of practice, formal/informal meetings, e-learning, workshops, seminars, etc.)	86.6
Encouraging staff to share knowledge through the provision of rewards/incentives, trust, teamwork, etc.	73.3
Using ICT to support the creation of and access to internal knowledge (ie, automation of library operations and services, creating knowledge repositories, creation of databases of best practices, and knowledge directories)	53.3
Extending access to external information/knowledge resources through library networks, or partnerships with other libraries, library portals including links to library professional groups and publications, etc.	40.0

[a] The overall percentage is greater than 100% because multiple answers were allowed.

networks or partnership with other libraries, library portals including links to library professional groups and publications, etc.

Potential Benefits of KM Practice

There is widespread recognition in the literature that the use of KM practice would help academic libraries to improve their overall performance and become more relevant to their parent organizations and the communities that they serve. To identify the perceptions of the librarians on potential benefits of KM practice in academic libraries, they were asked to indicate their views. The results are shown in Table 9.7.

Table 9.7 Potential benefits of KM practice in academic libraries

What benefits does KM provide for academic libraries?	%[a]
KM can add values to the library operations and services	93.3
KM can reduce the chances of duplication of work	73.3
KM can make academic libraries more relevant to their universities/ institutes	73.3
KM can help to transform academic library into a learning organization	53.3
KM can improve library's overall performance and future prospects	46.6

[a] The overall percentage is greater than 100% because multiple answers were allowed.

Barriers to KM Applications in Academic Libraries

As shown in Table 9.8, the respondents perceived a number of problems as barriers to the application of KM practice in academic libraries.

Some respondents have also expressed their own views regarding the problems of incorporating KM practice in academic libraries, which are summarized in Table 9.9.

Librarians' Involvement in KM Practice

Respondents were asked to specify the stage of KM initiatives in their libraries. As shown in Table 9.10, 40% of respondents indicated that they were currently evaluating the importance of KM for their libraries, 26.7% indicated that they have a plan to introduce KM in the near future, 20% were in the nascent stage and had initiated KM practice in some areas, while only 13.3% indicated that they have initiated KM in their libraries.

Table 9.8 Librarians' perceived challenges for incorporating KM practice in academic libraries

Barriers	%[a]
Lack of expertise to identify knowledge resources within or outside the library	93.3
Lack of understanding of the KM concept and its benefits	86.6
Lack of knowledge capture and a knowledge-sharing culture	80.0
Lack of top management commitment to initiate KM	66.6
Lack of rewards/incentives for innovative performance and knowledge sharing	60.0
Lack of financial resources to initiate KM	60.0
Reluctance of the library professionals to adopt the change	53.3
Lack of IT infrastructure to support the capture, storage, sharing, and distribution of information	46.6

[a] The overall percentage is greater than 100% because multiple answers were allowed.

Table 9.9 Barriers to the application of KM practice: relevant comments

KM is a new concept for librarians that needs some specialized training and motivation for the staff
Knowledge sharing is not part of performance evaluation and there are no incentives or recognition for knowledge sharing; therefore staff are neither willing to share knowledge nor take any extra responsibility
KM is usually misinterpreted as information management or content management. Because of this lack of understanding of KM, librarians or decision-makers often do not show any interest in KM
Unwillingness to adopt and initiate change

Table 9.10 Status of KM initiatives in academic libraries

Stages of KM initiatives	%
Evaluating the importance of KM for their libraries	40.0
Introduction stage (planning to initiate)	26.7
Nascent stage (initiated in some areas)	20.0
Growth stage (almost initiated)	13.3

Table 9.11 Use of KM practice in academic libraries

Are you aware of any KM practices in your library?	%
Yes	40.0
No	60.0

Table 9.12 Use of KM practice in academic libraries: relevant comments

Our library provides training to the subordinate staff
At many stages from acquisition to management of the library but fully in a systematic way by automation and digitization
In the technical section by maintaining an authority file to reduce duplication of efforts to save time
Library automation, creating a library website for availability of resources on the web
We archive the knowledge created in our institution in our digital repository
Creating a database of newspaper articles
Building an articles database of periodicals subscribed to in our library

With regard to the involvement of academic libraries in KM practice, respondents were asked to indicate if they were aware of any KM practice in their libraries: 53% of respondents answered "No" (see Table 9.11). Those who answered "Yes" to this question were further asked to specify such practices in their libraries. Their involvement is supported by comments of the respondents, which have been summarized in Table 9.12.

DISCUSSION

Using the data presented and interpreted above, this section discusses the major findings of the study based on five research questions.

RQ1: What Is the Concept of KM, as Understood by Librarians?

Examination of the responses received from librarians regarding the definitions of KM shows that the majority of them see KM as a management process, which enables the organization to create, store, share, and reuse organizational knowledge, while only 13% consider KM as an activity which is concerned with strategy and tactics of the management of people and their knowledge (Table 9.2). More than half of the respondents chose the same KM definition from the three definitions provided. This may be interpreted as meaning that there is a level of commonality among respondents on what KM means to them. The analysis of respondents' own definitions of KM indicates that they have conceptualized KM from three major viewpoints: an IM point of view, a tacit point of view, and a cultural point of view (Table 9.3). The analysis of those KM definitions that most respondents chose or those which they themselves provided shows that their views on KM are varied and most of them have shallow perceptions of KM dealing with the management of explicit knowledge alone rather than viewing KM as a holistic organization-wide strategy integrating people, process, and technology. They have mixed understandings of the concept of KM and most of them focused on the use of technology or specific processes for the capture and use of explicit knowledge rather than sharing and using the tacit knowledge embedded in the employees.

The librarians who have participated in the present research seemed aware of the concepts of KM, as most of them tried to define KM in their own words (Table 9.3). However, there is some level of uncertainty about the relationship between KM and IM and the difference between the two, as emerged from the analysis of definitions provided by the librarians. They focused largely on capturing, storing, and retrieving explicit knowledge rather than creating and sharing tacit knowledge.

RQ2: What Are the Potential Applications and Methods of Incorporating KM Practice in Academic Libraries?

The majority of the respondents believe that KM may be integrated into reference and information services. Other possible areas of KM practice in academic libraries, as indicated by the respondents, were technical services, planning and decision-making, and library administration

(Table 9.4). Additionally, they emphasized the role of KM in areas such as digital and online library services, e-learning, human resource management, and project management (Table 9.5). Based on the data presented in Table 9.6, the methods of KM application in academic libraries are discussed as follows.

Provision of Training and Learning Opportunities for Employees

As shown in Table 9.6, 86.6% of respondents agreed that "providing training and learning opportunities to employees to acquire new knowledge and develop competencies" can help academic libraries to adopt KM practice in academic libraries. There is support for this viewpoint in the literature too. For example, Wen (2005) points out that acquisition of knowledge by employees is one of the important steps of the KM implementation process. Further, he argues that knowledge can be acquired and enhanced by providing training or learning opportunities to the staff. Continuous learning through professional training courses or attending workshops and seminars are some important methods of acquiring knowledge and developing competencies for employees involved in KM practice, as identified and discussed by Sanchez (2001).

Promoting a Knowledge-Sharing Culture

There is a strong view expressed within the literature that knowledge which is embedded in employees has no value until it is utilized and shared among other employees of an organization. Knowledge in an organization can be shared through the formation of communities of practice, formal or informal meetings, face-to-face interactions, mentoring, apprenticeships, and use of best practices. According to White (2004), KM systems generally fail if there is no knowledge-sharing culture in place. Sharing of knowledge depends on the strategy of an organization which might best encourage and motivate employees to share their most valuable personally held knowledge (Hariharan, 2005). Gibbert and Krause (2002) argue that knowledge sharing cannot be forced, but can only be encouraged and facilitated. Further, they mention that knowledge sharing can be induced when there are perceived benefits for the employees in terms of incentives or rewards. Recognizing the importance of incentives and rewards for creating a knowledge-sharing culture, a high majority of respondents (73.3%) indicated that KM can be incorporated into academic library practice by "encouraging staff to share knowledge through the provision of rewards/incentives, trust, teamwork, etc.".

Use of ICT to Support the Creation of and Access to Internal Knowledge

It has been argued widely in the literature that ICT serves as a powerful enabler and provides effective and efficient tools for all facets of KM application, including capturing, storing, sharing, and access to knowledge (see, eg, Gandhi, 2004). ICT also supports the process of knowledge sharing by enabling people to locate as well as communicate with each other (Roknuzzaman et al., 2009). Academic libraries have a variety of knowledge sources available inside as well as outside the library. Availability and exploitation of both internal and external sources of knowledge are essential to improve the working efficiency of the staff, as well as reducing the chances of redundancy. Academic libraries can use ICT for the automation of library functions and services, creation of knowledge repositories, development of a database of best practices, library portals and intranets, which help to locate, capture, store, and share internal knowledge. More than half (53.3%) of the respondents indicated that the use of ICT to support access to internal knowledge is one of the most important aspects of KM application.

Networking and Partnerships With Other Libraries

Access to external information/knowledge resources through library networks or partnerships with other libraries, including links to professional library groups and publications, etc., is also recognized as an important method of KM application in academic libraries by 40% of respondents.

RQ3: What Are the Potential Benefits of Incorporating KM Into Academic Library Practice?

KM Helps to Improve Library Operations and Services

One reason for considering KM in academic libraries is to add value to libraries' operations and services, as indicated by 93.3% of respondents (Table 9.7). Due to the advancement in ICT and the changing needs of users, there is an increased need for approaches that incorporate the use of tools and services that are aligned with users' practices and expectations. KM enables librarians to capture, store, organize, share, and disseminate the right information to the right user at the right time. By using web applications such as Web 2.0 and social media, university librarians can empower their users with the right content at the right time in the right format. The use of social media can help librarians to know the requirements of their users, which ultimately leads to the delivery of more appropriate and timely services (Daneshgar and Bosanquet, 2010). Roknuzzaman and Umemoto (2009) rightly point out that if librarians are aware of the knowledge of their users and/or if they have better possibilities for sharing knowledge with them, then this is all beneficial for the services they provide for their users.

KM Helps to Improve a Library's Overall Performance and Future Prospects

KM helps to improve a library's overall performance and future prospects as indicated by 46.6% of respondents. There is a strong view expressed within the LIS literature that libraries are in danger of being left behind in competition with other information suppliers and KM has been seen as a survival factor for libraries, helping them to respond to the challenges librarians face in a continuously changing environment (Porumbeanu, 2010; Sarrafzadeh et al., 2010). Other major challenges for academic librarians, as observed, are: the downward trends in library support; erosion of acquisitions and operating budgets; an increase in user service demands; outdated management and organizational structure; and new technological developments (Wen, 2005). To deal with these issues, librarians are required to adopt new managerial processes that can adequately overcome these challenges and help academic libraries to survive by increasing efficiency and improving the quality of information products and user services (Shanhong, 2000; Teng and Hawamdeh, 2002). By capturing and utilizing knowledge, libraries can achieve a multitude of benefits, including savings in research and development costs, reduce duplication of work, transfer of best practices, increase employees' capabilities, and enhance employee satisfaction. This will ultimately improve the library's overall performance and future prospects.

KM Helps to Make Academic Libraries More Relevant to Their Parent Organizations

About 47% of respondents also think that KM helps academic libraries to become more relevant to their parent organizations. It is believed that implementation of KM practice in academic libraries can enhance their overall visibility within the organization. Librarians can benefit their institutions, their libraries, and themselves by undertaking a campus-wide role in managing organizational knowledge through the creation of knowledge repositories and management of content (Townley, 2001). Implementation of KM practice can also assist librarians in meeting user needs in the light of ultimate organizational goals (Sarrafzadeh et al., 2010). Thus KM provides academic libraries with an opportunity to collaborate with other units in their organizations, and hence to become more integrated into institutional operations and enhance their overall visibility within the organization.

KM Helps to Transform Academic Libraries Into Learning Organizations

According to 53% of respondents, implementation of KM practice can help academic libraries transform themselves into learning organizations. KM facilitates continuous and ongoing processes of learning and unlearning, thus ensuring that the need to impose top-down radical change is minimized (Malhotra, 2000). According to Parirokh et al. (2008), organizational learning in academic libraries can be improved by sharing their knowledge among employees. Organizational learning is essential for developing professional competencies and it must be fostered and enhanced continuously. Professional competencies based on activities such as knowledge organization and preservation, information search, retrieval and dissemination, and the creation of information products and services constitute essential organizational assets of academic libraries. Therefore librarians should identify and focus on those few processes which they do best, developing and improving them all the time. Through a variety of mechanisms of organizational learning, librarians can create, collect, and use the knowledge necessary for these processes. Based on this knowledge, they can develop new operating procedures and improve existing ones.

RQ4: What Are the Barriers to Incorporating KM Practice?

As shown in Tables 9.8 and 9.9, the respondents perceived a number of problems as barriers to incorporating KM into academic library practice, which are discussed below.

One of the major barriers to incorporating KM into academic library practice, as perceived by 93% of respondents (Table 9.8), is the lack of expertise among library professionals to identify knowledge resources within or outside the library. KM, as described by Amar (2002), is the effective use and reuse of both explicit and tacit knowledge of an organization. According to Nelson (2008), identification of knowledge resources is one of the most important steps in the KM implementation process. The success of KM in libraries, according to Abell and Oxbrow (2001), depends on the abilities of employees to "identify, acquire and evaluate internal and external sources of knowledge and integrate, organize and make relevant knowledge available to the right person at the right time" (p. 38). The results of the present study indicate that librarians are mostly involved in the management of information or explicit knowledge. They equate the concept of KM with information management, and do not recognize the importance of identifying, capturing, and sharing tacit knowledge due to the lack of expertise.

Although LIS professionals have been acknowledging for years that KM is a burgeoning field of great interest to them, they do not know what exactly is meant by KM and they are not aware of the benefits of KM in libraries. Misunderstanding of the concept of KM is also perceived as a barrier to incorporating KM into academic library practice by 87% of respondents in the present study. This finding confirms the results of a study by Roknuzzaman and Umemoto (2009), who in investigating the view of library practioners on KM found that KM is misinterpreted as information management or content management activities in libraries and, because of this lack of understanding of KM, library authorities or decision-makers often do not show any interest in KM.

Lack of knowledge capture and a knowledge-sharing culture was perceived as another major barrier to KM application in academic libraries by 80% of respondents. Sharing of knowledge is one of the most critical factors for the effectiveness of KM as cited in the literature. A group of previous studies (eg, Blair, 2002; Roknuzzaman and Umemoto, 2009) has also reported that the existing library environment and mechanism do not support and encourage staff to share and utilize their expertise, and there is a need for a favorable organizational culture for the creation and sharing of knowledge in libraries.

Lack of top management support and provision of rewards/incentives were perceived as barriers to KM application in academic libraries by 67% and 60% of respondents respectively. The impact of top management and leadership support is greater for KM as it is an emerging discipline, particularly in India, and employees may need the added incentives of total commitment from their organizations' top management and leadership. Top management support also influences other factors critical to the success of KM, such as organizational culture, as the role of leadership is crucial in fostering trust and promoting a knowledge-sharing culture. According to Bennett and Gabriel (1999), a structured reward system with well-defined policies helps the flow of information. Provision of fair performance measurements can also motivate employees to share their knowledge and to help others.

More than half (53.3%) of the respondents believe that LIS professionals' reluctance to accept change in their normal working life is also a hurdle to initiating KM practice in academic libraries. Financial constraints, including lack of IT infrastructure, are other major barriers discouraging LIS professionals to initiate KM in academic libraries, as indicated by 60% and 47% of respondents respectively.

RQ5: How Are Academic Librarians Involved With KM at Their Institutions?

The results of the present research indicate that librarians in India are still in the early stages of understanding the potential implications of KM. They have mostly been involved either evaluating the importance of KM or planning to introduce KM practice in their libraries (see Table 9.10). Fewer libraries have initiated the practices of KM, as seen from the responses of respondents presented in Table 9.10. On the basis of the KM maturity model proposed by Yang and Bai (2009), academic libraries in India may be situated at the first and second levels of the KM implementation stage.

Forty percent of respondents in the present study acknowledged that they are aware of at least one practice of KM in their libraries (Table 9.11), but these may be perceived as basic information management activities, as seen from the respondents' own views presented in Table 9.12. They have mostly been involved in KM through the use of their skills in organizing and retrieving information or the development of intranets, institutional repositories, management of content, and the training of users in the effective use of databases and other resources. However, no evidence has emerged from the views of respondents for the involvement of academic libraries in the creation and sharing of tacit knowledge, either through development knowledge directories or the formation or encouragement of communities of practice. Thus there seems to have been little impact of KM on academic library operations and services in India as reflected in the results of the present study. The results of the present research confirm the findings of an earlier study conducted by Jain (2007), who in investigating the practices of KM in academic libraries in East and South Africa found that their practices went little beyond traditional information management activities, and the majority of the participants considered themselves as information managers. A recent study on KM and its potential application in libraries by Sarrafzadeh et al. (2010) also reported similar findings.

SUMMARY

Although the concept of KM emerged from the business sector, its practices are now being applied in the domains of nonprofit and public sector organizations, including academic institutions. Increasingly, library practitioners have started to acknowledge the importance of KM in libraries. They commonly held the view that a library is a knowledge-based organization where the organization and maintenance of recorded knowledge is a practice as old as civilization itself, and therefore the concept of KM is nothing new for them as they have been managing knowledge for a long time. Arguably, libraries have always been involved with collecting, organizing, and disseminating recorded or explicit knowledge, which is defined as knowledge that can be captured and therefore easily communicated and shared with the help of IT systems. However, the focus of KM is largely on the creation and sharing of tacit knowledge, which is defined as unrecorded knowledge embedded in people (their skill and expertise). Thus KM is usually misinterpreted as the information management or content management activities in a library.

From the study's limited sample, it appears that the levels of understanding of KM concepts among librarians are varied, and most of them view KM as the management of information resources, services, and systems using various technologies and tools via activities such as information acquisition, storage and retrieval, data mining, and information use through the training of users in the effective use of databases and services. This may be due to the logical overlap between the concepts and tools involved in the management of information and knowledge.

However, most librarians agree that KM is applicable to academic library practice and its application is the best way to improve the functions and services of academic libraries. Although a KM framework is lacking in academic libraries, provision of training and education, a favorable organizational culture, use of ICT, and networking or partnerships with other libraries have been validated as important KM enablers by the respondents of this study, and may be used as a framework for incorporating KM practice as well as evaluating existing KM practice in academic libraries in India.

In spite of librarians' limited involvement in KM practice, there seems to be a developing interest among librarians towards KM. This conclusion may be drawn on the basis of three major sets of perceptions emerging from a review of the literature. First, librarians can and should enter into KM roles through the application of their traditional skills related to IM. Second, there are potential benefits for them from an involvement in KM, including personal career development and enhancement of their position and status within their parent organizations. Finally, KM offers potential benefits for the development of libraries.

The findings of the present study have a number of practical implications for both academics and library practitioners. In order to implement KM effectively in academic libraries in India, librarians need to clarify the concept of KM. Many people still associate KM with IM and, as such, are reluctant to take ownership of the concept. The implementation of KM in academic libraries will not succeed if librarians view KM as simply an application of some technology or specific processes along with the traditional practice of IM. Librarians therefore need to broaden their understanding, change their traditional mindset, and apply a holistic approach to KM focusing on the management of both explicit and tacit knowledge.

Since the focus of KM is on people's expertise, librarians must acquire competencies in the fields of communication, human resource management, change management, project management, teamwork, mentoring, presentation, and leadership. These competencies are necessary for the proper repositioning of academic librarians to face the challenges of present-day realities. A focus on the transfer of traditional LIS skills, for example, in knowledge organization to the management of tacit knowledge could greatly enhance the influence of librarians in the field of KM and contribute to their overall understanding of the need for knowledge both at organizational and personal levels.

Academic libraries work as a unit of the university system to support the objectives and mission of their parent organizations. Since an academic library is a unit in an organization (university or institute), implementing KM at its own level is a difficult task unless it has the support of the parent organization. Universities/institutes can support academic libraries by providing adequate financial support to develop KM systems, formulating a strategy for KM implementation, and offering a reward or promotion on the basis of the performance of employees.

REFERENCES

Abell, A., Oxbrow, N., 2001. Competing with Knowledge: The Information Professionals in the Knowledge Management Age. Library Association Publishing, London.

Ajiferuke, I., 2003. Role of information professionals in knowledge management programs: empirical evidence from Canada. Inf. Sci. J. 6, 247–257.

Amar, A.D., 2002. Managing Knowledge Workers. Quorum Books, Westport, CT.

Anderson, P., 2007. All that glisters in not gold: web 2.0 and the librarian. J. Librariansh. Inf. Sci. 39 (4), 195–198.

Aswath, L., Gupta, S., 2009. Knowledge management tools and academic library services. In: Proceedings of International Conference of Academic Libraries on Vision and Roles of Future Academic Libraries, 5–8 October 2009, New Delhi, India. Available from: http://crl.du.ac.in/ical09/papers/index_files/ical-51_250_732_3_RV.pdf (accessed 16.03.11).

Aurum, A., Daneshgar, F., Ward, J., 2008. Investigating knowledge management practices in software development organizations: an Australian experience. Inf. Softw. Technol. 50, 510–533.

Bejune, M., 2007. Wikis in libraries. Inf. Technol. Libr. 26, 26–38.

Bennett, R., Gabriel, H., 1999. Organizational factors and knowledge management within large marketing departments: an empirical study. J. Knowl. Manag. 3 (3), 212–225.

Bishop, K., 2001. Information Service Professionals in Knowledge-Based Organizations in Australia: What Will We Manage? University of Technology, Sydney. p. 65.

Blair, D.C., 2002. Knowledge management: hype, hope, or help? J. Am. Soc. Inf. Sci. Technol. 50 (12), 1019–1028.

Branin, J.J., 2003. Knowledge management in academic libraries: building the knowledge bank at the Ohio State University. J. Libr. Adm. 39 (4), 41–56.

Budd, J.M., 1998. The Academic Library: Its Context, Its Purpose and Its Operation. Libraries Unlimited, Englewood, CO.

Cao, Y., 1999. The reorientation of libraries in knowledge economy era. Libr. Work Res. 3, 24–26.

Chatzkel, J., 2004. Establishing a global KM initiative: the WIPRO story. J. Knowl. Manag. 8 (2), 6–18.

Chawla, D., Joshi, H., 2010. Knowledge management initiatives in Indian public and private sector organizations. J. Knowl. Manag. 14 (6), 811–827.

Chowdhury, G.G., Chowdhury, S.C., 2003. Introduction to Digital Libraries. Facet Publishing, London.

Chu Kai-Wah, S., 2009. Using wikis in academic libraries. J. Acad. Librariansh. 35, 170–176.

Chua, A.Y.K., 2009. The dark side of knowledge management initiatives. J. Knowl. Manag. 13 (4), 32–40.

Clarke, R., 2004. KM in the main library of the University of West Indies, Trinidad. Inf. Dev. 20 (1), 30–35.

Daneshgar, F., Bosanquet, L., 2010. Organizing customer knowledge in academic libraries. Electron. J. Knowl. Manag. 8 (1), 21–32.

Daneshgar, F., Parirokh, M., 2007. A knowledge schema for organizational learning in academic libraries. Knowl. Manag. Res. Pract. 5, 22–33.

Dickson, A., Holley, R.P., 2010. Social networking in academic libraries: the possibilities and the concerns. New Libr. World 111 (11/12), 468–479.

Farkas, M., 2007a. Your stuff, their space. Am. Libr. 38 (11), 36.

Farkas, M., 2007b. Who moved my e-mail? Am. Libr. 38 (10), 30.

Ferguson, S., 2004. The knowledge management myth: will the real knowledge managers please step forward? Available from: http://conferences.alia.org.au/alia2004/pdfs/ferguson.s.paper.pdf (accessed 05.11.15).

Foo, S., Ng, J., 2008. Library 2.0: libraries and library school. In: Paper Presented at the Library Association of Singapore Conference, 9 May 2008, Singapore. Available from: http://www.las.org.sg/pa_sfjn.pdf (accessed 17.01.14).

Foo, S., Chaudhry, A.S., Majid, S.M., Logan, E., 2002. Academic libraries in transition: challenges ahead. In: Proceedings of the World Library Summit, 22–26 April, Singapore. Available from: http://islab.sas.ntu.edu.sg:8000/user/schubert/publications/2002/02wls_fmt.pdf (accessed 15.12.15).

Gandhi, S., 2004. Knowledge management and reference services. J. Acad. Librariansh. 30 (5), 368–381.

Gibbert, M., Krause, H., 2002. Practice exchange in a best practice marketplace. In: Davenport, T., Probst, G. (Eds.), Knowledge Management Casebook: Best Practices. Publicis MCD, Berlin, pp. 68–84.

Goswami, C., 2004. Managing the technical, professional workforce: can knowledge management be the answer? In: Mallikarjun, M., Chugan, P.K. (Eds.), Managing Trade, Technology and Environment. Excel Books, New Delhi, India, pp. 362–372.

Gulati, A., Raina, R.L., 2000. Professional competencies among librarians and information professionals in the knowledge era. World Libr. 10 (1), 11–18.

Hariharan, A., 2005. Critical success factors for knowledge management. Knowl. Manag. Rev. 8 (2), 16–19.

Hashim, L., Mokohtar, H., 2012. Preparing new era librarians and information professionals: trends and issues. Int. J. Human. Soc. Sci. 2 (7), 151–156. Available from: http://www.ijhssnet.com/journals/Vol_2_No_7_April_2012/16.pdf (accessed 21.04.16).

Isaac, A.M., 2008. Transformation of India into a knowledge society. In: Paper Presented at PICMET '08 Conference, 27–31 July 2008, Cape Town, South Africa. Available from: http://www.knowledgecommission.gov.in/downloads/news/news314.pdf (accessed 28.06.15).

Jain, P., 2007. An empirical study of knowledge management in academic libraries in East and Southern Africa. Libr. Rev. 56 (5), 377–392.

Jain, P., 2012. An empirical study of knowledge management in university libraries in SADC countries. In: Tse Hou, H. (Ed.), New Research on Knowledge Management Applications and Lesson Learned. InTech, Shanghai, pp. 137–154. Available from: http://www.intechopen.com/books/new-research-on-knowledgemanagement-applications-and-lesson-learned/an-empirical-study-of-knowledge-management-inuniversitylibraries-in-sadc-countries (accessed 15.06.15).

Jantz, R., 2001. Knowledge management in academic libraries: special tools and processes to support information professionals. Ref. Serv. Rev. 29 (1), 33–39.

Judith, M., 2013. The impact of cloud computing on the future of academic library practices and services. New Libr. World 114 (3–4), 132–141.

Khanna, A., Mitra, D., Gupta, A., 2005. How shop-floor employees drive innovation at Tata Steel. Knowl. Manag. Rev. 8 (3), 20–23.

Khoo, C.S., 2005. Competencies for new era librarians and information professionals. Available from: http://www.ibrarian.net/navon/paper/COMPETENCIES_FOR_NEW_ERA_LIBRARIANS_AND_INFORMATI.pdf?paperid=11070448 (accessed 25.06.15).

Kidwell, J.J., Linde, K.M.V., Johnson, S.L., 2000. Applying corporate knowledge management practices in higher education. Educ. Q. 4, 28–33.

Kim, Y.-M., Abbas, J., 2010. Adoption of library 2.0 functionalities by academic libraries and users: a knowledge management perspective. J. Acad. Librariansh. 36 (3), 211–218.

Knowledge Management Research Report, 2002. London: Atos KPMG Consulting. Available from: http://www.kpmgconsulting.co.uk/research/othermedia/wf_8519kmrepo.pdf (accessed 25.06.15).

Lawal, O.O., 2004. Human capacity building for librarians in the university community. Gateway Libr. J. 7 (2), 1–2.

Lee, H.W., 2005. Knowledge management and the role of libraries. Chin. Librariansh. Int. Electron. J. 19. Available from: http://www.white-clouds.com/iclc/cliej/cl19.htm (accessed 26.05.12).

Levinge, L., 2005. Information management in the library: are we minding our own business? In: Huthwaite, A. (Ed.), Managing Information in the Digital Age: The Australian Technology Network Libraries Respond. University of South Australia Library for the Librarians of the Australian Technology Network, Adelaide, pp. 68–81.

Malhan, I.V., 2006. Strategic planning for developing Indian university libraries into knowledge resource and service centers. In: Paper Presented at World Library and Information Congress: 72nd IFLA General Conference and Council, 20–24 August 2006, Seoul. Available from: http://www.ifla.org/IV/ifla72/index.htm (accessed 17.06.12).

Malhan, I.V., Gulati, A., 2003. Knowledge management problems of developing countries with special reference to India. Inf. Dev. 9 (3), 209–213.

Malhotra, Y., 2000. Knowledge management for e-business performance: advancing information strategy to 'Internet Time'. Inf. Strat. Exec. J. 16 (4), 5–16.

Maponya, P., 2004. Knowledge management practices in academic libraries: a case study of the University of Natal, Pietermaritzburg Libraries. Available from: http://www.ukzn.ac.za/department/data/leap_scecsalpaper.pdf (accessed 17.06.12).

Markgren, S., Ascher, M.T., Crow, S.J., Lougee-Heimer, H., 2004. Asked and answered online: how two medical libraries are using OCLC's Question Point to answer reference questions. Med. Ref. Serv. 23 (1), 13–28.

Mehta, N., Oswald, S., Mehta, A., 2007. Infosys technologies: improving organizational knowledge flows. J. Inf. Technol. 22 (4), 456–464.

Mohanty, S.K., Chand, M., 2005. 5iKM3: Knowledge Management Maturity Model, Knowledge Management Practices. Tata Consultancy Services, Mumbai. Available from: www.tcs.com/SiteCollectionDocuments/WhitePapers/5iKM3KnowledgeManagement MaturiyModel.pdf (accessed 17.05.12).

Mphidi, H., Snyman, R., 2004. The utilization of an intranet as a knowledge management tool in academic libraries. Electron. Libr. 22 (5), 393–400.

National Knowledge Commission, Government of India, 2007. Libraries: gateways to knowledge. Available from: http://knowledgecommission.gov.in/downloads/documents/NKC_Library.pdf (accessed 28.06.13).

Nazim, M., 2008. Information searching behavior in the Internet age: a users' study of Aligarh Muslim University. Int. Inf. Libr. Rev. 40, 73–81.

Nazim, M., Mukherjee, B., 2011. Implementing knowledge management in Indian academic libraries. J. Knowl. Manag. Pract. 12 (3). Available from: http://www.tlainc.com/article1269.htm (accessed 28.06.13).

Nelson, E., 2008. Knowledge management for libraries. Libr. Adm. Manag. 22 (3), 135–137.

Parirokh, M., Daneshgar, F., Fattahi, R., 2008. Identifying knowledge sharing requirements in academic libraries. Libr. Rev. 57 (2), 107–122.

Porumbeanu, O.-L., 2010. Implementing knowledge management in Romanian academic libraries: identifying the elements that characterize their organizational culture. J. Acad. Librariansh. 36 (6), 549–552.

Rah, J.A., Gul, S., Wani, Z.A., 2010. University libraries: step towards a web based knowledge management system. J. Inf. Knowl. Manag. Syst. 40 (1), 24–38.

Raja, W., Ahmad, Z., Sinha, A.K., 2009. Knowledge management and academic libraries in IT era: problems and positions. In: Poster Paper Presented at International Conference on Academic Libraries at University of Delhi, 5–8 October 2009. Available from: http://crl.du.ac.in/ical09/papers/index_files/ical-124_198_418_2_RV.pdf (accessed 17.07.12).

Ralph, L.L., 2008. An Investigation of a Knowledge Management Solution for Reference Services. Ph.D. Thesis, Nova Southeastern University.

Ralph, L.L., Ellis, T.J., 2009. An investigation of a knowledge management solution for the improvement of reference services. J. Inf., Inf. Technol. Org. 4, 17–38.

Roknuzzaman, M., Umemoto, K., 2009. How library professionals view knowledge management in libraries: a qualitative study. Libr. Manag. 30 (8/9), 643–656.

Roknuzzaman, M., Kanai, H., Umemoto, K., 2009. Integration of knowledge management process into digital library system: a theoretical perspective. Libr. Rev. 58 (5), 372–386.

Rowley, J., 2007. The wisdom hierarchy: representations of the DIKW hierarchy. J. Inf. Sci. 33 (2), 163–180.

Rus, I., Lindvall, M., 2002. Knowledge management in software engineering. IEEE Softw. 19 (3), 26–38.

Sanchez, R., 2001. Knowledge Management and Organizational Competence. Oxford University Press, New York.

Santosus, M., Surmacz, J., 2001. The ABCs of knowledge management. CIO Magazine.

Sarrafzadeh, M., 2005. The implications of knowledge management for the library and information professions. actKM Online J. Knowl. Manag. 2 (1), 92–102. Available from: www.actkm.org/actkmjournal_vol2iss1.php (accessed 05.04.12).

Sarrafzadeh, M., Martin, B., Hazeri, A., 2010. Knowledge management and its potential applicability for libraries. Libr. Manag. 31 (3), 198–212.

Schwarzwalder, R., 1999. Librarians as knowledge management agents. EContent 22 (4), 63–65.

Seonghee, K., 1999. The roles of knowledge professionals for knowledge management. Available from: http://www.ifla.org/IV/ifla65/papers/042-115e.htm (accessed 15.12.15).

Shanhong, T., 2000. Knowledge management in libraries in the twenty-first century. In: World Library and Information Congress: 66th IFLA Council and General Conference, 13–18 August 2000, Jerusalem.

Singh, S.P., 2007. What are we managing: knowledge or information? VINE J. Inf. Knowl. Manag. Syst. 37 (2), 169–179.

Singh, J., 2009. Leadership competencies for change management in libraries: challenges and opportunities. In: Keynotes Address at International Conference on Academic Libraries at University of Delhi, 5–8 October 2009. Available from: http://crl.du.ac.in/ical09/papers/index_files/ical-51_250_732_3_RV.pdf (accessed 16.11.15).

Sinotte, M., 2004. Exploration of the field of knowledge management for the library and information professional. Libri 54 (3), 190–198.

Stover, M., 2004. Making tacit knowledge explicit: the ready reference database as codified knowledge. Ref. Serv. Rev. 32 (2), 164–173.

Subramanian, N., 2007. Knowledge and information management in libraries: a new challenge for the library and information professionals in the digital environment. Available from: http://library.igcar.gov.in/readit2007/conpro/s1/S1_5.pdf (accessed 19.04.12).

Suresh, J.K., Mahesh, K., 2008. Managing the knowledge supply chain at Infosys. KM Rev. 11 (4), 14–19.

Teng, S., Hawamdeh, S., 2002. Knowledge management in public libraries. Aslib Proc. 54 (3), 188–197.

Thanuskodi, S., 2010. Knowledge management in academic libraries: an overview. In: Paper Presented at 6th International Conference on Webometrics, Informetrics and Scientometrics & Eleventh COLLNET Meeting, 19–22 October 2010. University of Mysore.

Townley, C.T., 2001. Knowledge management and academic libraries. Coll. Res. Libr. 62 (1), 44–55.

Tripathi, M., Kumar, S., 2010. Use of Web 2.0 tools in academic libraries: a reconnaissance of the international landscape. Int. Inf. Libr. Rev. 42, 195–207.

Tripathy, J.K., Patra, N.K., Pani, M.R., 2007. Leveraging knowledge management: challenges for the information professional. DESIDOC Bull. Inf. Technol. 27 (6), 65–73.

Ugwu, C.I., Ezema, I.J., 2010. Competencies for successful knowledge management applications in Nigerian academic libraries. Int. J. Libr. Inf. Sci. 2 (9), 184–189.

Vijayakumar, J.K., Vijayakumar, M., 2003. Brief communication knowledge, connections and communities: a special reference to Indian university libraries. Int. Inf. Libr. Rev. 35 (2–4), 375–382.

Wen, S., 2005. Implementing knowledge management in academic libraries: a pragmatic approach. In: 3rd China-US Library Conference, 22–25 March, Shanghai.

White, T., 2004. Knowledge management in an academic library: based on the case study KM within OULS. In: World Library and Information Congress: 70th IFLA General Conference and Council, 22–27 August, Buenos Aires.

Yang, Z., Bai, H., 2009. Building a maturity model for college library. In: International Conference on Test and Measurement, 5–6 December 2007, Hong Kong, pp. 1–4.

Yi, Z., 2006. Knowledge management for library strategic planning: perceptions of applications and benefits. Libr. Manag. 29 (3), 229–240.

CHAPTER 10

Information Technology and Knowledge Management

INTRODUCTION

There is an increasing recognition of the value of knowledge and information to individuals, organisations and communities. As knowledge has become a central productive and strategic asset, the success of all types of organisations is increasingly dependent on their ability to acquire, create, store, share and utilise knowledge. That is why developing procedures and routines to optimise the acquisition, creation, protection and sharing of knowledge and information in the organisations has become one of the most important activities. Knowledge management (KM) is viewed as 'the creation and subsequent management of an environment which encourages knowledge to be created, shared, learnt, enhanced, organised and utilised for the benefit of the organisation and its customers' (Abell and Oxbrow, 2001, p. 267). The overall objective of KM is to enable organisations to create value from their intellectual and knowledge-based assets, and thereby achieve organisational effectiveness (Dalkir, 2005). Creating value from such assets involves sharing and use of knowledge for solving problems. Knowledge sharing is used to transform individual knowledge into organisational knowledge (Foss et al., 2010) and is therefore recognised as one of the most important aspects of KM (Kebede, 2010). The success of KM initiatives in every organisation depends on creation, sharing and utilisation of knowledge (Gandhi, 2004), because effective transfer and use of knowledge within an organisation can reduce the chances of duplication of work, saves costs, improves innovation capacity, and therefore sustains competitive advantage, while lack of transfer and use can lead to information overload and confusion, as well as wasted manpower (Adamovic et al., 2012; Clarke, 2004).

KM has been heavily influenced by the growth and application of information and communication technologies (ICT). ICT provides organisations with a wide range of tools to support their employees in organising, searching and sharing knowledge. ICT can be used to support KM activities by allowing people to search for and identify people with expertise that they are looking for. This can be done by creating databases of expertise, searchable web portals or electronic yellow pages.

Academic libraries have been established to support teaching, learning, research activities and development of a culture of sharing and imparting knowledge to fulfil the mission and objectives of their parent institutions. Academic libraries also play a pivotal role in ensuring the success of higher degrees of research. Important activities of academic libraries include collection development, reference services, document delivery, access to organised collections held by the library and assisting users in information search and retrieval (Cholin, 2005; Malhan, 2006). With the recent developments in ICT, especially the Internet and the World Wide Web, academic libraries are expected to initiate the next level of much desired services, that is, just-in-time delivery of the most appropriate and high-quality information at a place where it is desired using state-of-the art ICT-based tools. The advantages offered by ICT have led most academic libraries to provide ICT-based information services to meet the needs of their users (Badar, 2008; Woodward, 2009). The ICT approach has been used in academic libraries to deliver numerous applications such as local/wide area network applications, online information services, online journals and databases, library databases, online access catalogues, automated circulation facilities and digital online archives (Ghuloum and Ahmed, 2011).

Recent advances in ICT have not only increased tremendously the ability to access, store and process information within an academic library, but also have brought significant changes to the concept, organisation, functioning and management of library and information systems and services. In most academic libraries in developed countries, online public access catalogues (OPACs) have largely replaced card catalogues, offering enhanced search capabilities for accessing local collections; they often include the holdings of other area or regional libraries as well. Many libraries are also providing a web interface to their library and information system, often including direct links to electronic journals, books and Internet resources (Mohsenzadeh and Isfandyari-Moghaddam, 2009). ICT can support KM in academic libraries in two ways: by providing the means to acquire, organise, store, retrieve and disseminate information (Sabashini et al., 2012); and by connecting library users with librarians and library services through the use of web-based tools to communicate with library users and share information and knowledge (Jain, 2007; Yuan et al., 2013).

The most common applications of ICT-based KM tools include:

- *communication tools* such as e-mail, instance messaging, telephones, teleconferencing, intranets and video-conferencing;
- *long-standing tools* such as databases and institutional archives;
- *social media tools* such as wikis, blogs, online communities and social networking sites (SNSs).

KM systems are (generally information technology (IT)-based) systems for managing knowledge in organisations, supporting the creation, capture, storage and dissemination of information (Rah et al., 2010). They are designed to facilitate the implementation of KM instruments in support of knowledge processes with the aim of increasing organisational effectiveness. Among existing technologies that are being incorporated into IT-based KM solutions are: expert systems, intelligent agents, decision-support systems, natural language processing, information retrieval, electronic document management, knowledge warehousing, KM software, learning-management platforms, learning-management systems and learning-management portals (Brogan et al., 2001).

A KM system can be any of the following:

- *Document based.* Any technology that permits creation/management/sharing of formatted documents such as Lotus Notes, web, distributed databases, etc.
- *Ontology/taxonomy based.* These are similar to document technologies in the sense that a system of terminologies (ie, ontology) is used to summarise the document, for example, author, subject, organisation, etc., as in DHTML and other XML-based ontologies.
- *Based on artificial intelligence technologies.* These are used as a customised representation scheme to represent the problem domain.
- *Integrated digital library systems.* These consist of digital resources, technological infrastructure, experience and expertise, digital library services and a KM process.
- *Web-based KM systems.* These support the creation, organisation, storage, dissemination and utilisation of the institution's digital knowledge assets.

ICT-BASED KM SYSTEMS

ICT-based KM systems include web-based applications (blogs, wikis, Really Simple Syndication (RSS)), Instant Messaging (IM), social networking applications (Facebook, MySpace, etc.), social media applications (YouTube, Flickr, etc.), social bookmarking (Delicious, LibraryThing) and web discovery services (WDS). They are being used by libraries and librarians all over the world to promote information services, share information, interact and communicate with users and colleagues. ICT-based KM systems are being used to deliver online library services to users wherever they desire. This chapter outlines how library professionals working in libraries of higher education institutions integrate these systems into their traditional library services.

Web-Based Applications

Web-based applications or services refer to dynamic tools that include blogs, wikis, RSS feeds and IM. With the great popularity and use of these tools, all types of libraries have explored them as a method of communication to promote their library collections and services to potential users. This new method of providing library services, according to Dickson and Holley (2010), is referred to as library 2.0.

Really Simple Syndication

RSS, also known as Rich Site Summary, is designed to feed users with regularly changing web content of news-like sites, news-oriented community sites, and even personal weblogs without requiring the users to visit multiple sites to receive these updates (Stephens, 2006). RSS allows library users to subscribe to the library's content, so they can be automatically informed whenever a library adds new information to any section of the website. A university library may apply this technology to provide updates to library users on new items in a collection, services provided and content in subscription databases (Maness, 2006). RSS in a university library may also be used as a form of advertisement to push library information to users who would not otherwise utilise the resources provided by libraries. This service enables users to reduce any unnecessary steps it takes to access the relevant databases. Cornell University offers MyUpdates, which is a tool to help scholars stay informed of new resources provided by the library (Kim and Abbas, 2010). The library of the University of Southampton provides news feed on RSS to inform users about activities and events held in the university (Tripathi and Kumar, 2010).

Blogs

Blogs offer another social platform for libraries to reach university students with new services. A blog is a type of web page, usually maintained by an individual, that contains regular entries of commentary, descriptions of events or other materials such as videos (Tripathi and Kumar, 2010; Wikipedia, 2014a). Blogs have several potential uses in university libraries. Blogs encourage user interaction through their comment feature, which allows students to provide feedback regarding information services. In one form, librarians can post news about the library as well as events occurring at the library. Blogs are also used to create subject guides, as they can be easily updated to reflect the most current sources for a particular class or department. Tripathi and Kumar (2010) suggest that academic libraries use blogs to communicate with staff and users; to facilitate academic debate; to post hourly changes, events, new resources lists, deadlines, etc.; to teach basic search tips; and to provide links to the library websites. Michigan State University Libraries exemplify a more interactive use of blogs, where librarians regularly respond to comments by its followers, even if the goal is only to market their services to students and not answer reference questions (Dickson and Holley, 2010).

Wikis

A wiki is defined as 'a collection of web pages which allows users to add and edit content collectively' (University of Southampton, 2014). Wikis have great potential to leverage knowledge creation and sharing in the library context. According to Kim and Abbas (2010), wikis may be used in an academic library for knowledge sharing, collaborative authoring and online discussion. Although an initial survey on the use of wikis shows that academic libraries make little use of this function (Long, 2006), the overall use of this functionality in academic libraries has increased during the last few years, as reported in the findings of a recent study. Bejune (2007) observed that academic libraries mostly use wikis for collaboration between libraries. However, wikis are also used to leverage knowledge creation and sharing in a library. For example, the Ohio University Library created a Biz Wiki of business information resources for students where library users as well as librarians are allowed to create and edit content (Kim and Abbas, 2010). This Biz Wiki research portal includes embedded catalogue records for books, instructional videos by the liaison librarian and links to the liaison librarian's Facebook and Twitter accounts, which has enhanced collaboration between librarians and users, as well as diversified its uses (Chu Kai-Wah, 2009). Another example of collaboration among users is Columbia University Library, which initiated student-developed projects on social justice movements using a wiki. This project aims to encourage students to discover knowledge on social movements and share it with the community (Kim and Abbas, 2010).

Instant Messaging

IM is defined as 'a synchronous communication technology that allows users to send real-time messages to other users' (Chua et al., 2008). The most striking feature of IM is the communication that takes place between users in real time. IM may be used in academic libraries to provide chat-reference services so that users can ask questions and receive responses directly from librarians during specified contact times. Foley (2002) considers IM as an alternative for librarians seeking to reshape the delivery of reference services. Using IM, it is possible for libraries to reach remote users across campuses and around the world as physical boundaries do not stand in the way of communication. Most academic libraries offer some form of digital reference service through e-mail or web formats. Now many libraries are moving towards an almost-immediate form of virtual reference through IM. For example, Texas Christian University's Mary Couts Burnett Library started an IM reference service, allowing faculty, staff, students and guests to send questions and receive replies using six different IM protocols, including the MeeboMe widget. The MeeboMe widget is an IM box on the library's web pages that users type questions into without the need of special software or messenger accounts, and has proven to be a very popular part of the new reference service (Texas Christian University, 2014).

Social Media

The concept of social media is defined as 'a collection of internet websites, services and practices that support collaboration, community building, participation and sharing' (Reynol et al., 2011). In the last few years, social media websites have appeared to encourage users to share multimedia objects from photographs to videos. As part of Web 2.0 applications, social media tools range from networking platforms such as Facebook to video-sharing sites such as YouTube (Stoeckel and Sinkinson, 2013). Most social media tools allow users to create individual profiles where team-based and collaborative learning are possible through sharing of content. The findings of a study on the use of social media in faculties across the United States conducted by Pearson Learning Solutions and the Babson Survey Research Group show that two-thirds of the 2000 faculties surveyed use social media in class contexts (Mike et al., 2011). The use of social media in academic libraries is widespread in terms of marketing and broadcasting. Libraries commonly use Facebook fan pages, Twitter accounts, YouTube channels or blogs to distribute news about events, services or resources; to alert users about new additions to collections; and to provide links to articles, videos and other web content that might be relevant for users. Libraries have also actively used these mechanisms to foster relationships with users by allowing them to ask questions and providing feedback about library services (American Library Association, 2014). Librarians can also post videos of library tours as well as bibliographic instruction for students, as described by the librarian at the University of South Florida who created a video for students demonstrating how to use a database (Ariew, 2008).

Social Bookmarking/Cataloguing

Social bookmarking is a form of link management that allows 'users to collect and label information resources for both their own use and for sharing with other users' (Gilmour and Strickland, 2009). In simple terms, the process of describing public documents and web page content by assigning keywords (tags) is called social bookmarking/cataloguing. Delicious is one of the most popular social bookmarking websites. By collecting, analysing and describing web content, social bookmarking websites generate valuable metadata about public documents and resources available over the Internet. Dickson and Holley (2010) suggested that librarians could use social bookmarking to create resource lists for different departments and classes that can be viewed by students. Social bookmarking is also used to create class reading lists and bibliographies by tagging the resources with the department and class number (Kroski, 2007). A link to Delicious can also be added to the library catalogue for assigning the tags from its Delicious account to the library catalogue in order to create access points for materials that are not adequately described by the existing Library of Congress Subject Headings (Dickson and Holley, 2010).

Social bookmarking is also used to enhance the features of library catalogues. LibraryThing, 'a social cataloguing application for book catalogue and various types of metadata' (Wikipedia, 2014b), offers libraries a solution for the enhancement of the features of their catalogues by incorporating user-generated book reviews and recommendations, and providing a customisable mobile application called Library Anywhere (MacManus, 2012). LibraryThing was created by Tim Spalding in Portland in 2005. As of October 2014 it had more than 1,800,000 users and more than 95 million books catalogued (http://www.librarything.com). The key feature of LibraryThing is the cataloguing of books by importing data from libraries through Z39.50 connections and from six Amazon.com stores. Library sources supply MARC and Dublin Core records to LibraryThing and users can import catalogue records from 700 libraries, including the Library of Congress, the National Library of Australia, the British Library, the Canadian National Catalogue and Yale University Library. For a nominal fee, LibraryThing allows member libraries to use its collective wisdom in local library catalogues. Libraries can also use LibraryThing tags to generate links between related books on their own collections by incorporating LibraryThing widgets into their OPACs (Wenzler, 2007).

Web Discovery Services

The term 'web discovery' emerged from a seminar entitled 'Returning the researcher to the library, defining web-scale discovery: the promise of a unified search index for libraries', sponsored by Serials Solutions and the *Library Journal* (Infomotions Inc., 2009). Resource discovery service (RDS) may be defined as a preharvested central index coupled with a richly featured discovery layer that provides a single search interface across a library's local content, open access and licenced databases. In simple terms, RDS eliminates the need to search a library's local and remote (open access and subscription) content separately. RDS, with the help of its preharvested index, gathers data from multiple sources and processes into the central index and provides a quick search of a vast range of local and remote content with relevancy ranked results. Several commercial web discovery products have recently appeared on the market. Encore from Innovative Interfaces, Primo Central from Ex Libris, Summon from Serials Solutions, EBSCO Discovery Service from EBSCO and WorldCat Local from the online computer library center (OCLC) are some of the resource discovery products used in libraries the world over.

Many studies have been published in recent years that examine the impact of RDS on usage of online databases and journals. O'Hara (2012) examines the impact of the implementation of WDS at the University of Manitoba by studying 3 years' usage statistics of journals and found an increase in full-text journal requests. Lam and Sum (2013) also noted an increase in access to full-text content at the Open University of Hong Kong by comparing the usage of a range of databases, journals and e-books during the 12-month period before and after the implementation of RDS. However, they were uncertain whether this was due to the implementation of the RDS. Preliminary findings of a large-scale comparative study of RDS on online journal usage in the United Kingdom indicate a mixed picture of usage, where some libraries experienced increased usage while other saw a decrease (Levine-Clark et al., 2013).

USE OF ICT-BASED KM SYSTEMS IN LIBRARIES

ICT-based tools and applications are widely used in libraries to facilitate networking and resource sharing, eliminate duplication of efforts, improve the speed of operations, increase access to information resources and improve the quality of information services (Peyala, 2011). Use of ICT applications can also assist libraries in creating, storing, transferring and using tacit and explicit knowledge. Libraries can use numerous ICT-based tools including integrated library management systems, competency databases, decision-support systems, online retrieval and search systems, expert networks, e-mail, groupware, teleconferencing, intranets, the World Wide Web, document management systems, video-conferencing, metadata and data mining (Okumus, 2012; Peyala, 2011; Rah et al., 2010; Shanhong, 2000).

Mohsenzadeh and Isfandyari-Moghaddam (2009) performed a study to define the status of the application of ICT in academic libraries in Kerman, Iran. The results showed that the level of application of ICT in Kerman academic libraries was acceptable, but efforts should be made to improve their status to match the ever-increasing demand for better library services at universities. The most important problem and a serious difficulty was lack of educated librarians, which requires suitable investment and planning. Ramzan and Singh (2009) investigated the levels of ICT application in academic libraries across Pakistan and found a lack of ICT infrastructure, especially the absence of computers, e-mail and the Internet. It was revealed that the respondent libraries needed to be fully automated using standard library software. However, access to online resources was found to be extensive and comprehensive.

Parirokh et al. (2008), on the basis of a survey in the United States, report how sharing of knowledge through the use of ICT among librarians can improve organisational learning in academic libraries. The findings of the study show that almost all libraries use e-mail and library websites as part of their communication system. Intranets and telephone lines have also been used by most libraries. However, the traditional face-to-face communication method is also widely used. Virtual reference desks and user mailing lists, which are relatively new developments, had been used by about half of the participating libraries, and probably await a wider acceptance in the future.

Gandhi (2004) describes the value of capturing the tacit knowledge of reference librarians and explains the early efforts of reference librarians to capture tacit knowledge through old information tools like card files of frequently asked questions (FAQs). However, with the recent developments in ICT, these practices have been replaced by the use of common knowledge databases (CKDBs) (Jantz, 2001), web-based ready-reference databases (RRDs) (Stover, 2004) and knowledge banks (Branin, 2003). Both Jantz (2001) and Stover (2004) described the introduction of a new tool that has been developed by a team of reference librarians. Jantz (2001) examined how reference librarians could become more effective with the use of ICT tools and shared his experience of the development and use of CKDB within the New Brunswick Campus Libraries of Rutgers University. Stover (2004) described the development of a web-based RRD for reference services at San Diego State University to capture and reuse the tacit and informal knowledge of reference librarians.

Some scholars suggest creating and maintaining a digital library or institutional repository as a tool for storing, retrieving and sharing all the intellectual assets of a university in a range of formats, including those that are unpublished, unstructured and unique (Ayanbode, 2011; Branin, 2003; Kao and Wu, 2012; Rah et al., 2010; Robertson and Sullivan, 2000). This is because technology in digital libraries is an enabler in the modern information supply chain (Abell, 2000; Jain, 2007; Singh, 2007) and librarians must be skilled at the technical aspects of the job.

Based on a review of the literature, Bem and Coelho (2013) identified the trends and applications of modern ICT-based tools in libraries and found that libraries often developed ICT-based applications (especially regarding the sharing of knowledge through Web 2.0 features). Modern ICT-based tools, such as blogs, wikis, shared classification systems (tagging), social networks, etc., are mostly used in libraries. Xu et al. (2009) investigated the use of Web 2.0 functionalities in academic libraries by visiting 81 academic library websites in New York. The findings reveal that 42% of libraries adopted one or more Web 2.0 functionalities such as blogs, while the implementation of these in individual libraries varies greatly. They have also proposed a conceptual model of Academic Library 2.0 in their report. Redden (2010) explored the potential utilisation of social bookmarking websites by academic libraries. He argues that these websites allow users and organisations to create accounts for bookmarking online content to facilitate academic libraries in collaboration and networking, organisation and sharing of electronic resources, and teaching information literacy. Mphidi and Snyman (2004) focused on the utilisation of intranets in academic libraries, especially in South Africa. The purpose of the study was to report the extent to which academic libraries in South Africa are utilising these intranets. The study found that there was a strong awareness of the importance of ICT as knowledge-sharing tool. Though the content and use of intranets varies from library to library, it was observed from the findings that academic libraries did not utilise the full potential of intranets. Based on a questionnaire survey of 20 library directors working in the academic libraries of the eastern United States, Kim and Abbas (2010) investigated the use of Web 2.0 tools in academic libraries. Based on 230 randomly selected academic library websites and 184 users, they investigated the adoption of Web 2.0/Library 2.0 functionalities by academic libraries and their users. It was found that RSS and blogs have been widely adopted by academic libraries, while the bookmark function was rarely used by users.

USE OF ICT-BASED KM SYSTEMS: A CASE STUDY OF INDIAN ACADEMIC LIBRARIES[1]

Over the past two decades, academic libraries in India have witnessed the impact of ICT on the structure of their services. Academic libraries in India are at various stages of development regarding the applications of ICT in their day-to-day activities. Many academic libraries in India are already using computers and advanced telecommunication systems, and many more are currently implementing such systems. Libraries in India have explored ICT for computerising a wide range of administrative and technical processes, building databases, developing networks and providing innovative and intelligent information services. The widespread use of ICT in libraries has created a profound impact on library operations, information resources, information services and staff competencies, and expectations of users (Peyala, 2011). Recently, some academic libraries have also started to use Internet and Web 2.0 functionalities to communicate with users and to share knowledge within or outside libraries. Increasingly, libraries around the world are using blogs, wikis, RSS, social media and other web applications for knowledge-sharing purposes (Bejune, 2007; Chu Kai-Wah, 2009; Dickson and Holley, 2010; Kim and Abbas, 2010; Tripathi and Kumar, 2010). These tools are being used to improve the exchange and flow of information in libraries (Nelson, 2008), and meeting information needs by being useful for knowledge sharing between librarians and library users and communication with library users (Mavodza and Ngulube, 2011). However, there is uncertainty about whether and to what extent these ICT tools are being used in Indian academic libraries. Accordingly, the present study is

[1]This section of the chapter is based on an article by Husain and Nazim (2015).

an attempt to examine the use of different ICT-based KM tools in Indian academic libraries at various levels.

Studies on the use of ICT in India indicate that computerisation of library systems and services in India started in the mid-1970s. However, this trend has accelerated during the past two decades, especially in institutions of higher education, due to the increased number of students, greater demand for the use of library material within and outside the library, the increasing amount of materials being published and the development of new and cheaper computers. Over the past three decades, libraries in India have witnessed an impact of ICT on the structure and functioning of services. Many libraries in India are already using ICT and advanced communication systems, and many more are currently in the process of implementing such systems. The Information Library Network Centre, an interuniversity centre of the University Grants Commission, has been supporting, funding and providing the necessary assistance to university libraries as regards automation and networking for the past several years.

Kumar (1987) was the first to survey the status of ICT applications in university libraries in India and found that Delhi University Library conducted stocktaking using computers in 1970, Andhra University Library produced a list of new additions in the 1970s, SNDT University Library obtained computers in 1985, and Marathwada University Library acquired minicomputers for library operations in 1985. Raman and Rao (2003) made a useful study on the use of ICT in central university libraries in India. Their survey provided a useful summary of the current state of the art of ICT in libraries in India. The survey confirmed that ICT has become deeply embedded in the management of information in university libraries. It has become a powerful tool in the handling of routine library operations and services. The analysis shows that the use of ICT in libraries is increasing steadily and significantly, and university libraries have developed an infrastructure for the use of ICT for housekeeping operations and online services for users. Moreover, the study revealed an awareness of current developments concerned with end-users. Vyas (2003) conducted a survey of 12 university libraries in Rajasthan and Indian Institutes of Technology, and found that most of these libraries have implemented ICT in their in-house activities and services, to automate and digitise resources and to share resources at local and national levels.

Haneefa (2007) carried out a study to examine the application of ICT in special libraries in Kerala, India. The results indicate that library automation in special libraries in Kerala largely commenced during 1990–2000.

Computerized documentation system-integrated set for information system (CDS-ISIS) was used more in libraries than any other software. The library catalogue was found to be the most popular area for automation. Most of these libraries were hampered by lack of funds, lack of infrastructure and lack of skilled professionals to embark on automation of all library management activities and applications of ICT. Raza and Nath (2007) measured the use of ICT in the university libraries of Punjab, Himachal Pradesh and Chandigarh (India), with an ulterior objective to establish some co-relation between quality in libraries and the use of ICT. They have also highlighted the access of networks, information services and barriers in ICT applications. Ultimately, it was emphasised that although quality depends on merging print culture with digital culture, the results confirm that print culture is still dominant in university libraries in this region. The central library of Jammu was the first university library in India to implement modern ICT, including radio-frequency identification (RFID) technology (Malhan, 2006). Tiwari and Sahoo (2013) conducted a survey of the university libraries of Rajasthan to explore the availability of ICT infrastructure, applications of ICT in housekeeping operations and user services, requirements of training and problems encountered during the implementation of ICT. The findings revealed that ICT activities are in the development stage in the university libraries of Rajasthan. The lack of basic management and proper planning and frequent changes in ICT are the basic hurdles to overcome for successful implementation and development of ICT.

Madhusudhan and Nagabhushanam (2013) examined how some university libraries in India provide web access to their collections and user support for that access, and the problems faced by users in accessing web-based library services. The findings show that a few surveyed university libraries offer innovative web-based library services in different sections and many are yet to exploit the full potential of the web forms, and are lagging behind in the effective use of a library website. Preedip and Kumar (2011) found that web information services are not widespread and have yet to take off widely in academic libraries in India; the diffusion rate of Web 2.0 information services is relatively low. Tyagi (2012) observed that a large number of respondents had knowledge about Web 2.0 tools and were more inclined to adopt the Web 2.0 technologies in their personal lives. However, libraries are lagging behind in using social networking technologies. Bhardwaj (2014) investigated how library and information science (LIS) professionals working in higher education institutions in India integrate SNS into their routine work. The findings revealed that information professionals use SNS to socialise, keep themselves up to date, find jobs and acquire information about conferences and seminars in their respective fields.

Need and Objectives of Study

Academic libraries contribute to educational and research activities in many ways through exploiting ICT and electronic information resources, such as e-books, online journals/databases and web-based information services. Over the years, several ICT-based applications and services have evolved which are being used in libraries to support the process of knowledge capture, storing and sharing. Modern ICT-based tools such as the Internet, Web 2.0 and social media are increasingly used in libraries as information-sharing tools. They are also used in libraries to connect library users with libraries and to establish relationships between librarians and library users. Many studies have been done in developed countries to investigate the impact of these ICT-based tools on libraries and library services, but no research has been conducted on the use of different types of ICT-based tools in academic libraries in India. According to Haneefa (2007), libraries procure expensive ICT equipment, but this may not be utilised in an optimal way. This is a major concern for libraries around the world. There may be several reasons for this state of affairs, such as a lack of qualified and trained library staff. In view of these facts, an attempt has been made to study the use of ICT-based tools and services in academic libraries in India.

The purpose of the study was to examine the use of different ICT-based tools in Indian academic libraries. However, the more specific objectives of the study are to

- explore the implementation of ICT in housekeeping operations and services;
- identify the use of different ICT-based tools for knowledge sharing; and
- to examine the librarians' perceived challenges of ICT application.

Methodology

We conducted a survey of academic libraries in India to address these objectives. The survey method defined by Powell and Connaway (2004) was used as a research strategy that encompasses any measurement procedures that involve asking questions from the respondents concerning the current status of the subject under study. The survey method helps to collect primary data to describe a population too large to observe directly. Academic institutions and their libraries in India are too numerous to consider in total as a sample for any research. Therefore only the libraries of the central universities were included in this study, keeping in mind that these are funded by the central government of India and may have advanced library infrastructure and facilities. Of the total of 42 central universities in India, 12 have been established since 2009 and are in the process of developing an infrastructure, academic programmes and libraries. Therefore 30 central universities, established before 2009, were selected on the basis of collections, infrastructure and services at various locations within India. A purposive sampling method was used to explore the use of different ICT-based tools in academic libraries in India. The university librarians of these universities were selected as respondents. However, in the absence of the university librarian, any official up to the level of assistant librarian was allowed to participate in the survey.

A questionnaire that included closed-ended questions was used as the data collection instrument. The questions in the questionnaire were grouped into five sections. The first section aimed at gaining basic information such as the name of the library, year of establishment, total collections, number of sanctioned posts and number of staff currently working, etc. The second section explored the implementation of ICT in various library operations and services. The third section was to examine the use of ICT-based interactive tools used for sharing knowledge in the respondents' library. The fourth section aimed to find the requirements of training for library staff in handling ICT-based systems. The fifth section examined the barriers related to the use of ICT-based applications.

A total of 30 questionnaires were delivered by post. Two months after sending the questionnaires, 12 completed questionnaires were received. After that, the first follow-up letter was sent as a reminder to the librarians who were yet to return the questionnaires. Then three more duly filled questionnaires were received. A second follow-up letter was sent as a reminder to the librarians who had not yet returned the questionnaires. But there were no more responses. The number of returned questionnaires was 15, with a response rate of 50%. The libraries that participated in the study were from nine different states of the country: four from Uttar Pradesh, four from Delhi, and one each from Andhra Pradesh, West Bengal, Kerala, Chhattisgarh, Manipur, Mizoram and Meghalaya. These libraries were spread over an area of 4000 km and represented an extended community of users. They are very different libraries in terms of staff and users. As there was not a large amount of data, data analysis was done by a simple frequency count and is presented in tables. The details of libraries participating in the study are shown in Table 10.1. Column A denotes the serial number. Column B identifies the name of the university. Column C provides the year each

Table 10.1 Profile of the participating libraries

A	B	C		D	E	
Serial no.	Name of the university library	Year of establishment University	Library	Total collection	Library staff NPS[a]	NSW[b]
1	Aligarh Muslim University (AMU), Aligarh	1920	1960	1,186,139	121	100
2	Allahabad University (ALU), Allahabad	1837	1913	653,164	88	44
3	Babasaheb Bhimrao Ambedkar University (BBAU), Lucknow	1996	1996	13,000	9	7
4	Banaras Hindu University (BHU), Varanasi	1916	1917	1,061,378	159	122
5	Guru Ghasidas University (GGS),	1983	1984	110,000	22	19
6	Indira Gandhi National Open University (IGNOU), New Delhi	1985	1986	130,000	17	17
7	Jamia Millia Islamia University (JMIU), New Delhi	1920	1920	340,000	59	50
8	Jawaharlal Nehru University (JNU), New Delhi	1968	1969	560,000	99	78
9	Manipur University (MPU), Imphal	1980	1980	160,000	25	18
10	Maulana Azad National Urdu University (MANUU), Hyderabad	1998	1998	32,498	22	22
11	Mizoram University (MU), Mizoram	2001	2001	87,431	26	20
12	North Eastern Hill University (NEHU), Shillong	1973	1973	250,000	73	63
13	Pondicherry University (PU), Pondicherry	1985	1986	251,000	53	36
14	University of Delhi (UOD), Delhi	1922	1922	1,475,729	416	126
15	Visva Bharati (VB), Shanti Niketan, West Bengal	1921	1925	376,511	42	28
	Total				1122	700

[a] Number of posts sanctioned.
[b] Number of staff working.

university and its library were established. Column D provides an indication of the relative size of each library based on total collections. Column E indicates the total number of sanctioned posts and the number of staff currently working in the participating libraries.

This research is limited as regards to the generalisation of the findings. Although the intention of researchers was to cover different types of academic libraries in India, the investigation succeeded mainly in obtaining responses from the librarians of the central universities due to time and financial constraints. Thus the results of this study are not representative of all types of academic libraries and therefore cannot be generalised to other libraries. Moreover, despite the questionnaires being distributed to 30 librarians, the sample size is still relatively small. Thus both the quantity and variety of responses may be too small in some instances for meaningful comparisons and conclusions.

Results

Library Collection

Library collection forms a sound foundation for efficient services. The details of the total collections of the responded libraries are presented in Table 10.1. As may be observed from Table 10.1, Delhi University Library System (DULS) has the largest collection with more than 1.47 million books, including back volumes of periodicals, followed by Aligarh Muslim University (AMU) with about 1.18 million and Banaras Hindu University (BHU) with over 1.06 million. On the other hand, Babasaheb Bhimrao Ambedkar University and Mizoram University have the smallest collections of books and other reading materials (0.01 and 0.08 million respectively).

Library Staff

Human resources play a prominent role in the successful management of any library. The details of human resources available in academic libraries are presented in Table 10.1. The table, as per the study, demonstrates that there are 1122 sanctioned posts in 15 academic libraries (15 central university libraries). It is surprising to note that of the 1122 sanctioned posts, 422 posts were vacant and 700 staff members were currently working in these libraries. Of the 15 libraries, DULS has the largest number of sanctioned posts and staff presently working (416 sanctioned, 126 working), followed by BHU (159 sanctioned, 122 working) and AMU (121 sanctioned, 100 working).

Computerised Library Operations and Services

The availability of ICT or software in a library alone is not sufficient unless these technologies or systems are put to use solving problems in the working environment. The respondents were asked to indicate the functions and services of their library which are based on ICT applications. To obtain a benchmark on the progress of implementing integrated library management systems for housekeeping operations, the survey offered a list of functions and asked the respondents to mark the computerised operations in their libraries. Although the question asked for a list of operations currently in use, responses appear to include planned and current operations. As Table 10.2 shows, automation of library catalogues has been implemented in almost all libraries, followed by circulation systems (85%), serial control (85%) and acquisitions and budget (75%). Other applications were management information (45%) and RFID (20%). Three libraries indicated that RFID systems for theft control in their libraries are in development. The data analysis reveals that the majority of libraries surveyed have various operations automated.

Further, respondents were asked to indicate the use of ICT-based services provided by the libraries to their users. As shown in Table 10.3, 80% of libraries provide access to in-house-developed library databases, 75% provide access to electronic resources (e-books, e-journals, e-databases, etc.) and 55% provide web-based reference or other information services. However, as shown in Table 10.3, other technology-based services such as online tutorials (40%), subject gateways/web portals (35%), automatic (electronic) mailing alert systems (10%) and FAQ databases (15%) are among the least used ICT-based methods for sharing knowledge between librarians and users. It seems that participating libraries have not used ICT effectively for this activity.

Table 10.2 Automated library functions/activities

Serial no.	Library functions/activities	Yes (%)	No (%)
1	Acquisitions and budget	15 (75%)	5 (25%)
2	Circulation	17 (85%)	3 (15%)
3	Serial control	17 (85%)	3 (85%)
4	Library catalogues (OPAC)	20 (100%)	0 (0%)
5	Management information	9 (45%)	11 (55%)
6	Security system (RFID, etc.)	4 (20%)	16 (80%0

Table 10.3 ICT-based information services

Serial no.	Services	Frequency	%
1	Access to in-house developed library databases/ OPACs/web OPACs	16	80.0
2	Online tutorials on how to use information resources/services	8	40.0
3	Access to electronic resources (e-books, e-journals, e-databases, etc.)	15	75.0
4	Access to open-access information sources through in-house-developed subject gateways/web portals	7	35.0
5	Web-based reference or other information services	11	55.0
6	FAQ database	3	15.0
7	Automatic (electronic) mailing alert system	2	10.0

Table 10.4 ICT-based tools for sharing knowledge

Serial no.	ICT-based KM tools	Frequency	%
1	E-mail	20	100
2	Phone calls/teleconferencing	20	100
3	Intranets	16	10
4	Video-conferencing	3	15
5	Data mining/resource discovery tools	4	20
6	Institutional repositories/digital libraries	13	65
7	Wikis	7	35
8	RSS	6	30
9	Blogs	2	10
10	Social networking sites	5	25
11	Bookmarking	2	10

Use of ICT-Based Tools for Communication and Knowledge Sharing in Academic Libraries

Various ICT-based tools that are currently used by librarians for communication with their staff, library users or other libraries are shown in Table 10.4.These technologies correspond to the communication channels, repositories, databases and the new generation of interactive social media that enable a pair of roles to collaborate in performing their collaborative tasks. As shown in Table 10.4, almost all libraries use e-mail and telephone calls as part of their communication system. However, video-conferencing, which is an effective interactive communication method, has been used by some of the participating libraries (15%). Intranets (80%) and institutional repositories/digital libraries (65%) have also been used by the majority of libraries. However, resource discovery tools, which are relatively new techniques for searching massive metadata for easier navigation and retrieval, are used by some libraries (20%).

With the emergence of Web 2.0 and social media tools, the relationship between a library and its users has changed dramatically. These tools may be used by libraries to personalise outreach services. The application of these technologies may help libraries offer their resources and services to users in a proactive manner. With the use of these tools, users can also participate in activities that were once the sole purview of the library, such as cataloguing via folksonomy or providing comments on books via blogging (Casey and Savastinuk, 2006). The use of blogs, wikis, RSS feeds, social networking and social bookmarking in academic libraries in India is uncommon, as indicated by the respondents (Table 10.4).

Availability of Trained Staff for Handling ICT-Based Systems and Services in Libraries

As examined in an earlier study by Nazim and Mukherjee (2013), ICT is perceived as the most required competency among LIS professionals for involvement in KM practice. Therefore respondents in the present study were asked to indicate whether staff in their libraries were adequately trained or require training in various ICT-based applications. The results are presented in Table 10.5. It may be observed from the table that all the respondents indicated that trained staff are not available in their libraries for handling ICT-based systems and services, and that they required training. Areas where respondents indicated a requirement for training were computer programming (80%), website or portal development (75%), hardware maintenance (65%), metadata or e-resource management and content management (50%). Database creation and management is the only area where the majority of respondents indicated that trained staff are available. However, 35% of respondents indicated that training is needed in this area too.

Table 10.5 Need for training in ICT-based information management systems

Serial no.	ICT-based information/knowledge management system	Need training (%)	Trained staff available (%)
1	Database creation and management	6 (30%)	14 (70%)
2	Content management	12 (60%)	8 (40%)
3	Metadata/e-resource management	13 (65%)	7 (35%)
4	Web/portal development	15 (75%)	5 (20%)
5	Hardware maintenance	14 (70%)	6 (30%)
6	Computer programming	17 (85%)	3 (15%)

Table 10.6 Barriers related to the use of ICT in academic libraries

Challenges in ICT application	Rank	%
Lack of trained staff in IT	1	85.0
Low levels of IT skills among library users	2	75.0
Lack of awareness of the potential benefits of IT	3	75.0
Lack of funding for IT	4	70.0
Inadequate IT infrastructure	5	55.0
Resistance of library staff to use IT	6	45.0
Lack of updated IT policy or strategy	7	35.0

Librarians' Perceived Challenges of ICT-Based Systems and Services

Table 10.6 indicates the ranked order of the number of constraints faced by librarians in the use of ICT-based systems and services. The highly ranked constraints were lack of trained staff in ICT, low levels of ICT skills among library users, lack of awareness of the potential benefits of ICT and inadequate ICT infrastructure. Similar constraints have been identified in earlier studies by Raman and Rao (2003) and Cholin (2005). Inadequate funding for ICT infrastructure development was identified as the major problem by these researchers. However, in the present study, it was ranked fifth by the respondents. This may be due to an overemphasis on the development of ICT infrastructure by universities during the past 10 years. The lowest ranked constraints were resistance of library staff to use ICT and lack of updated ICT policy and strategy.

MAJOR OUTCOMES

- The majority of the libraries of the central universities in India have implemented ICT in housekeeping operations such as library catalogues, circulation systems, serial control and acquisitions and budget. However, libraries lack ICT implementation in the areas of management information systems and RFID.
- ICT-based information services such as access to in-house-developed library databases, access to electronic resources (e-books, e-journals, e-databases, etc.), and web-based reference services are offered by the majority of the libraries of the central universities. However, other ICT-based services such as online tutorials, subject gateways/web portals, automatic (electronic) mailing alert systems, and FAQ databases are among the least used methods for delivery of information services to users.

- Among the communication tools, e-mail, telephone calls and intranets are being used as part of their communication system by most libraries. However, video-conferencing, which is an effective communication system, has been little used in libraries.
- The majority of academic libraries in India have either created an institutional repository or maintain a digital library for providing online access to a variety of information resources. However, resource discovery tools, which are used for searching and locating a library's local and remote content at a single search interface, have not gained momentum in Indian academic libraries.
- The use of social media tools such as blogs, wikis, RSS feeds, social networking and social bookmarking in academic libraries in India is also uncommon, as seen from the results of the present study.
- Almost all the respondents indicated a need for trained staff in various areas of ICT applications, including computer programming, website or portal development, hardware maintenance, metadata or e-resource management and content management.
- Lack of trained staff in ICT, low levels of ICT skills among library users, lack of awareness of the potential benefits of ICT and inadequate ICT infrastructure are observed to be the major constraints in the application of ICT in academic libraries in India.

SUMMARY

People are still using libraries, but the ways in which they are interacting with libraries is changing. While many library users are still visiting library buildings to borrow materials and use resources, there are a growing number of library users who prefer to use library services online on their personal devices. In order to successfully reach and interact with library users and provide library services online, librarians must be willing to adapt new and innovative technologies. The use of web-based tools and services such as blogs, wikis, RSS feeds, IM (online chat services), social media and social bookmarking combined with web discovery tools may help academic libraries to reach out to their users with next-generation library services. These technologies provide a new platform for reaching library users beyond the traditional library buildings and website by allowing students to access librarians and the library's resources and services without leaving the comfort of the websites they use the most. The ultimate goal of librarians is to make library resources available to library users. Some of the roles of librarians in a web environment include: understanding and articulating the nature of SNSs, creating web pages and content, establishing a friendly user interface over the network, creating online database management, evaluating and applying information, and assisting users with skill acquisition. But librarians need the training and skills to search and navigate the web, create social network space, teach and provide quality online library services.

It is important to mention here that libraries spend a huge amount of money on the subscription of print and online resources, but it is obvious that users are not aware of the availability of resources and services which are available in the library, as well as how to search for the required information with the available resources. A web discovery tool/service must be implemented by libraries to provide access to both libraries' local and remote content on a single search platform.

The findings of the study indicate that academic libraries in India have mostly been involved in applying ICT-based solutions for the management of various library functions and services, including computerisation of library catalogues, circulation systems, serial control, acquisitions and budget, access to in-house-developed library databases, access to electronic resources (e-books, e-journals, e-databases, etc.) and web-based reference services. Generally, most academic libraries in India are using ICT-based applications to organise and retrieve information. As the need for the delivery of information services within or outside a campus emerged, their involvement towards the development of intranets and institutional archives or digital libraries increased. Additionally, librarians are using traditional tools of knowledge transfer and sharing such as e-mail and teleconferencing. The reason for the extensive use of telephone calls may be due to the fact that these technologies have been available for decades and librarians are familiar with them. Use of these tools is often the employees' first and instinctive reaction when looking for help or advice. However, videoconferencing, which is an effective interactive communication method, was not used much in practice, probably due to lack of sufficient funding. Modern ICT-based tools of knowledge creation, identification and sharing like web discovery tools, blogs, wikis, RSS feeds, social networking and social bookmarking are being used very commonly by libraries in developed countries (Tripathi and Kumar, 2010). It may be observed from a review of the literature that LIS professionals in India are aware of Web 2.0 and SNS and are active on SNS to socialise and keep themselves up to date, find jobs and acquire information about conferences and seminars in their respective fields (Bhardwaj, 2014; Tyagi, 2012), but their involvement at institutional level for promoting library services and communication with users is rare, as seen from the findings of the present study.

Although there is an indication of the use of various ICT-based communication and knowledge-sharing tools (such as intranets and institutional repositories, content management, etc.), academic libraries in India are still in the early stages of the implementation of these technologies. Some of the roles of librarians in an ICT environment include understanding and articulating the nature of social media, creating websites or blogs, establishing a friendly user interface over the network, and content management. Most academic libraries in India are struggling to incorporate modern ICT-based tools, resources and services due to inadequate skills and expertise of library staff. There is a need for the authorities to recruit multiskilled library staff familiar with the implementation of ICT-based tools, resources and services. As the development of ICT infrastructure depends on the availability of funds, lack of ICT infrastructure and lack of funds were identified as the major challenges of implementing ICT-based resources and services in an earlier study of academic libraries in Kerala (India) by Haneefa (2007). But during the past 10 years, libraries, particularly central university libraries in India, have received sufficient funds and assistance for the development of ICT infrastructure. That is why, although a lack of funding and lack of ICT infrastructure were still perceived as barriers to ICT use by the majority of the respondents, they have ranked them fourth and fifth respectively in the order of priority (Table 10.6).

It may be concluded that the level of application of ICT in Indian academic libraries is acceptable, but they should improve their status to match the ever-increasing demand for better library and information services by utilising the full potential of their knowledge resources. Academic libraries should renovate their existing library environments and develop knowledge and skills among their staff in the fields of computer programming, website or portal development, hardware maintenance, and metadata or e-resource management for handling ICT-based information systems and providing quality information services to their respected user community. They also need to develop skills of searching and navigating the web, creating social network space, teaching and providing quality online library services.

The posts which are lying vacant should be filled on an urgent basis. Librarians must recruit adequately trained staff to work with modern ICT-based information systems. It is essential for academic libraries to initiate training programmes in collaboration with the computer centres of the university, departments of LIS and library associations.

The present research is significant because it sheds light on the current level of adoption and use of modern ICT-based tools in library functions and services in the selected university libraries. Thus the findings of the study will help practicing librarians, policymakers, management, and the University Grants Commission of India to promote the use of different ICT-based information systems in academic libraries, to design courses of ICT, and to introduce training programmes for working staff. This research also has some limitations. As it surveyed only 15 university libraries, the sample may not accurately represent the whole population. For future research, a broad study should include more university libraries, as well as expanding the study to other types of libraries, to gain a broader perspective on the implementation of ICT.

REFERENCES

Abell, A., 2000. Skills for knowledge environments. Inf. Manag. J. 34 (3), 10–12.

Abell, A., Oxbrow, N., 2001. Competing with Knowledge: The Information Professional in the Knowledge Management Age. Library Association Publishing, London.

Adamovic, D., Potgieter, A., Mearns, M., 2012. Knowledge sharing through social media: investigating trends and technologies in global marketing and advertising research company. SA J. Inf. Manag. 14 (1), 1–7.

American Library Association, 2014. The 2012 state of America's libraries: a report from American Library Association. American Libraries, 2012. (special issue). Available at: http://www.ala.org/news/sites/ala.org.news/files/content/StateofAmericas LibrariesReport2012Finalwithcover.pdf (accessed 24.10.14).

Ariew, S., 2008. Joining the YouTube conversation to teach information literacy. In: Godwin, P., Parker, J. (Eds.), Information Literacy Meets Library 2.0. Facet Publications, London, pp. 125–132.

Ayanbode, O., 2011. Library digitisation: a strategy to bridge information and knowledge divides'. Eur. J. Sci. Res. 56 (2), 212–218.

Badar, A., 2008. Academic Libraries, second ed. House Strange Printing and Publishing, Cairo.

Bejune, M., 2007. Wikis in libraries. Inf. Technol. Libr. 26, 26–38.

Bem, R.M.D., Coelho, C.C.S.R., 2013. Applications of knowledge management in the area of librarianship and information science: a systematic review. Braz. J. Inf. Sci. 7 (1), 67–93.

Bhardwaj, R.K., 2014. Use of social networking sites by LIS professionals in higher education institutions in India: a study. Ref. Libr. 55 (1), 74–88.

Branin, J.J., 2003. Knowledge management in academic libraries: building the knowledge bank at the Ohio State University. J. Libr. Adm. 39 (4), 41–56.

Brogan, M., Hingston, P., Wilson, V., 2001. A bounded or unbounded universe? knowledge management in postgraduate LIS education. In: 67th IFLA Council and General Conference, August 16–25, 2001.

Casey, M., Savastinuk, L., 2006. Library 2.0: service for the next generation library. Libr. J. 131, 40–42.

Cholin, V.S., 2005. Study of the application of information technology for effective access to resources in Indian university libraries. Int. Inf. Libr. Rev. 37 (3), 189–197.

Chu Kai-Wah, S., 2009. Using Wikis in academic libraries. J. Acad. Librariansh. 35 (2), 170–176.

Chua, A.Y.-K., Hoe-Lian Goh, D., Lee, C.S., 2008. The prevalence and use of Web 2.0 in libraries. In: Proceedings of ICADL. Lecture Notes in Computer Science, vol. 5362. Springer, Berlin, Heidelberg, pp. 22–30.

Clarke, R., 2004. KM in the main library of the University of West Indies. Trinidad. Inf. Dev. 20 (1), 30–35.

Dalkir, K., 2005. Knowledge Management in Theory and Practice. Elsevier, Boston, MA.

Dickson, A., Holley, R.P., 2010. Social networking in academic libraries: the possibilities and concerns. New Libr. World 111 (11/12), 468–479.

Foley, M., 2002. Instant messaging reference in an academic library: a case study. Coll. Res. Libr. 63 (1), 36–45.

Foss, N.J., Husted, K., Michailova, S., 2010. Governing knowledge sharing in organizations: levels of analysis, governance mechanisms and research directions. J. Manag. Stud. 47 (3), 455–482.

Gandhi, S., 2004. Knowledge management and reference service. J. Acad. Librariansh. 30 (5), 368–381.

Ghuloum, H., Ahmed, V., 2011. The implementation of new ICT services in Kuwaiti academic libraries. Built Hum. Environ. Rev. 4 (1), 74–86.

Gilmour, R., Strickland, J., 2009. Social bookmarking for library services: bibliographic access through delicious. Coll. Res. Libr. News 70 (4), 234–723.

Haneefa, M., 2007. Application of information and communication technologies in special libraries in Kerala (India). Libr. Rev. 56 (7), 603–620.

Husain, S., Nazim, M., 2015. Use of different information and communication technologies in Indian academic libraries. Libr. Rev. 64 (1/2), 135–153.

Infomotions Inc., 2009. Web-scale discovery indexes and next generation's library catalogs. Available at: http://infomotions.com/musings/web-scale/ (accessed 12.07.14).

Jain, P., 2007. An empirical study of knowledge management in academic libraries in East and Southern Africa. Libr. Rev. 56 (5), 377–392.

Jantz, R., 2001. Knowledge management in academic libraries: special tools and processes to support information professionals. Ref. Serv. Rev. 29 (1), 33–39.

Kao, S.C., Wu, C.H., 2012. A personalized information and knowledge integration platform for DL service. Libr. Hi Tech 30 (3), 490–512.

Kebede, G., 2010. Knowledge management: an information science perspective. Int. J. Inf. Manag. 30, 416–424.

Kim, Y.-M., Abbas, J., 2010. Adoption of Library 2.0 functionalities by academic libraries and users: a knowledge management perspective. J. Acad. Librariansh. 36 (3), 211–218.

Kroski, E., 2007. The social tools of Web 2.0: opportunities for academic libraries. Choice 44 (12), 2011–2021.

Kumar, P.S.G., 1987. Computerization of Indian Libraries. B.R. Publishing Corporation, New Delhi.

Lam, M.S., Sum, M., 2013. Enhancing access and usage: the OUHK's experience in resource discovery service. In: Paper Presented at IFLA World Library Information Congress, 17–23 August 2013, Singapore. Available at: http://library.ifla.org/76/1/106-lam-en.pdf (accessed 12.12.14).

Levine-Clark, M., McDonald, J., Price, J., 2013. Discovery or displacement? A large scale longitudinal study of the effect of discovery systems on online journal usage. In: Paper Presented at Charleston Conference, November 7, 2013. Available at: http://wwwslideshare.net/MichaelLevineClark/mlc-jdm-jsp-charleston-2013-slideshare-28161600 (accessed 24.10.14).

LibraryThing, 2014. A home for your books. Available at: www.librarything.com (accessed 12.12.14).

Long, S.A., 2006. Exploring the wiki world: the new face of collaboration. New Libr. World 157, 157–159.

MacManus, R., 2012. The social library: how public libraries are using social media. Available at: http://readwrite.com/author/richard-macmanus (accessed 18.09.14).

Madhusudhan, M., Nagabhushanam, V., 2013. Use of web-based library services in select university libraries in India: a study. Int. J. Libr. Inf. Stud. 2 (1), 1–20.

Malhan, I.V., 2006. Strategic planning for developing Indian university libraries into knowledge resource and service centers. In: World Library and Information Congress: 72nd

IFLA general Conference and Council, 20–24 August, Seoul. Available at: www.ifla.org/IV/ifla72/index.htm (accessed 17.05.14).
Maness, J.M., 2006. Library 2.0: the next generation of web-based library services. LOGOS: J. World Book Community 17 (3), 139–145.
Mavodza, J., Ngulube, P., 2011. The use of technology-based mechanisms and knowledge management techniques in library practices in academic environment: a case study. Mousaion 29 (2), 95–116.
Mike, M., Seaman, J., Tinti-Kane, H., 2011. Teaching, Learning, and Sharing: How Today's Higher Education Faculty Use Social Media. Pearson, Boston, MA.
Mohsenzadeh, F., Isfandyari-Moghaddam, A., 2009. Application of information technologies in academic libraries. Electron. Libr. 27 (6), 986–998.
Mphidi, H., Snyman, R., 2004. The utilization of an intranet as a knowledge management tool in academic libraries. Electron. Libr. 22 (5), 393–400.
Nazim, M., Mukherjee, B., 2013. Knowledge management competencies required among library and information science professionals: an Indian perspective. Libr. Rev. 62 (6/7), 375–387.
Nelson, E., 2008. Knowledge management for libraries. Libr. Admin. Manag. 22 (3), 135–137.
O'Hara, L., 2012. Collection usage pre- and post-summon implementation at the University of Manitoba libraries. Evid. Based Libr. Inf. Pract. 7 (4), 25–34.
Okumus, F., 2012. Facilitating knowledge management through information technology in hospitality organizations. J. Hosp. Tour. Technol. 4 (1), 64–80.
Parirokh, M., Daneshgar, F., Fattahi, R., 2008. Identifying knowledge sharing requirements in academic libraries. Libr. Rev. 57 (2), 107–122.
Peyala, V., 2011. Impact of using information technology in central university libraries in India: results of a survey. Program: Electron. Libr. Inf. Syst. 45 (3), 308–322.
Powell, R.R., Connaway, L.S., 2004. Basic Research Methods for Librarians. Libraries Unlimited, London.
Preedip, B.B., Kumar, V., 2011. Use of web technology in providing information services by south Indian technological universities as displayed on library websites. Libr. Hi Tech 29 (3), 470–495.
Rah, J.A., Gul, S., Wani, Z.A., 2010. University libraries: step towards a web based knowledge management system. VINE: J. Inf. Knowl. Manag. Syst. 40 (1), 24–38.
Raman, P.V., Rao, V.C., 2003. Use of information technology in central university libraries of India. DESIDOC Bull. Inf. Technol. 23 (2), 25–42.
Ramzan, M., Singh, D., 2009. Status of information technology applications in Pakistani libraries. Electron. Libr. 27 (4), 573–584.
Raza, M.M., Nath, A., 2007. Use of IT in university libraries of Punjab, Chandigarh and Himachal Pradesh: a comparative study. Int. Inf. Libr. Rev. 39 (3/4), 211–227.
Redden, C.S., 2010. Social bookmarking in academic libraries: trends and applications. J. Acad. Librariansh. 36 (3), 219–227.
Reynol, J., Heiberger, G., Loken, E., 2011. The effect of twitter on college student engagement and grades. J. Comput. Assist. Learn. 27 (2), 119–132.
Robertson, S., Sullivan, S., 2000. The rediscovered agents of change: librarians working with academics to close the information gap. In: Paper Presented at the Australian Library and Information Association on Capitalizing on Knowledge: The Information Profession in the 21st Century, Canberra, 23–26 October. Available at: http://eric.ed.gov/PDFS/ED452877.pdf (accessed 13.04.14).
Sabashini, R., Rita, S., Vivek, M., 2012. The role of ICTs in knowledge management for organizational effectiveness. In: Krishna, P.V., Babu, M.R., Ariwa, E. (Eds.), Global Trends in Information Systems and Software Applications. Springer-Verlag, Berlin, Heidelberg, pp. 542–549.
Shanhong, T., 2000. Knowledge management in libraries in the twenty first century. In: World Library and Information Congress: 66th IFLA Council and General Conference, 13–18 August, Jerusalem.
Singh, S.P., 2007. What are we managing: knowledge or information? VINE: J. Inf. Knowl. Manag. Syst. 37 (2), 169–179.

Stephens, M., 2006. Web 2.0 & Libraries: Best Practices for Social Software. American Library Association, Chicago, IL.

Stoeckel, K.S., Sinkinson, C., 2013. 'Social media', tips and trends. Summer. Available at: http://www.ala.org/acrl/sites/ala.org.acrl/files/content/aboutacrl/directoryofleadership/sections/is/iswebsite/projpubs/tipsandtrends/2013summer.pdf (accessed 24.10.14).

Stover, M., 2004. Making tacit knowledge explicit: the ready reference database as codified knowledge. Ref. Serv. Rev. 32 (2), 164–173.

Texas Christian University, 2014. Using instant messaging at an academic library reference desk: successes, challenges, and future directions. Available at: http://www.lib.lsu.edu/sci/chem/vbulletin_real/bond.pdf (accessed 12.07.14).

Tiwari, B.K., Sahoo, K.C., 2013. Infrastructure and use of ICT in University Libraries of Rajasthan (India). Libr. Philos. Pract. (e-journal), Paper 883. Available at: http://digitalcommons.unl.edu/libphilprac/883 (accessed 12.08.14).

Tripathi, M., Kumar, S., 2010. Use of Web 2.0 tools in academic libraries: a reconnaissance of the international landscape. Int. Inf. Libr. Rev. 42, 195–207.

Tyagi, S., 2012. Use of web 2.0 technology by library professionals: study of selected engineering colleges in western Uttar Pradesh. DESIDOC J. Libr. Inf. Technol. 32, 439–445.

University of Southampton, 2014. Using wikis within blackboard. Available at: http://www.southampton.ac.uk/isolutions/computing/elearn/wikis/ (accessed 22.10.14).

Vyas, S.D., 2003. Application of information technology in university libraries of Rajasthan: a survey report. In: Paper Presented at First International Convention on Automation of Libraries in Education and Research Institutions (CALIBER), Ahmedabad, 13–15 February. Available at: http://ir.inflibnet.ac.in/bitstream/1944/191/2/03cali_22.pdf (accessed 29.07.14).

Wenzler, J., 2007. LibraryThing and the library catalogue: adding collective intelligence to the OPAC. In: Paper Presented in a Workshop on Next Generation Libraries CARL, NITIG, September 7, 2007. Available at: http://wff1.ff.unilj.si/oddelki/biblio/oddelek/osebje/dokumenti/MercunZumer08_New_generation_of_catalogues_for_the_new_generation_of_users.pdf (accessed 25.12.14).

Wikipedia, 2014a. Definition of blog. Available at: http://en.wikipedia.org/wiki/Blog (accessed 25.12.14).

Wikipedia, 2014b. LibraryThing. Available at: http://en.wikipedia.org/wiki/LibraryThing (accessed 25.12.14).

Woodward, J.A., 2009. Creating the Customer-Driven Academic Library. American Library Association, Chicago, IL.

Xu, C., Ouyang, F., Chu, H., 2009. The academic library meets web 2.0: applications and implications. J. Acad. Librariansh. 35 (4), 324–331.

Yuan, Y.C., Zhao, X., Liao, Q., Chi, C., 2013. The use of different information and communication technologies to support knowledge sharing in organizations: from e-mail to micro-blogging. J. Am. Soc. Inf. Sci. Technol. 64 (8), 1659–1670.

FURTHER READING

Isaac, A.M., 2008. Transformation of India into a knowledge society. In: Paper Presented at PICMET Conference on Technology Management for a Sustainable Economy, Cape Town, 27–31 July. Available at: www.knowledgecommission.gov.in/downloads/news/news314.pdf (accessed 29.07.14).

National Knowledge Commission, Government of India, 2007. Libraries: gateways to knowledge. Available at: http://knowledgecommission.gov.in/downloads/documents/NKC_Library.pdf (accessed 29.07.14).

CHAPTER 11

Factors Critical to the Success of Knowledge Management

INTRODUCTION

Despite the best efforts of organizations, many face challenges in implementing and sustaining successful knowledge management (KM) initiatives. This may be due to a variety of reasons, such as unrealistic expectations, a one-size-fits-all approach to KM, lack of understanding of KM concepts, lack of or overemphasis on technology, or a lack of strategic alignment or information. The ultimate aim of KM is to increase the effectiveness and sustainability of growth of an organization. In the context of libraries, the objective of KM is to promote knowledge innovation, closer relationships in and between libraries, and between a library and its users, to strengthen knowledge internetworking and to quicken knowledge flow (Shanhong, 2000). KM provides new opportunities for librarians and information specialists to expand their existing roles and utilize the skills they have honed to meet corporate objectives (Hayes, 2004). Therefore KM can be used as a way to expand the library's role to areas such as administration or support services, where libraries have had little impact in the past (Townley, 2001). The success of KM is believed to be dependent on various factors, as they provide a platform which facilitates knowledge sharing among individuals, whose actions in turn are influenced by their environment. An appropriate organizational environment enables an organization to execute better, faster, and adopt change more easily. This chapter provides an overview of the different factors that contribute to the success of KM initiatives with specific reference to academic libraries.

KM SUCCESS FACTORS

Successful implementation of KM systems in an organization depends on several factors. First, people do not like to share their knowledge, because they may be afraid of being replaced if they share what they know. Organizations should encourage knowledge sharing by providing tangible rewards and creating a culture that supports that. Second, employees may be resistant to the new system or new process due to time limitations, and lack of knowledge about it. Proper training in a new system is necessary to reduce employees' anxiety (Milam, 2005).

Several authors have attempted to identify the factors that are critical to the success of KM implementation. However, the list differs because of the multidisciplinary nature of KM. Skyrme and Amidon (1997) identified six factors that are critical for the success of KM systems:

1. the need to have a strategic link between KM and business objectives;
2. developing a compelling vision for KM;
3. the existence of KM leadership;
4. possessing a knowledge-creating and -sharing culture;
5. having a well-developed technology infrastructure; and
6. putting systematic organizational knowledge processes (KPs) in place.

Other factors outlined by authors on KM include: (1) the need for measurement of KM activities and outcomes; (2) adequate control and coordination of KM activities; (3) provision of enabling resources and training; (4) possessing a KM ontology and repository; (5) introducing new structures, roles, and responsibilities; (6) employee empowerment and teamwork; and (7) providing motivational incentives (Davenport et al., 1998; Holsapple and Joshi, 2000; Hasanali 2002; Ryan and Prybutok, 2001; Alavi and Leidner, 2001; Bellaver and Lusa, 2001; Chong and Choi, 2005).

The terminology used to describe KM systems may be different or presented under broader headings or broken down into smaller units, but overall these authors agreed on the importance of people, process, and technology. Butler and Murphy (2007) proposed a framework of critical success factors for implementing KM in public sector organizations. They identified various factors and grouped them into the following three broad categories: (1) strategy-based success factors, (2) organizational success factors, and (3) institutional success factors. Gold et al. (2001) analyzed KM success factors from the perspective of organizational capabilities. Organizational capabilities have two aspects: (1) knowledge infrastructure capabilities and (2) KP capabilities. Knowledge infrastructure capabilities include technology, organizational structure (OS), and culture, while KP capabilities cover acquisition, conversion, application, and protection of knowledge. The model proposed by Gold et al. (2001) matches the principles of the KM success model developed by Hostler (2005), which includes technology, people, and process. Technology focuses on the application of technological resources to maximize the KM functions. In fact, KM involves change management and requires organizational culture (OC) and structure to support the new change.

Hostler's principles of KM success are similar to the knowledge maturity model developed and used by Tata Consultancy Services (TCS), which consists of three basic pillars: people, technology, and process. TCS believes that states of knowledge maturity can be achieved by systematically addressing these three pillars.

People and culture address the "mindsets" and relate to attributes of assessing people and culture.

Technology and infrastructure are the enablers that help people to harness the maximum out of the KM initiative.

Process, policy, and strategy facilitate and guide the efforts of people to capture and use the knowledge in the organization to achieve benefits for the business (Mohanty and Chand, 2005).

SUCCESS FACTORS OF KM IN LIBRARIES

Recently Conley and Zheng (2009) grouped KM success factors into two categories: organizational factors and factors related to the KM initiative. Organizational factors capture the general characteristics of the organization, such as top management and leadership support, OC, structure, technology infrastructure, and strategy. KM initiative-related factors encompass those that are targeted to KM practices, including processes, training and education, measurement and incentives. Some important success factors are described in the next section.

Organizational Culture

OC is often cited as one of the most important aspects to achieve as well as one of the biggest barriers to KM success. An OC that encourages knowledge sharing, creation, and contribution to organizational knowledge structures is critical to the success of KM (Ralph and Tijerino, 2009). As Octavia-Luciana Porumbeanu (2010) rightly stressed, an organization should develop a culture which is open to change, encourages learning, creativity and quality, and helps to garner new abilities and knowledge.

The success of an organization depends a lot on its culture, which in turn influences the employees' attitudes and behavior. In the context of the discussion on the process of KM implementation in academic libraries, the change of culture at organizational level is extremely important. If libraries and other information services are to survive in the contemporary information marketplace, the creation of a culture oriented towards performance, which appreciates and encourages communication, collaboration, and that rewards creativity and new ideas is essential. This also has to be a culture oriented towards people, employees, and users, one which meets their information needs and one of permanent change, oriented towards learning and continuous professional training, and one that stimulates knowledge sharing and development. Thus a knowledge- and learning-oriented culture would facilitate the creation of knowledge and innovation that is extremely important for organizations like academic libraries.

Organizational Structure

The OS provides guidance in determining who people interact with when conducting organizational tasks. The existence of a favorable environment for communication, collaboration, knowledge sharing, and transfer, as well as easy identification of the organization's knowledge assets, are essential for this approach and to facilitate it. An effective OS allows and encourages employees to collaborate and share knowledge in an organization. Bennett and Gabriel (1999) explained that flexible and informal structures facilitate internal communication within an organization, enhance people's willingness to change, encourage more adventure in information-gathering activities, cultivate a critical attitude in interpretation of information, and encourage individual initiatives. In additional to the formal OS, reward and incentive systems should also be well structured. A structured reward system with well-defined policies clarifies the flow of information and how it should be accessed. An incentive program can also motivate employees to share their knowledge and to help others.

Technology Infrastructure

KM needs an infrastructure that allows employees to transfer, communicate, and integrate information and knowledge from different departments. Technology has provided a number of possible solutions for sharing recorded human knowledge via e-mail, intranets, and knowledge bases. Thus technology is vital in enabling and facilitating many KM processes and initiatives. With the use of proper technological tools, organizations can extract and organize knowledge, make it accessible to employees, and even speed up the knowledge transfer process. The technology must be accessible to everyone, training must be provided for its use, and, above all, it must be used. Lack of use contributes to failure. Although technology is essential for the success of KM, alone it does not ensure successful KM.

Knowledge Sharing

Knowledge sharing has been recognized as the most important factor in the success of KM. Knowledge sharing means the exchange of employees' knowledge, skills, and experiences. It ensures that the knowledge within an organization is available for employees whenever they need it, and its benefits include retaining intellectual assets and improving productivity. Previous studies have identified three elements that have a critical impact on knowledge sharing: a knowledge-sharing culture, information technology (IT), and employee motivation (Jones et al., 2006). Knowledge residing in the minds of people has no value until it is utilized and shared among other employees of an organization, as Davenport et al. (1998) rightly stressed that "knowledge is created invisibly in the human brain and only right organizational climate can persuade people to create, reveal, share and use it." Organizations and their authorities can provide a natural and friendly environment that may encourage employees to share their ideas and knowledge. IT capability is a necessary foundation for knowledge sharing.

Knowledge Processes

KPs must be effective to capture, store, and transform knowledge for KM to be successful. The fundamental meaning of a KP is the integration of knowledge for organizational learning. Nonaka and Takeuchi (1995) put forward a well-known knowledge conversion framework that proposed a knowledge conversion process consisting of four major elements: socialization, internalization, externalization, and combination. Socialization relates to the situation of going from tacit to tacit knowledge and is a process of transferring personal experiences and knowledge to others. Internalization is the transfer of explicit knowledge to tacit knowledge. Externalization relates to transfer from tacit to explicit knowledge and is the process of converting knowledge and experience into explicit concepts via dialog and collective reflection. Combination relates to transfer from explicit to explicit knowledge and intends to systemize different types of explicit knowledge into a KM system. Training and formal education are examples of combination. Each of the four transformations results in some kind of learning or creation of new knowledge.

Training and Education

The role of ongoing training and education in successful KM programs is also an important consideration. For the success of KM programs, ongoing training and education should take place to keep employees abreast of how they can contribute and how they can take advantage of the new tools and processes that have been put in place. Libraries are no exception, especially as in their case the pace and the volume of changes which they have to deal with is doubled by the complexity of satisfying the information needs and requests of users through up-to-date products and services.

ASSESSING SUCCESS FACTORS FOR KM: A CASE STUDY OF INDIAN ACADEMIC LIBRARIES

Successful implementation of KM in an organization depends on several factors. For example, a favorable organizational environment enables an organization to execute better, learn faster, and change more easily. Information technologies facilitate the process of knowledge capture, storage, and sharing. Therefore it was important to identify those factors that contribute to the success of KM in terms of its implementation in academic libraries. Some library experts (eg, Keeling and Lambert, 2000; McManus and Loughridge, 2002; Malhan, 2006a,b; Pinto, 2006; Ralph and Tijerino, 2009; Siddike and Islam, 2011) described and proposed several factors in the context of libraries. After an extensive review of the literature, 21 factors were identified and grouped into five broad categories: OS, OC, education and training (ET), KP, and IT. Respondents were asked to indicate the degree of importance as well as the actual implementation of these factors in their academic libraries.

We employed a quantitative research method using a structured questionnaire with closed-ended questions. Academic institutions and their libraries in India are too numerous to consider in total as a sample for any research. Therefore only central university libraries were included in this study, keeping in mind that these are funded by the central government and might have advanced library infrastructures and facilities. Of the total of 42 central university libraries in India, 30 libraries were selected on the basis of collections, infrastructure, and services at various locations within India. The university librarians of these universities were selected as respondents. However, in the absence of the university librarian, an official up to the rank of assistant librarian was allowed to participate in the survey. A total of 30 questionnaires were delivered by post, of which only 15 were returned (50% response rate). The libraries that participated in the study were from nine different states of the country: four from Uttar Pradesh, four from Delhi, one each from Andhra Pradesh, West Bengal, Kerala, Chhattisgarh, Manipur, Mizoram, and Meghalaya. These libraries are spread around a 4000 km area and serve an extended community of users. They are very different libraries in terms of staff and users. The details of the libraries participating in the study are shown in Table 10.1 of Chapter 10.

Success Factors: Degree of Importance

The respondents were asked to indicate their perceptions of the degree of importance of each factor on a five-point Likert scale, where 1 represented "not important" and 5 denoted "very important." For validation purposes, a mean value of 3.45 was fixed as the cut-off point, meaning that a factor would be considered "important" if it received a mean score of 3.45 or more. Two statistical approaches were applied to analyze the data: (1) analysis of individual factors and (2) analysis of success factors based on the grouping of 21 factors into five categories: OS, OC, ET, KP, and IT.

Table 11.1 illustrates the mean scores of the degree of importance of 21 factors belonging to the five KM success factors. The mean scores of the degree of importance held by respondents for all factors ranged from 3.55 to 4.81, with an average mean of 4.22. The highest rated factor was "provision of rewards for innovative performance and sharing of knowledge," with a mean score of 4.81. Other factors that received higher perceptions of importance by librarians include "a spirit of cooperation and teamwork" and "access to the internal knowledge (operating rules, policies, and procedures) for all employees in the library," with mean scores of 4.68 and 4.64 respectively.

Table 11.1 Mean scores of the degree of importance (individual factors)

	Factors	Mean	Overall mean[a]
ET1	KM awareness training for employees	4.62	Very important
ET2	Providing employees with adequate information on KM-related principles through training	4.31	Important
ET3	Encouraging employees to participate in internal and external new learning opportunities such as conferences, training, seminars, other courses, etc.	3.80	Important
OS1	Reformulation of a policy regarding staff and organizational development (recruitment of staff with more qualifications and experience, timely or performance-based promotion, etc.)	4.35	Important

Continued

Table 11.1 Mean scores of the degree of importance (individual factors)—cont'd

	Factors	Mean	Overall mean
OS2	Adequate budgeting or funding to support KM implementation	4.17	Important
OS3	Promoting ongoing employee contributions	4.15	Important
OS4	Top management commitment towards utilization of KM systems	3.91	Important
OS5	Policies to improve quality of working life	3.73	Important
OC1	Provision of rewards/incentives for innovative performance and sharing of knowledge	4.81	Very important
OC2	Encouraging experienced workers to share their knowledge with new or less experienced workers	4.22	Important
OC3	A spirit of cooperation and teamwork	4.68	Very important
OC4	Acceptance of change as part of working life (adoption of new technologies, introducing new services, continuous improvement in services, etc.)	4.20	Important
OC5	A formal system that allows for contributions from every employee's opinions or suggestions	4.19	Important
KP1	Access to the internal knowledge (operating rules, policies, and procedures) for all employees in the library	4.64	Very important
KP2	Access to external knowledge resources (online catalogs, expert databases, publications, etc.)	3.55	Important
KP3	Cooperation with other libraries, membership of library networks or consortia to share and enhance information sources	4.55	Very important
KP4	Documentation of the operating rules, policies, and procedures for KM implementation processes	4.52	Very important
KP5	Capture and codification of knowledge related to library operations and information sources (automation of catalog records, authority files, FAQ database in reference, etc.)	4.05	Important

Table 11.1 Mean scores of the degree of importance (individual factors)—cont'd

	Factors	Mean	Overall mean
IT1	Use of IT to facilitate storage and access to the library's internal records (document management system)	4.28	Important
IT2	Use of hardware and software for automation, digital library development, and online training	4.10	Important
IT3	Effectiveness and user friendliness of information systems that enable employees to retrieve and apply knowledge in their job	3.92	Important

[a]For the purpose of marking the overall perceptions of respondents, the following scoring system designed by Sarrafzadeh et al. (2010) was used: mean 1–1.44 = Not Important; mean 1.45–2.44 = Minor Importance; mean 2.45–3.44 = Moderately Important; mean 3.45–4.44 = Important; mean 4.55–5 = Very Important. A mean value of 3.45 was fixed as the cut-off point, meaning that a factor would be considered "important" if it received a mean score of 3.45 or more.

The lowest rated factor was "access to external knowledge resources (online catalogs, expert databases, publications, etc.)," with a mean score of 3.55; however, this still lies between moderately important and important. Other factors receiving lower ratings were "policies to improve quality of working life" (mean 3.73), "encouraging employees to participate in internal and external new learning opportunities such as conferences, training, seminars, other courses, etc." (mean 3.80), and "top management commitment towards utilization of the KM systems" (mean 3.91). All 21 factors scored a mean higher than 3.45, meaning that all factors were perceived to be important or very important for the success of KM implementation in academic libraries in India.

Table 11.2 shows the mean scores of the five success factors on the basis of grouping of 21 individual factors into five categories. The respondents had similar attitudes towards IT, ET, and KP (means 4.10, 4.24, and 4.26). It may be noted that all the factors were considered "important" because the minimum mean score of any factor was not less than 3.45. However, OC achieved the highest rating of the five, with a mean score of 4.34. The lowest rated factor was OS, with a mean score of 4.06. It may be observed that IT, as a success factor for the implementation of KM in academic libraries, was not rated as important by the respondents as it was recognized that the foundations of KM resided in the acquisition, organization, and exchange of information.

Table 11.2 Descriptive statistics of five success factors (degree of importance)

Factors	Mean	Overall mean[a]
Education and training	4.24	Important
Organizational strategy	4.06	Important
Organizational culture	4.34	Important
Knowledge process	4.26	Important
Information technology	4.10	Important

[a] For the purpose of marking the overall perceptions of respondents, the following scoring system designed by Sarrafzadeh et al. (2010) was used: mean 1–1.44 = Not Important; mean 1.45–2.44 = Minor Importance; mean 2.45–3.44 = Moderately Important; mean 3.45–4.44 = Important; mean 4.55–5 = Very Important. A mean value of 3.45 was fixed as the cut-off point, meaning that a factor would be considered "important" if it received a mean score of 3.45 or more.

Success Factors: Degree of Implementation

For the purpose of investigating the degree of implementation of these factors in academic libraries, perceptions of the respondents for the same 21 factors were measured using a five-point Likert scale, where 1 represented "not implemented" and 5 denoted "extensively implemented." For the purpose of knowing whether a factor is implemented, a mean value of 3.45 was fixed as the cut-off point, meaning that a factor would be considered "implemented" if it received a mean score of 3.45 or more. Descriptive statistics were applied to analyze the individual factors concerning the level of implementation of these factors in the libraries under study, as well as five success factors on the basis of the grouping of these 21 factors into the five categories mentioned earlier.

Table 11.3 shows the mean scores of the degree of implementation of 21 factors. The mean scores of the degree of implementation of these factors ranged between 2.05 and 3.38, with an average mean score of 2.83. The factor achieving the highest mean was "encouraging employees to participate in internal and external new learning opportunities," with a mean rating of 3.38. It was followed by "Access to external knowledge resources (online catalogs, expert databases, publications, etc.) (mean 3.23) and "A spirit of cooperation and teamwork" (mean 3.16)." The factor "a spirit of cooperation and teamwork" received higher scores in both degree of importance and degree of implementation. It may be observed from the results that no factor crossed the cut-off point, that is, 3.45, meaning that no factor was considered as "implemented" in the libraries under study.

The least implemented factor was "provision of rewards for innovative performance and sharing of knowledge," with a mean score of 2.05. Other factors that obtained low mean scores were "KM awareness training for employees" (mean 2.09) and "providing employees with adequate information on KM-related principles through training" (mean 2.30). The factor "KM awareness

Table 11.3 Mean scores of the degree of implementation (individual factors)

	Factors	Mean	Overall mean[a]
ET1	KM awareness training for employees	2.09	Little implemented
ET2	Providing employees with adequate information on KM-related principles through training	2.30	Little implemented
ET3	Encouraging employees to participate in internal and external new learning opportunities such as conferences, training, seminars, other courses, etc.	3.38	Moderately implemented
OS1	Reformulation of a policy regarding staff and organizational development (recruitment of staff with more qualifications and experience, timely or performance-based promotion, etc.)	2.71	Moderately implemented
OS2	Adequate budgeting or funding to support KM implementation	2.95	Moderately implemented
OS3	Promoting ongoing employee contributions	2.66	Moderately implemented
OS4	Top management commitment towards utilization of KM systems	2.51	Moderately implemented
OS5	Policies to improve quality of working life	2.85	Moderately implemented
OC1	Provision of rewards/incentives for innovative performance and sharing of knowledge	2.05	Little implemented
OC2	Encouraging experienced workers to share their knowledge with new or less experienced workers	2.92	Moderately implemented
OC3	A spirit of cooperation and teamwork	3.16	Moderately implemented
OC4	Acceptance of change as part of working life (adoption of new technologies, introducing new services, continuous improvement in services, etc.)	2.97	Moderately implemented
OC5	A formal system that allows for contributions from every employee's opinions or suggestions	2.85	Moderately implemented
KP1	Access to the internal knowledge (operating rules, policies, and procedures) for all employees in the library	3.00	Moderately implemented

Continued

Table 11.3 Mean scores of the degree of implementation (individual factors)—cont'd

	Factors	Mean	Overall mean
KP2	Access to external knowledge resources (online catalogs, expert databases, publications, etc.)	3.23	Moderately implemented
KP3	Cooperation with other libraries, membership of library networks or consortia to share and enhance information sources	3.01	Moderately implemented
KP4	Documentation of the operating rules, policies, and procedures for KM implementation processes	2.98	Moderately implemented
KP5	Capture and codification of knowledge related to library operations and information sources (automation of catalog records, authority files, FAQ database in reference, etc.)	2.78	Moderately implemented
IT1	Use of IT to facilitate storage and access to the library's internal records (document management system)	3.08	Moderately implemented
IT2	Use of hardware and software for automation, digital library development, and online training	3.03	Moderately implemented
IT3	Effectiveness and user friendliness of information systems that enable employees to retrieve and apply knowledge in their job	3.00	Moderately implemented

[a] For the purpose of marking the overall perceptions of respondents, the following scoring system designed by Sarrafzadeh et al. (2010) was used: mean 1–1.44 = Not implemented; mean 1.45–2.44 = Little Implemented; mean 2.45–3.44 = Moderately Implemented; mean 3.45–4.44 = Implemented; mean 4.55–5 = Extensively implemented. A mean value of 3.45 was fixed as the cut-off point, meaning that a factor would be considered "implemented" if it received a mean score of 3.45 or more.

training for employees" received the lowest mean for the degree of implementation but received the highest mean for the degree of importance. Of the 21 factors, eight had means between 3.00 and 3.38; this suggests that these factors were implemented moderately while the rest were little implemented.

With respect to the success factors concerning the degree of implementation, the respondents had similar attitudes towards ET, OC, and OS (means 2.59, 2.79, and 2.73). Respondents are agreed that their libraries were equipped with KP and IT to some extent, but there was a lack of trained staff and favorable OC for the capture and sharing of knowledge. The mean scores of the five success factors (degree of implementation) are shown in Table 11.4.

Table 11.4 Descriptive statistics of five success factors (degree of implementation)

Factors	Mean	Overall mean[a]
Education and training	2.59	Moderately implemented
Organizational strategy	2.73	Moderately implemented
Organizational culture	2.79	Moderately implemented
Knowledge process	3.00	Moderately implemented
Information technology	3.03	Moderately implemented

[a] For the purpose of marking the overall perceptions of respondents, the following scoring system designed by Sarrafzadeh et al. (2010) was used: mean 1–1.44 = Not implemented; mean 1.45–2.44 = Little Implemented; mean 2.45–3.44 = Moderately Implemented; mean 3.45–4.44 = Implemented; mean 4.55–5 = Extensively implemented. A mean value of 3.45 was fixed as the cut-off point, meaning that a factor would be considered "implemented" if it received a mean score of 3.45 or more.

Both IT and KP are important for the implementation of KM, but IT alone cannot function without the support of OS. Among the five success factors, IT had the highest mean (mean 3.03) while ET had the lowest (mean 2.59). This may be interpreted as the academic libraries surveyed not having a provision of training for employees to participate in KM practice despite the availability of IT infrastructure.

Comparison Between the Degree of Importance and the Degree of Implementation

The mean scores of both the degree of importance and the degree of implementation were compared. Results of the differences in means are shown in Table 11.5. The major difference in the means between the degree of importance and the degree of actual implementation was found in the factors related to OC: "provision of rewards/incentives for innovative

Table 11.5 Comparison of means: degree of importance and implementation

	Factors	Md[a]
ET1	KM awareness training for employees	2.53
ET2	Providing employees with adequate information on KM-related principles through training	2.01
ET3	Encouraging employees to participate in internal and external new learning opportunities such as conferences, training, seminars, other courses, etc.	0.42
OS1	Reformulation of a policy regarding staff and organizational development (recruitment of staff with more qualifications and experience, timely or performance-based promotion, etc.)	1.64
OS2	Adequate budgeting or funding to support KM implementation	1.22

Continued

Table 11.5 Comparison of means: degree of importance and implementation—cont'd

	Factors	Md
OS3	Promoting ongoing employee contributions	1.49
OS4	Top management commitment towards utilization of KM systems	1.4
OS5	Policies to improve quality of working life	0.88
OC1	Provision of rewards/incentives for innovative performance and sharing of knowledge	2.76
OC2	Encouraging experienced workers to share their knowledge with new or less experienced workers	1.3
OC3	A spirit of cooperation and teamwork	1.52
OC4	Acceptance of change as part of working life (adoption of new technologies, introducing new services, continuous improvement in services, etc.)	1.23
OC5	A formal system that allows for contributions from every employee's opinions or suggestions	1.34
KP1	Access to the internal knowledge (operating rules, policies, and procedures) for all employees in the library	1.64
KP2	Access to external knowledge resources (online catalogs, expert databases, publications, etc.)	0.32
KP3	Cooperation with other libraries, membership of library networks or consortia to share and enhance information sources	1.54
KP4	Documentation of the operating rules, policies, and procedures for KM implementation processes	1.54
KP5	Capture and codification of knowledge related to library operations and information sources (automation of catalog records, authority files, FAQ database in reference, etc.)	1.27
IT1	Use of IT to facilitate storage and access to the library's internal records (document management system)	1.2
IT2	Use of hardware and software for automation, digital library development, and online training	1.09
IT3	Effectiveness and user friendliness of information systems that enable employees to retrieve and apply knowledge in their job	0.92

[a] *Md*, mean difference.

performance and sharing of knowledge" (mean difference, Md = 2.76); ET: "KM awareness training for employees" (Md = 2.53) and "providing the employees with adequate information of KM-related principles through training" (Md = 2.01). These factors were not implemented to the same extent as their perception of importance.

The lowest difference between the means of the degree of importance and the degree of actual implementation was "access to external knowledge resources (online catalogs, expert databases, publications, etc.)" (Md = 0.32), "encouraging employees to participate in internal and external new learning opportunities such as conferences, training, seminars, other courses, etc." (Md = 0.42), "policies to improve quality of working life" (Md = 0.88), and "effectiveness and user friendliness of information systems that enable employees to retrieve and apply knowledge in their job" (Md = 0.92).

As shown in Table 11.5, there is a significant difference between the means of the degree of importance and the degree of actual implementation for all factors. The perceived degree of importance was much greater than the degree of implementation, indicating a lack of KM implementation in the academic libraries.

ROLE OF OC IN KM

OC, according to Schein (2010), is a pattern of common assumptions, values, beliefs, and attitudes that influence organizational behavior. Thus a knowledge- and learning-oriented culture can facilitate the implementation and development of KM systems, which are extremely important in organizations such as academic libraries. Highlighting knowledge sharing as an important feature of a KM system, Ackerman et al. (2003) stated that the reuse of knowledge created by knowledge workers is a common reason for initiating KM practices. Parirokh et al. (2008) reported how sharing of knowledge among librarians can improve organizational learning in academic libraries. Organizations and management should provide a natural and friendly environment that enables employees to share their ideas and knowledge. According to Wen (2005), an OC for sharing knowledge and expertise should be established with appropriate rewards and incentives. Those staff members who share their personal knowledge and experiences through writing, publishing, lecturing, tutoring, or mentoring should be appropriately recognized and rewarded. An empirical study by Babalhavaeji and Kermani (2011) on the knowledge-sharing behavior of library and information science (LIS) professionals in Iran suggested that intention and intrinsic motivation influence the knowledge-sharing behavior of library professionals. These studies also support the view of Barquin (2001), who believes in giving incentives to employees to encourage their participation in KM activities.

OC is one of the most cited factors in the literature which contributes to the success of KM irrespective of the type and nature of organizations.

Many researchers believe that a rich OC contributes to the effective and successful application of KM practices in academic libraries (Davenport and Prusak, 1998; Carter, 2004; Chong and Choi, 2005). According to Davenport and Prusak (1993), for KM to succeed it is essential to have a knowledge-oriented culture; that is, a culture that encourages and rewards knowledge sharing. Alavi and Leidner (2001) also believe that an effective KM application needs a culture that supports the sharing of knowledge and skills. Researchers who have carried out empirical studies on the role of OC in KM presented similar opinions. Porumbeanu (2010) analyzed the elements that characterize the OC in Romanian academic libraries to investigate whether the OC supported the implementation of KM. Based on a survey of library professionals from five university libraries, she reviewed some of the elements such as the OC in the institution, the values promoted by this culture, the policies concerning staff and organizational development, the managerial style, and the provision of incentives for knowledge sharing. The findings of the study show fairly favorable conditions for future implementation of KM practices in Romanian academic libraries. Based on the findings of this research, she proposed a model of successful implementation of KM in academic libraries. This model, in addition to the requirement of a favorable OC, focuses on systematic management and deployment of knowledge and expertise, human resources management, technology infrastructure, networking and partnership with other organizations, and creation of a position of Chief Knowledge Officer (CKO).

Sheng and Sun (2007) also emphasized the need to create a knowledge innovation culture (KIC) in libraries for the success of KM. They defined KIC as a value, behavioral, and institutional system, which leads to competitive advantages and sustainable development for libraries through knowledge creation. According to them, this kind of culture is different from traditional library culture and has several specific functions. Some factors, like environment, resources, and business, may affect the development of KIC in libraries. Therefore it is necessary for libraries to establish an environment beneficial to knowledge innovation, to enhance trust and cooperation within staff, to create a learning culture, shape knowledge-based team organization, enhance human resource development, and cultivate knowledge innovation talents in order to build up KIC in libraries. Further, they discussed the development of KIC in the Library of the Chinese Academy of Sciences as a case study. The library initiated KIC as a project to (i) create a change of service idea and modes in the institutes, (ii) enhance institute leaders' cognition and assistance in documentation and information services, (iii) further the understanding of institutes' information demands and library services, (iv) shape the trademarks and characteristics of services, and (v) improve the staff's professional competencies.

McManus and Loughridge (2002) have also highlighted the requirement of a corporate information culture for the effectiveness of KM in university libraries in the United Kingdom. Based on the results of a small-scale pilot interview-based survey of senior library professionals working in university libraries, they reviewed some of the reasons why KM was apparently so unpopular in university libraries, where the culture and OS were found to be the major factors affecting the perception of the relevance of KM programs in university libraries.

As Jantz (2001) pointed out, a change in culture requires active involvement of management. Agreeing with this view, Graham et al. (2005), on the basis of a case study at the Alabama library, stressed the need for liaison in order to create interest among the rest of the community of colleges or universities and to encourage their involvement. This is a point also raised by Skyrme (2004) on the need for information professionals to stay connected to organizational decision-making. Similar issues have been raised by Nelke (2010), with special emphasis on the importance of leadership. According to him, as knowledge managers, librarians must be able to persuade people to contribute and share their knowledge for the benefit of not only themselves and their department, but for the whole organization. Further, he stressed the need for strong support from top management and the role of librarians as consultants working in close connection with their colleagues. Addressing the participants of an International Conference on Academic Libraries held at New Delhi in 2009, Singh (2009) suggested that academic librarians should develop leadership competencies for leading and managing change in the present competitive and challenging environment where libraries are facing fierce competition from other information providers and companies like Google, and ever-increasing and diversified demand from users.

ASSESSMENT OF ORGANIZATIONAL CULTURE IN BANARAS HINDU UNIVERSITY LIBRARY SYSTEM

In the specific context of Indian academic libraries, identification and analysis of the characteristic elements of their culture has not received any special attention despite the fact that one of the priorities clearly recognized by most of those involved in this field is the cultural change needed in the organizations themselves. If there is to be a change of OC in Indian academic libraries, there is a need to recognize certain aspects that will lead to the implementation of change in the entire organization, a different management style, and the involvement of employees in the development of the new culture, as well as a new attitude towards KM.

Keeping this view in mind, we decided to undertake a study aimed at analyzing the elements that characterize the OC in one of the largest academic library systems in India, Banaras Hindu University Library System (BHULS), by evaluating the librarians' perception of

- the OC in the institution where they work;
- the values promoted by this culture;
- their policies concerning staff and organizational development;
- their managerial style;
- knowledge sharing.

For this study we chose BHULS, the largest academic library system in the country. By choosing BHULS as an example, we aimed to obtain a picture of the current situation in Indian academic libraries. The BHULS developed from a small but precious collection donated by Prof. P. K. Telang in memory of his father Justice K. T. Telang in 1917, housed in the Telang Hall of the Central Hindu College, Kamachha. It was nurtured in its infancy by the renowned historian, Sir Jadunath Sarkar. With the university taking shape at its current location, the library was also shifted in 1921 to the Central Hall of the Arts College (now Faculty of Arts) and then in 1941 to its present majestic building built with a munificent donation from Maharaja Sayajirao Gaekwad of Baroda, based on the design of a great library, the British Museum in London, on the suggestion of Pandit Madan Mohan Malaviya, the founder of the university, after his return from the Round Table Conference in London in 1931.

The BHULS serves users from the whole university with three institute libraries, eight faculty libraries, and 25 departmental libraries. The BHULS currently has 911,036 book titles, 135,350 periodicals (bound volumes), 941 current periodical titles, and approximately 5000 other rare documents which are digitized and can be accessed through a local area network. There are more than 14,000 active users of the library. The library has provided several electronic information resources (9816 online journals, 516 e-books, 10 bibliographic databases) since 1995. There are 20 computers with access to the Internet. The staff of the library consists of 175 persons.

A questionnaire consisting of 15 open- and closed-ended questions was designed to collect the required data and opinions for this study. Fifty questionnaires were nonrandomly distributed to the library staff of BHULS. Of the 50 respondents, 4 were deputy librarians, 8 were assistant librarians, 14 were professional assistants, and 24 were semiprofessional assistants. We approached each respondent personally and therefore we were able to get a 100% response rate. Staff completing the questionnaire were aged between 25 and 54 years, with the majority (80%) aged between 25 and 45 years. Their length of service was between 2 and 27 years, with the majority (75%) having between 2 and 18 years of employment in libraries, 75% having a master's degree in LIS, 15% a bachelor's degree in LIS, and 10% a doctoral degree in LIS.

Results

When respondents were asked about their organization's willingness to accept change, the majority of participants (73%) responded positively, giving examples of continuous improvement of library operations and services, development of information and human resources, and the fast adoption of new technologies. Twenty-seven percent answered in the negative, mentioning that lack of recognition and receptivity for change in their organization are serious obstacles to change. When asked about their work environment and what they think about it, 33% of the participants considered that it was one that encouraged the development of communities of practice and organizational learning, 21% mentioned collaboration, 13% mentioned communication, and 9% teamwork. With respect to the ways that staff performance was encouraged in their organization, a majority of the participants (57%) considered that performance was insufficiently rewarded or not encouraged at all.

However, 19% of the participants in this study indicated that this was by material reward, 14% by advancement in careers, and 10% by appreciation from senior fellows. On the question whether the organization provides support for professional training courses or workshops, an overwhelming majority (69%) of respondents asserted that their organization encouraged them to participate in professional conferences, workshops, and other related events; 17% responded that they participated in such events on their own initiative, and 21% said that their organization sends them to such activities. In addition, 31% noted that their organization initiated their own professional seminars, training, or other events. These high percentages show that BHULS understands very well the importance of trained staff with up-to-date knowledge. Further, when they were asked to mention areas where they would like to gain more knowledge to overcome future challenges, 21% mentioned knowledge of e-resources, 37% knowledge of library automation and digitization, and 19% said metadata.

To characterize the nature of the OS of BHULS, respondents were asked to explain in a few words the managerial style of their organization; 26% of the participants characterize it as being one that creates a stimulating environment. Phrases and words such as open for change, dynamic, flexible, democratic, and communicative competitive climate were used. On the contrary, 49% characterize their managerial style adversely as being authoritative, and they used terms such as rigid, dictatorial, bureaucratic, disorganized, noncommunicative, nontransparent, and reluctant to change. Twenty-five percent of respondents remained silent on this important issue by choosing the option "not sure." These varying perceptions show that no major change has taken place at management level at BHULS. On the question regarding employees' perception of their library policy concerning the staff and the organizational development, 57% of the participants perceived the priority of the library as part of organizational development being one orientated towards continuous professional development. However, 9% of respondents remarked on the fact that hiring staff with more qualifications in the LIS field constitutes one of the priorities for the institutions where they work.

Although technology is essential for the success of KM, the literature also reveals that technology alone does not ensure successful KM. BHULS is equipped with the latest technology to store and disseminate information resources to their users. The library recently installed integrated library software to integrate information and knowledge of resources and users in different sections. Expert and best practice databases, portals, and knowledge repositories have not yet been designed and maintained by BHULS. However, most of the participants (79%) use the Internet and Web 2.0 tools to share knowledge to keep them abreast with the latest developments in their field.

Asked about their understanding of the importance of knowledge sharing, 63% of staff mentioned that sharing of knowledge and experiences is important for organizational as well as personal development. When asked about the staff's willingness to share knowledge, the majority of staff (69%) again responded positively, indicating their willingness to share knowledge and professional experience. In response to the question of why to share knowledge, the following reasons were mentioned by the respondents: professional cooperation (14%), increase of working efficiency (21%), loss of knowledge when a member of staff leaves the organization (31%), and exchange of professional experience (25%). Among the respondents not willing to share their knowledge, the reasons mentioned were: lack of rewards and incentives, fear of negative consequences, and insecurity about the value of their knowledge.

Asked about the KP in their organization, the majority of respondents (65%) were less sure about KP activities in the library. However, 10% of respondents mentioned that the structure of their library facilitates exchange or transfer of knowledge, 15% mentioned that knowledge required for day-to-day work is easily accessible in the library, and 11% mentioned that they apply knowledge learned from their experiences. When respondents were asked to indicate the requirements of knowledge needed in the future to facilitate their working practices, 41% of staff specified the requirement of IT skills, 11% specified their willingness to enhance their knowledge level in routine work and process assigned to them, and 42% specified no requirements to enhance their level of knowledge as they are equipped with IT skills.

SUMMARY

OC, KP, ET, IT, and OS are all important factors which influence the success of KM initiatives in all types of organizations, including libraries. The results of our survey show that there is a considerable difference between the perceived importance and actual implementation of these factors in academic libraries in India. The perceived degree of importance is much higher than the degree of implementation of these factors. This gap indicates that academic libraries are not adopting the practices which are perceived to be important for the success of KM initiatives. Sharing of knowledge is one of the most critical success factors for KM, as discussed in the KM literature. Three elements that can facilitate knowledge sharing are a knowledge-sharing culture, information and communication technology, and employee motivation.

Given the critical role that OC plays in the implementation of KM practices, the results of our research on BHULS show that some of the elements of OC already exist and there are fairly favorable conditions for adopting KM practices at BHULS. Staff in the library that participated in this study seem to be motivated and ready to grasp the challenges. A KM program, once put into practice, can lead to an improvement in their performances and greater security for the organization to survive in a highly competitive age. Based on the results obtained from the study, it is recommended that academic libraries adopt the following strategies for the success of KM initiatives by

- creating an environment beneficial to knowledge innovation, an organizational learning culture, shaping a knowledge-based team, and improving trust and cooperation;
- enhancing human resource development, and development and utilization of innovative talents;
- creating a position of knowledge manager to increase the chances of success in the implementation of KM practice;
- developing a better communication strategy, which would provide a coherent context for systems and people in the organization;
- encouraging the development of communities of practice, communication, innovation, and exchange of ideas.

REFERENCES

Ackerman, M., Pipek,V., Wulf,V., 2003. Sharing Expertise: Beyond Knowledge Management. MIT Press, Cambridge, MA.

Alavi, M., Leidner, D., 2001. Knowledge management and knowledge management systems: conceptual foundations and research issues. MIS Q. 25 (1), 107–136.

Babalhavaeji, F., Kermani, Z.J., 2011. Knowledge sharing behavior influences: a case of Library and Information Science faculties in Iran. Malays. J. Libr. Inf. Sci. 16 (1), 1–14.

Barquin, R., 2001. What is knowledge management? Knowledge and innovation. J. KMCI 1 (2), 127–143.

Bellaver, R.F., Lusa, J.M., 2001. Knowledge Management Strategy and Technology. Artech House, Norwood, MA.

Bennett, R., Gabriel, H., 1999. Organizational factors and knowledge management within large marketing departments: an empirical study. J. Knowl. Manag. 3 (3), 212–225.

Butler, T., Murphy, C., 2007. Implementing knowledge management systems in public sector organizations: a case study of critical success factors. Available at: http://is2.Isc.ac.uk/asp/aspecis/20070021.pdf (accessed 15.12.15).

Carter, C., 2004. When your gurus walk out the door. KM Rev. 7 (3), 16–19.

Chong, S., Choi, Y.S., 2005. Critical factors in the successful implementation of knowledge management. J. Knowl. Manag. Pract. 6. Available at: http://www.tlainc.com/articl90.html (accessed 05.05.11).

Conley, C.A., Zheng, W., 2009. Factors critical to knowledge management success. Adv. Dev. Hum. Resour. 11, 334–348.

Davenport, T.H., Prusak, L., 1993. Blow up the corporate library. Int. J. Inf. Manag. 16 (6), 405–412.

Davenport, T.H., DeLong, D.W., Beer, C., 1998. Successful knowledge management project. MIT Sloan Manag. Rev 39 (2), 43–57.

Davenport, T.H., Prusak, L., 1998. Working Knowledge: How Organisations Manage What They Know. Harvard Business School Press, Boston, MA.

Gold, H., Malhotra, A., Segars, H., 2001. Knowledge management: an organizational capabilities perspective. J. Manag. Inf. Syst. 18 (1), 215–233.

Graham, J.-B., Skaggs, B.L., Stevens, K.W., 2005. Digitizing a gap: a state-wide institutional repository project. Ref. Serv. Rev. 33 (3), 337–345.

Hasanali, F., 2002. Critical success factors of knowledge management. Available at: www.providersedge.com/docs/km_articles/Critical_Success_Factors_of_KM.pdf (accessed 09.08.10).

Hayes, H., 2004. The role of libraries in the knowledge economy. Serials 17 (3), 231–238.

Holsapple, C.W., Joshi, K.D., 2000. An investigation of factors that influence the management of knowledge in organisations. J. Strateg. Inf. Syst. 9, 235–261.

Hostler, J., 2005. The path to advancement-centered knowledge management: transforming advancement services. Available at: http://www.supportingadvancement.com/potpourri/trans_as_km/trans_as_km_presentation.pdf (accessed 22.11.10).

Jantz, R., 2001. Knowledge management in academic libraries: special tools and processes to support information professionals. Ref. Serv. Rev. 29 (1), 33–39.

Jones, M.C., Cline, M., Ryan, S., 2006. Exploring knowledge sharing in ERP implementation: an organisational culture framework. Decis. Support. Syst. 41 (2), 411–434.

Keeling, C., Lambert, S., 2000. Knowledge management in the NHS: positioning the healthcare librarian at the knowledge intersection. Health Libr. Rev. 17, 136–143.

Malhan, I.V., 2006a. Strategic planning for developing Indian university libraries into knowledge resource and service centers. In: World Library and Information Congress: 72nd IFLA General Conference and Council, 20–24 August 2006, Seoul. Available at: http://www.ifla.org/IV/ifla72/index.htm (accessed 17.06.10).

Malhan, I.V., 2006b. Developing corporate culture in the Indian university libraries: problems and challenges of change management. Libr. Manag. 27 (6/7), 486–493.

McManus, D., Loughridge, B., 2002. Corporate information, institutional culture and knowledge management: a UK university library perspective. New Libr. World 103 (9), 320–327.

Milam, J.H., 2005. Organizational learning through knowledge workers and infomediaries. N. Dir. High. Educ 131, 51–73 (Fall 2005).

Mohanty, S.K., Chand, M., 2005. 5iKM3: Knowledge Management Maturity Model, Knowledge Management Practices. Tata Consultancy Services, Mumbai. Available at: www.tcs.com/SiteCollectionDocuments/WhitePapers/5iKM3KnowledgeManagementMaturityModel.pdf (accessed 17.05.10).

Nelke, M., 2010. Knowledge management and leadership. In: World Library and Information Congress: 76th IFLA Council and General Conference, 10–15 August 2010, Gothenburg, Sweden. Available at: http://www.ifla.org/files/hq/papers/ifla76/95-nelke-en.pdf (accessed 16.01.13).

Nonaka, I., Takeuchi, H., 1995. The Knowledge-Creating Company: How Japanese Companies Create the Dynamics of Innovations. Oxford University Press, New York, NY.

Parirokh, M., Daneshgar, F., Fattahi, R., 2008. Identifying knowledge-sharing requirements in academic libraries. Libr. Rev. 57 (2), 107–122.

Pinto, L.G., 2006. Building a culture of assessment in Lisbon public libraries: a knowledge management approach. In: World Library and Information Congress: 72nd IFLA General Conference and Council, 20–24 August 2006, Seoul, Korea.

Porumbeanu, O.-L., 2010. Implementing knowledge management in Romanian academic libraries: identifying the elements that characterize their organisational culture. J. Acad. Librariansh. 36 (6), 549–552.

Ralph, L.L., Tijerino, C., 2009. Knowledge management and library culture. Coll. Undergrad. Libr. 16 (4), 329–337.

Ryan, S.D., Prybutok, V.R., 2001. Factors affecting knowledge management technologies: a discriminative approach. J. Comput. Inf. Syst. 41 (3), 31–37.

Schein, E.H., 2010. Organisational Culture and Leadership, fourth ed. Jossey-Bass Publishers, San Francisco, CA.

Shanhong, T., 2000. Knowledge management in libraries in the twenty-first century. In: World Library and Information Congress: 66th IFLA Council and General Conference, 13–18 August 2000, Jerusalem.

Sheng, X., Sun, L., 2007. Developing knowledge innovation culture of libraries. Libr. Manag. 28 (1/2), 36–52.

Siddike, M.A.K., Islam, M.S., 2011. Exploring the competencies of information professionals for knowledge management in the information institutions of Bangladesh. Int. Inf. Libr. Rev. 43, 130–136.

Singh, J., 2009. Leadership competencies for change management in libraries: challenges and opportunities. In: Keynotes Address at International Conference on Academic Libraries at University of Delhi, 5–8 October 2009. Available at: http://crl.du.ac.in/ical09/papers/index_files/ical-51_250_732_3_RV.pdf (accessed 16.01.13).

Skyrme, D.J., Amidon, D., 1997. The knowledge agenda. J. Knowl. Manag. 1 (1), 27–37.

Skyrme, D.J., 2004. Information managers: do we need them? In: Online Information Proceedings, December 2004, pp. 149–155. Available at: http://www.skyrme.com/pubs/online04.htm (accessed 16.01.13).

Townley, C.T., 2001. Knowledge management and academic libraries. Coll. Res. Libr. 62 (1), 44–55.

Wen, S., 2005. Implementing knowledge management in academic libraries: a pragmatic approach. In: 3rd China-US Library Conference, Shanghai, 22–25 March.

INDEX

Note: Page numbers followed by *f* indicate figures and *t* indicate tables.

L

M

N

O

P

Q

R

S

T

W

Printed in the United States
By Bookmasters